Python Text Processing with NLTK 2.0 Cookbook

Over 80 practical recipes for using Python's NLTK suite of libraries to maximize your Natural Language Processing capabilities.

Jacob Perkins

[PACKT] PUBLISHING

open source*
community experience distilled

BIRMINGHAM - MUMBAI

Python Text Processing with NLTK 2.0 Cookbook

First published: November 2010

Production Reference: 1031110

Published by Packt Publishing Ltd.
32 Lincoln Road
Olton
Birmingham, B27 6PA, UK.

ISBN 978-1-849513-60-9

www.packtpub.com

Cover Image by Sujay Gawand (sujay0000@gmail.com)

Credits

Author
Jacob Perkins

Reviewers
Patrick Chan

Herjend Teny

Acquisition Editor
Steven Wilding

Development Editor
Maitreya Bhakal

Technical Editors
Bianca Sequeira

Aditi Suvarna

Copy Editor
Laxmi Subramanian

Indexer
Tejal Daruwale

Editorial Team Leader
Aditya Belpathak

Project Team Leader
Priya Mukherji

Project Coordinator
Shubhanjan Chatterjee

Proofreader
Joanna McMahon

Graphics
Nilesh Mohite

Production Coordinator
Adline Swetha Jesuthas

Cover Work
Adline Swetha Jesuthas

About the Author

Jacob Perkins has been an avid user of open source software since high school, when he first built his own computer and didn't want to pay for Windows. At one point he had five operating systems installed, including Red Hat Linux, OpenBSD, and BeOS.

While at Washington University in St. Louis, Jacob took classes in Spanish and poetry writing, and worked on an independent study project that eventually became his Master's project: WUGLE—a GUI for manipulating logical expressions. In his free time, he wrote the Gnome2 version of Seahorse (a GUI for encryption and key management), which has since been translated into over a dozen languages and is included in the default Gnome distribution.

After receiving his MS in Computer Science, Jacob tried to start a web development studio with some friends, but since no one knew anything about web development, it didn't work out as planned. Once he'd actually learned about web development, he went off and co-founded another company called Weotta, which sparked his interest in Machine Learning and Natural Language Processing.

Jacob is currently the CTO/Chief Hacker for Weotta and blogs about what he's learned along the way at `http://streamhacker.com/`. He is also applying this knowledge to produce text processing APIs and demos at `http://text-processing.com/`. This book is a synthesis of his knowledge on processing text using Python, NLTK, and more.

Thanks to my parents for all their support, even when they don't understand what I'm doing; Grant for sparking my interest in Natural Language Processing; Les for inspiring me to program when I had no desire to; Arnie for all the algorithm discussions; and the whole Wernick family for feeding me such good food whenever I come over.

About the Reviewers

Patrick Chan is an engineer/programmer in the telecommunications industry. He is an avid fan of Linux and Python. His less geekier pursuits include Toastmasters, music, and running.

Herjend Teny graduated from the University of Melbourne. He has worked mainly in the education sector and as a part of research teams. The topics that he has worked on mainly involve embedded programming, signal processing, simulation, and some stochastic modeling. His current interests now lie in many aspects of web programming, using Django. One of the books that he has worked on is the *Python Testing: Beginner's Guide.*

I'd like to thank Patrick Chan for his help in many aspects, and his crazy and odd ideas. Also to Hattie, for her tolerance in letting me do this review until late at night. Thank you!!

Table of Contents

Preface

Natural Language Processing is used everywhere—in search engines, spell checkers, mobile phones, computer games, and even in your washing machine. Python's Natural Language Toolkit (NLTK) suite of libraries has rapidly emerged as one of the most efficient tools for Natural Language Processing. You want to employ nothing less than the best techniques in Natural Language Processing—and this book is your answer.

Python Text Processing with NLTK 2.0 Cookbook is your handy and illustrative guide, which will walk you through all the Natural Language Processing techniques in a step-by-step manner. It will demystify the advanced features of text analysis and text mining using the comprehensive NLTK suite.

This book cuts short the preamble and lets you dive right into the science of text processing with a practical hands-on approach.

Get started off with learning tokenization of text. Receive an overview of WordNet and how to use it. Learn the basics as well as advanced features of stemming and lemmatization. Discover various ways to replace words with simpler and more common (read: more searched) variants. Create your own corpora and learn to create custom corpus readers for data stored in MongoDB. Use and manipulate POS taggers. Transform and normalize parsed chunks to produce a canonical form without changing their meaning. Dig into feature extraction and text classification. Learn how to easily handle huge amounts of data without any loss in efficiency or speed.

This book will teach you all that and beyond, in a hands-on learn-by-doing manner. Make yourself an expert in using the NLTK for Natural Language Processing with this handy companion.

What this book covers

Chapter 1, Tokenizing Text and WordNet Basics, covers the basics of tokenizing text and using WordNet.

Chapter 2, Replacing and Correcting Words, discusses various word replacement and correction techniques. The recipes cover the gamut of linguistic compression, spelling correction, and text normalization.

Chapter 3, Creating Custom Corpora, covers how to use corpus readers and create custom corpora. At the same time, it explains how to use the existing corpus data that comes with NLTK.

Chapter 4, Part-of-Speech Tagging, explains the process of converting a sentence, in the form of a list of words, into a list of tuples. It also explains taggers, which are trainable.

Chapter 5, Extracting Chunks, explains the process of extracting short phrases from a part-of-speech tagged sentence. It uses Penn Treebank corpus for basic training and testing chunk extraction, and the CoNLL 2000 corpus as it has a simpler and more flexible format that supports multiple chunk types.

Chapter 6, Transforming Chunks and Trees, shows you how to do various transforms on both chunks and trees. The functions detailed in these recipes modify data, as opposed to learning from it.

Chapter 7, Text Classification, describes a way to categorize documents or pieces of text and, by examining the word usage in a piece of text, classifiers decide what class label should be assigned to it.

Chapter 8, Distributed Processing and Handling Large Datasets, discusses how to use execnet to do parallel and distributed processing with NLTK. It also explains how to use the Redis data structure server/database to store frequency distributions.

Chapter 9, Parsing Specific Data, covers parsing specific kinds of data, focusing primarily on dates, times, and HTML.

Appendix, Penn Treebank Part-of-Speech Tags, lists a table of all the part-of-speech tags that occur in the treebank corpus distributed with NLTK.

What you need for this book

In the course of this book, you will need the following software utilities to try out various code examples listed:

- NLTK
- MongoDB
- PyMongo
- Redis
- redis-py
- execnet
- Enchant
- PyEnchant
- PyYAML
- dateutil
- chardet
- BeautifulSoup
- lxml
- SimpleParse
- mxBase
- lockfile

Who this book is for

This book is for Python programmers who want to quickly get to grips with using the NLTK for Natural Language Processing. Familiarity with basic text processing concepts is required. Programmers experienced in the NLTK will find it useful. Students of linguistics will find it invaluable.

Conventions

In this book, you will find a number of styles of text that distinguish between different kinds of information. Here are some examples of these styles, and an explanation of their meaning.

Code words in text are shown as follows: "Now we want to split `para` into sentences. First we need to import the sentence tokenization function, and then we can call it with the paragraph as an argument."

A block of code is set as follows:

```
>>> para = "Hello World. It's good to see you. Thanks for buying this
book."
>>> from nltk.tokenize import sent_tokenize
>>> sent_tokenize(para)
```

New terms and **important words** are shown in bold.

Warnings or important notes appear in a box like this.

Tips and tricks appear like this.

Reader feedback

Feedback from our readers is always welcome. Let us know what you think about this book—what you liked or may have disliked. Reader feedback is important for us to develop titles that you really get the most out of.

To send us general feedback, simply send an e-mail to `feedback@packtpub.com`, and mention the book title via the subject of your message.

If there is a book that you need and would like to see us publish, please send us a note in the **SUGGEST A TITLE** form on `www.packtpub.com` or e-mail `suggest@packtpub.com`.

If there is a topic that you have expertise in and you are interested in either writing or contributing to a book, see our author guide on `www.packtpub.com/authors`.

Customer support

Now that you are the proud owner of a Packt book, we have a number of things to help you to get the most from your purchase.

Downloading the example code for this book

You can download the example code files for all Packt books you have purchased from your account at `http://www.PacktPub.com`. If you purchased this book elsewhere, you can visit `http://www.PacktPub.com/support` and register to have the files e-mailed directly to you.

Errata

Although we have taken every care to ensure the accuracy of our content, mistakes do happen. If you find a mistake in one of our books—maybe a mistake in the text or the code— we would be grateful if you would report this to us. By doing so, you can save other readers from frustration and help us improve subsequent versions of this book. If you find any errata, please report them by visiting http://www.packtpub.com/support, selecting your book, clicking on the **errata submission form** link, and entering the details of your errata. Once your errata are verified, your submission will be accepted and the errata will be uploaded on our website, or added to any list of existing errata, under the Errata section of that title. Any existing errata can be viewed by selecting your title from http://www.packtpub.com/support.

Piracy

Piracy of copyright material on the Internet is an ongoing problem across all media. At Packt, we take the protection of our copyright and licenses very seriously. If you come across any illegal copies of our works, in any form, on the Internet, please provide us with the location address or website name immediately so that we can pursue a remedy.

Please contact us at copyright@packtpub.com with a link to the suspected pirated material.

We appreciate your help in protecting our authors, and our ability to bring you valuable content.

Questions

You can contact us at questions@packtpub.com if you are having a problem with any aspect of the book, and we will do our best to address it.

1
Tokenizing Text and WordNet Basics

In this chapter, we will cover:

- ▶ Tokenizing text into sentences
- ▶ Tokenizing sentences into words
- ▶ Tokenizing sentences using regular expressions
- ▶ Filtering stopwords in a tokenized sentence
- ▶ Looking up synsets for a word in WordNet
- ▶ Looking up lemmas and synonyms in WordNet
- ▶ Calculating WordNet synset similarity
- ▶ Discovering word collocations

Introduction

NLTK is the **Natural Language Toolkit**, a comprehensive Python library for natural language processing and text analytics. Originally designed for teaching, it has been adopted in the industry for research and development due to its usefulness and breadth of coverage.

This chapter will cover the basics of tokenizing text and using WordNet. **Tokenization** is a method of breaking up a piece of text into many pieces, and is an essential first step for recipes in later chapters.

WordNet is a dictionary designed for programmatic access by natural language processing systems. NLTK includes a WordNet corpus reader, which we will use to access and explore WordNet. We'll be using WordNet again in later chapters, so it's important to familiarize yourself with the basics first.

Tokenizing text into sentences

Tokenization is the process of splitting a string into a list of pieces, or *tokens*. We'll start by splitting a paragraph into a list of sentences.

Getting ready

Installation instructions for NLTK are available at `http://www.nltk.org/download` and the latest version as of this writing is 2.0b9. NLTK requires Python 2.4 or higher, but is **not compatible with Python 3.0**. The **recommended Python version is 2.6**.

Once you've installed NLTK, you'll also need to install the data by following the instructions at `http://www.nltk.org/data`. We recommend installing everything, as we'll be using a number of corpora and pickled objects. The data is installed in a data directory, which on Mac and Linux/Unix is usually `/usr/share/nltk_data`, or on Windows is `C:\nltk_data`. Make sure that `tokenizers/punkt.zip` is in the data directory and has been unpacked so that there's a file at `tokenizers/punkt/english.pickle`.

Finally, to run the code examples, you'll need to start a Python console. Instructions on how to do so are available at `http://www.nltk.org/getting-started`. For Mac with Linux/Unix users, you can open a terminal and type **python**.

How to do it...

Once NLTK is installed and you have a Python console running, we can start by creating a paragraph of text:

```
>>> para = "Hello World. It's good to see you. Thanks for buying this
book."
```

Now we want to split `para` into sentences. First we need to import the sentence tokenization function, and then we can call it with the paragraph as an argument.

```
>>> from nltk.tokenize import sent_tokenize
>>> sent_tokenize(para)
['Hello World.', "It's good to see you.", 'Thanks for buying this
book.']
```

So now we have a list of sentences that we can use for further processing.

How it works...

`sent_tokenize` uses an instance of `PunktSentenceTokenizer` from the `nltk.tokenize.punkt` module. This instance has already been trained on and works well for many European languages. So it knows what punctuation and characters mark the end of a sentence and the beginning of a new sentence.

There's more...

The instance used in `sent_tokenize()` is actually loaded on demand from a pickle file. So if you're going to be tokenizing a lot of sentences, it's more efficient to load the `PunktSentenceTokenizer` once, and call its `tokenize()` method instead.

```
>>> import nltk.data
>>> tokenizer = nltk.data.load('tokenizers/punkt/english.pickle')
>>> tokenizer.tokenize(para)
['Hello World.', "It's good to see you.", 'Thanks for buying this
book.']
```

Other languages

If you want to tokenize sentences in languages other than English, you can load one of the other pickle files in `tokenizers/punkt` and use it just like the English sentence tokenizer. Here's an example for Spanish:

```
>>> spanish_tokenizer = nltk.data.load('tokenizers/punkt/spanish.
pickle')
>>> spanish_tokenizer.tokenize('Hola amigo. Estoy bien.')
```

See also

In the next recipe, we'll learn how to split sentences into individual words. After that, we'll cover how to use regular expressions for tokenizing text.

Tokenizing sentences into words

In this recipe, we'll split a sentence into individual words. The simple task of creating a list of words from a string is an essential part of all text processing.

How to do it...

Basic word tokenization is very simple: use the `word_tokenize()` function:

```
>>> from nltk.tokenize import word_tokenize
>>> word_tokenize('Hello World.')
['Hello', 'World', '.']
```

How it works...

`word_tokenize()` is a wrapper function that calls `tokenize()` on an instance of the `TreebankWordTokenizer`. It's equivalent to the following:

```
>>> from nltk.tokenize import TreebankWordTokenizer
>>> tokenizer = TreebankWordTokenizer()
>>> tokenizer.tokenize('Hello World.')
['Hello', 'World', '.']
```

It works by separating words using spaces and punctuation. And as you can see, it does not discard the punctuation, allowing you to decide what to do with it.

There's more...

Ignoring the obviously named `WhitespaceTokenizer` and `SpaceTokenizer`, there are two other word tokenizers worth looking at: `PunktWordTokenizer` and `WordPunctTokenizer`. These differ from the `TreebankWordTokenizer` by how they handle punctuation and contractions, but they all inherit from `TokenizerI`. The inheritance tree looks like this:

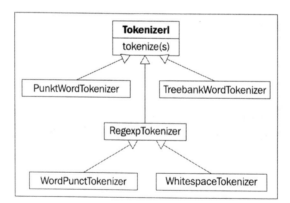

Contractions

`TreebankWordTokenizer` uses conventions found in the Penn Treebank corpus, which we'll be using for training in *Chapter 4, Part-of-Speech Tagging* and *Chapter 5, Extracting Chunks*. One of these conventions is to separate contractions. For example:

```
>>> word_tokenize("can't")
['ca', "n't"]
```

If you find this convention unacceptable, then read on for alternatives, and see the next recipe for tokenizing with regular expressions.

PunktWordTokenizer

An alternative word tokenizer is the `PunktWordTokenizer`. It splits on punctuation, but keeps it with the word instead of creating separate tokens.

```
>>> from nltk.tokenize import PunktWordTokenizer
>>> tokenizer = PunktWordTokenizer()
>>> tokenizer.tokenize("Can't is a contraction.")
['Can', "'t", 'is', 'a', 'contraction.']
```

WordPunctTokenizer

Another alternative word tokenizer is `WordPunctTokenizer`. It splits all punctuations into separate tokens.

```
>>> from nltk.tokenize import WordPunctTokenizer
>>> tokenizer = WordPunctTokenizer()
>>> tokenizer.tokenize("Can't is a contraction.")
['Can', "'", 't', 'is', 'a', 'contraction', '.']
```

See also

For more control over word tokenization, you'll want to read the next recipe to learn how to use regular expressions and the `RegexpTokenizer` for tokenization.

Tokenizing sentences using regular expressions

Regular expression can be used if you want complete control over how to tokenize text. As regular expressions can get complicated very quickly, we only recommend using them if the word tokenizers covered in the previous recipe are unacceptable.

Getting ready

First you need to decide how you want to tokenize a piece of text, as this will determine how you construct your regular expression. The choices are:

- Match on the tokens
- Match on the separators, or gaps

We'll start with an example of the first, matching alphanumeric tokens plus single quotes so that we don't split up contractions.

How to do it...

We'll create an instance of the `RegexpTokenizer`, giving it a regular expression string to use for matching tokens.

```
>>> from nltk.tokenize import RegexpTokenizer
>>> tokenizer = RegexpTokenizer("[\w']+")
>>> tokenizer.tokenize("Can't is a contraction.")
["Can't", 'is', 'a', 'contraction']
```

There's also a simple helper function you can use in case you don't want to instantiate the class.

```
>>> from nltk.tokenize import regexp_tokenize
>>> regexp_tokenize("Can't is a contraction.", "[\w']+")
["Can't", 'is', 'a', 'contraction']
```

Now we finally have something that can treat contractions as whole words, instead of splitting them into tokens.

How it works...

The `RegexpTokenizer` works by compiling your pattern, then calling `re.findall()` on your text. You could do all this yourself using the `re` module, but the `RegexpTokenizer` implements the `TokenizerI` interface, just like all the word tokenizers from the previous recipe. This means it can be used by other parts of the NLTK package, such as corpus readers, which we'll cover in detail in *Chapter 3, Creating Custom Corpora*. Many corpus readers need a way to tokenize the text they're reading, and can take optional keyword arguments specifying an instance of a `TokenizerI` subclass. This way, you have the ability to provide your own tokenizer instance if the default tokenizer is unsuitable.

There's more...

`RegexpTokenizer` can also work by matching the gaps, instead of the tokens. Instead of using `re.findall()`, the `RegexpTokenizer` will use `re.split()`. This is how the `BlanklineTokenizer` in `nltk.tokenize` is implemented.

Simple whitespace tokenizer

Here's a simple example of using the `RegexpTokenizer` to tokenize on whitespace:

```
>>> tokenizer = RegexpTokenizer('\s+', gaps=True)
>>> tokenizer.tokenize("Can't is a contraction.")
 ["Can't", 'is', 'a', 'contraction.']
```

Notice that punctuation still remains in the tokens.

See also

For simpler word tokenization, see the previous recipe.

Filtering stopwords in a tokenized sentence

Stopwords are common words that generally do not contribute to the meaning of a sentence, at least for the purposes of information retrieval and natural language processing. Most search engines will filter stopwords out of search queries and documents in order to save space in their index.

Getting ready

NLTK comes with a stopwords corpus that contains word lists for many languages. Be sure to unzip the datafile so NLTK can find these word lists in `nltk_data/corpora/stopwords/`.

How to do it...

We're going to create a set of all English stopwords, then use it to filter stopwords from a sentence.

```
>>> from nltk.corpus import stopwords
>>> english_stops = set(stopwords.words('english'))
>>> words = ["Can't", 'is', 'a', 'contraction']
>>> [word for word in words if word not in english_stops]
["Can't", 'contraction']
```

How it works...

The stopwords corpus is an instance of `nltk.corpus.reader.WordListCorpusReader`. As such, it has a `words()` method that can take a single argument for the file ID, which in this case is `'english'`, referring to a file containing a list of English stopwords. You could also call `stopwords.words()` with no argument to get a list of all stopwords in every language available.

There's more...

You can see the list of all English stopwords using `stopwords.words('english')` or by examining the word list file at `nltk_data/corpora/stopwords/english`. There are also stopword lists for many other languages. You can see the complete list of languages using the `fileids()` method:

```
>>> stopwords.fileids()
['danish', 'dutch', 'english', 'finnish', 'french', 'german',
'hungarian', 'italian', 'norwegian', 'portuguese', 'russian',
'spanish', 'swedish', 'turkish']
```

Any of these `fileids` can be used as an argument to the `words()` method to get a list of stopwords for that language.

See also

If you'd like to create your own stopwords corpus, see the *Creating a word list corpus* recipe in *Chapter 3, Creating Custom Corpora*, to learn how to use the `WordListCorpusReader`. We'll also be using stopwords in the *Discovering word collocations* recipe, later in this chapter.

Looking up synsets for a word in WordNet

WordNet is a lexical database for the English language. In other words, it's a dictionary designed specifically for natural language processing.

NLTK comes with a simple interface for looking up words in WordNet. What you get is a list of **synset** instances, which are groupings of synonymous words that express the same concept. Many words have only one synset, but some have several. We'll now explore a single synset, and in the next recipe, we'll look at several in more detail.

Getting ready

Be sure you've unzipped the `wordnet` corpus in `nltk_data/corpora/wordnet`. This will allow the `WordNetCorpusReader` to access it.

How to do it...

Now we're going to lookup the `synset` for `cookbook`, and explore some of the properties and methods of a synset.

```
>>> from nltk.corpus import wordnet
>>> syn = wordnet.synsets('cookbook')[0]
>>> syn.name
'cookbook.n.01'
>>> syn.definition
'a book of recipes and cooking directions'
```

How it works...

You can look up any word in WordNet using `wordnet.synsets(word)` to get a list of synsets. The list may be empty if the word is not found. The list may also have quite a few elements, as some words can have many possible meanings and therefore many synsets.

There's more...

Each synset in the list has a number of attributes you can use to learn more about it. The `name` attribute will give you a unique name for the synset, which you can use to get the synset directly.

```
>>> wordnet.synset('cookbook.n.01')
Synset('cookbook.n.01')
```

The `definition` attribute should be self-explanatory. Some synsets also have an `examples` attribute, which contains a list of phrases that use the word in context.

```
>>> wordnet.synsets('cooking')[0].examples
['cooking can be a great art', 'people are needed who have experience
in cookery', 'he left the preparation of meals to his wife']
```

Hypernyms

Synsets are organized in a kind of inheritance tree. More abstract terms are known as **hypernyms** and more specific terms are **hyponyms**. This tree can be traced all the way up to a root hypernym.

Hypernyms provide a way to categorize and group words based on their similarity to each other. The synset similarity recipe details the functions used to calculate similarity based on the distance between two words in the hypernym tree.

```
>>> syn.hypernyms()
[Synset('reference_book.n.01')]
>>> syn.hypernyms()[0].hyponyms()
[Synset('encyclopedia.n.01'), Synset('directory.n.01'),
Synset('source_book.n.01'), Synset('handbook.n.01'),
Synset('instruction_book.n.01'), Synset('cookbook.n.01'),
Synset('annual.n.02'), Synset('atlas.n.02'), Synset('wordbook.n.01')]
>>> syn.root_hypernyms()
[Synset('entity.n.01')]
```

As you can see, `reference book` is a *hypernym* of `cookbook`, but `cookbook` is only one of many *hyponyms* of `reference book`. All these types of books have the same root hypernym, `entity`, one of the most abstract terms in the English language. You can trace the entire path from `entity` down to `cookbook` using the `hypernym_paths()` method.

```
>>> syn.hypernym_paths()
[[Synset('entity.n.01'), Synset('physical_entity.n.01'),
Synset('object.n.01'), Synset('whole.n.02'), Synset('artifact.n.01'),
Synset('creation.n.02'), Synset('product.n.02'), Synset('work.n.02'),
Synset('publication.n.01'), Synset('book.n.01'), Synset('reference_
book.n.01'), Synset('cookbook.n.01')]]
```

This method returns a list of lists, where each list starts at the root hypernym and ends with the original `Synset`. Most of the time you'll only get one nested list of synsets.

Part-of-speech (POS)

You can also look up a simplified part-of-speech tag.

```
>>> syn.pos
'n'
```

There are four common POS found in WordNet.

Part-of-speech	Tag
Noun	n
Adjective	a
Adverb	r
Verb	v

These POS tags can be used for looking up specific `synsets` for a word. For example, the word `great` can be used as a noun or an adjective. In WordNet, `great` has one noun synset and six adjective synsets.

```
>>> len(wordnet.synsets('great'))
7
>>> len(wordnet.synsets('great', pos='n'))
1
>>> len(wordnet.synsets('great', pos='a'))
6
```

These POS tags will be referenced more in the *Using WordNet for Tagging* recipe of *Chapter 4, Part-of-Speech Tagging*.

See also

In the next two recipes, we'll explore lemmas and how to calculate synset similarity. In *Chapter 2, Replacing and Correcting Words*, we'll use WordNet for lemmatization, synonym replacement, and then explore the use of antonyms.

Looking up lemmas and synonyms in WordNet

Building on the previous recipe, we can also look up lemmas in WordNet to find **synonyms** of a word. A **lemma** (in linguistics) is the canonical form, or morphological form, of a word.

How to do it...

In the following block of code, we'll find that there are two lemmas for the cookbook synset by using the lemmas attribute:

```
>>> from nltk.corpus import wordnet
>>> syn = wordnet.synsets('cookbook')[0]
>>> lemmas = syn.lemmas
>>> len(lemmas)
2
>>> lemmas[0].name
'cookbook'
>>> lemmas[1].name
'cookery_book'
>>> lemmas[0].synset == lemmas[1].synset
True
```

How it works...

As you can see, `cookery_book` and `cookbook` are two distinct `lemmas` in the same `synset`. In fact, a lemma can only belong to a single synset. In this way, a synset represents a group of lemmas that all have the same meaning, while a lemma represents a distinct word form.

There's more...

Since lemmas in a synset all have the same meaning, they can be treated as synonyms. So if you wanted to get all synonyms for a `synset`, you could do:

```
>>> [lemma.name for lemma in syn.lemmas]
['cookbook', 'cookery_book']
```

All possible synonyms

As mentioned before, many words have multiple `synsets` because the word can have different meanings depending on the context. But let's say you didn't care about the context, and wanted to get all possible synonyms for a word.

```
>>> synonyms = []
>>> for syn in wordnet.synsets('book'):
...     for lemma in syn.lemmas:
...         synonyms.append(lemma.name)
>>> len(synonyms)
38
```

As you can see, there appears to be 38 possible synonyms for the word `book`. But in fact, some are verb forms, and many are just different usages of `book`. Instead, if we take the set of synonyms, there are fewer unique words.

```
>>> len(set(synonyms))
25
```

Antonyms

Some lemmas also have **antonyms**. The word `good`, for example, has 27 `synsets`, five of which have `lemmas` with antonyms.

```
>>> gn2 = wordnet.synset('good.n.02')
>>> gn2.definition
'moral excellence or admirableness'
>>> evil = gn2.lemmas[0].antonyms()[0]
>>> evil.name
'evil'
>>> evil.synset.definition
```

```
'the quality of being morally wrong in principle or practice'
>>> ga1 = wordnet.synset('good.a.01')
>>> ga1.definition
'having desirable or positive qualities especially those suitable for
a thing specified'
>>> bad = ga1.lemmas[0].antonyms()[0]
>>> bad.name
'bad'
>>> bad.synset.definition
'having undesirable or negative qualities'
```

The `antonyms()` method returns a list of `lemmas`. In the first case here, we see that the second `synset` for `good` as a noun is defined as `moral excellence`, and its first antonym is `evil`, defined as `morally wrong`. In the second case, when `good` is used as an adjective to describe positive qualities, the first antonym is `bad`, which describes negative qualities.

See also

In the next recipe, we'll learn how to calculate `synset` similarity. Then in *Chapter 2, Replacing and Correcting Words*, we'll revisit lemmas for lemmatization, synonym replacement, and antonym replacement.

Calculating WordNet synset similarity

Synsets are organized in a *hypernym* tree. This tree can be used for reasoning about the similarity between the synsets it contains. Two synsets are more similar, the closer they are in the tree.

How to do it...

If you were to look at all the hyponyms of `reference book` (which is the hypernym of `cookbook`) you'd see that one of them is `instruction_book`. These seem intuitively very similar to `cookbook`, so let's see what WordNet similarity has to say about it.

```
>>> from nltk.corpus import wordnet
>>> cb = wordnet.synset('cookbook.n.01')
>>> ib = wordnet.synset('instruction_book.n.01')
>>> cb.wup_similarity(ib)
0.91666666666666663
```

So they are over 91% similar!

How it works...

`wup_similarity` is short for *Wu-Palmer Similarity*, which is a scoring method based on how similar the word senses are and where the synsets occur relative to each other in the hypernym tree. One of the core metrics used to calculate similarity is the shortest path distance between the two synsets and their common hypernym.

```
>>> ref = cb.hypernyms()[0]
>>> cb.shortest_path_distance(ref)
1
>>> ib.shortest_path_distance(ref)
1
>>> cb.shortest_path_distance(ib)
2
```

So cookbook and instruction book must be very similar, because they are only one step away from the same hypernym, reference book, and therefore only two steps away from each other.

There's more...

Let's look at two dissimilar words to see what kind of score we get. We'll compare dog with cookbook, two seemingly very different words.

```
>>> dog = wordnet.synsets('dog')[0]
>>> dog.wup_similarity(cb)
0.38095238095238093
```

Wow, dog and cookbook are apparently 38% similar! This is because they share common hypernyms farther up the tree.

```
>>> dog.common_hypernyms(cb)
[Synset('object.n.01'), Synset('whole.n.02'), Synset('physical_
entity.n.01'), Synset('entity.n.01')]
```

Comparing verbs

The previous comparisons were all between nouns, but the same can be done for verbs as well.

```
>>> cook = wordnet.synset('cook.v.01')
>>> bake = wordnet.synset('bake.v.02')
>>> cook.wup_similarity(bake)
0.75
```

The previous synsets were obviously handpicked for demonstration, and the reason is that the hypernym tree for verbs has a lot more breadth and a lot less depth. While most nouns can be traced up to `object`, thereby providing a basis for similarity, many verbs do not share common hypernyms, making WordNet unable to calculate similarity. For example, if you were to use the `synset` for `bake.v.01` here, instead of `bake.v.02`, the return value would be `None`. This is because the root hypernyms of the two synsets are different, with no overlapping paths. For this reason, you also cannot calculate similarity between words with different parts of speech.

Path and LCH similarity

Two other similarity comparisons are the path similarity and **Leacock Chodorow (LCH)** similarity.

```
>>> cb.path_similarity(ib)
0.33333333333333331
>>> cb.path_similarity(dog)
0.071428571428571425
>>> cb.lch_similarity(ib)
2.5389738710582761
>>> cb.lch_similarity(dog)
0.99852883011112725
```

As you can see, the number ranges are very different for these scoring methods, which is why we prefer the `wup_similarity()` method.

See also

The recipe on *Looking up synsets for a word in WordNet,* discussed earlier in this chapter, has more details about hypernyms and the hypernym tree.

Discovering word collocations

Collocations are two or more words that tend to appear frequently together, such as "United States". Of course, there are many other words that can come after "United", for example "United Kingdom", "United Airlines", and so on. As with many aspects of natural language processing, context is very important, and for collocations, context is everything!

In the case of collocations, the context will be a document in the form of a list of words. Discovering collocations in this list of words means that we'll find common phrases that occur frequently throughout the text. For fun, we'll start with the script for *Monty Python and the Holy Grail*.

Getting ready

The script for *Monty Python and the Holy Grail* is found in the `webtext` corpus, so be sure that it's unzipped in `nltk_data/corpora/webtext/`.

How to do it...

We're going to create a list of all lowercased words in the text, and then produce a `BigramCollocationFinder`, which we can use to find **bigrams**, which are pairs of words. These bigrams are found using association measurement functions found in the `nltk.metrics` package.

```
>>> from nltk.corpus import webtext
>>> from nltk.collocations import BigramCollocationFinder
>>> from nltk.metrics import BigramAssocMeasures
>>> words = [w.lower() for w in webtext.words('grail.txt')]
>>> bcf = BigramCollocationFinder.from_words(words)
>>> bcf.nbest(BigramAssocMeasures.likelihood_ratio, 4)
[("'", 's'), ('arthur', ':'), ('#', '1'), ("'", 't')]
```

Well that's not very useful! Let's refine it a bit by adding a word filter to remove punctuation and stopwords.

```
>>> from nltk.corpus import stopwords
>>> stopset = set(stopwords.words('english'))
>>> filter_stops = lambda w: len(w) < 3 or w in stopset
>>> bcf.apply_word_filter(filter_stops)
>>> bcf.nbest(BigramAssocMeasures.likelihood_ratio, 4)
[('black', 'knight'), ('clop', 'clop'), ('head', 'knight'), ('mumble',
'mumble')]
```

Much better—we can clearly see four of the most common bigrams in *Monty Python and the Holy Grail*. If you'd like to see more than four, simply increase the number to whatever you want, and the collocation finder will do its best.

How it works...

The `BigramCollocationFinder` constructs two frequency distributions: one for each word, and another for bigrams. A **frequency distribution**, or `FreqDist` in NLTK, is basically an enhanced dictionary where the keys are what's being counted, and the values are the counts. Any filtering functions that are applied, reduce the size of these two `FreqDists` by eliminating any words that don't pass the filter. By using a filtering function to eliminate all words that are one or two characters, and all English stopwords, we can get a much cleaner result. After filtering, the collocation finder is ready to accept a generic scoring function for finding collocations. Additional scoring functions are covered in the *Scoring functions* section further in this chapter.

In addition to `BigramCollocationFinder`, there's also `TrigramCollocationFinder`, for finding triples instead of pairs. This time, we'll look for **trigrams** in Australian singles ads.

```
>>> from nltk.collocations import TrigramCollocationFinder
>>> from nltk.metrics import TrigramAssocMeasures
>>> words = [w.lower() for w in webtext.words('singles.txt')]
>>> tcf = TrigramCollocationFinder.from_words(words)
>>> tcf.apply_word_filter(filter_stops)
>>> tcf.apply_freq_filter(3)
>>> tcf.nbest(TrigramAssocMeasures.likelihood_ratio, 4)
[('long', 'term', 'relationship')]
```

Now, we don't know whether people are looking for a long-term relationship or not, but clearly it's an important topic. In addition to the stopword filter, we also applied a frequency filter which removed any trigrams that occurred less than three times. This is why only one result was returned when we asked for four—because there was only one result that occurred more than twice.

Scoring functions

There are many more scoring functions available besides `likelihood_ratio()`. But other than `raw_freq()`, you may need a bit of a statistics background to understand how they work. Consult the NLTK API documentation for `NgramAssocMeasures` in the `nltk.metrics` package, to see all the possible scoring functions.

Scoring ngrams

In addition to the `nbest()` method, there are two other ways to get **ngrams** (a generic term for describing *bigrams* and *trigrams*) from a collocation finder.

1. `above_score(score_fn, min_score)` can be used to get all ngrams with scores that are at least `min_score`. The `min_score` that you choose will depend heavily on the `score_fn` you use.

2. `score_ngrams(score_fn)` will return a list with tuple pairs of `(ngram, score)`. This can be used to inform your choice for `min_score` in the previous step.

See also

The `nltk.metrics` module will be used again in *Chapter 7, Text Classification*.

2
Replacing and Correcting Words

In this chapter, we will cover:

- ► Stemming words
- ► Lemmatizing words with WordNet
- ► Translating text with Babelfish
- ► Replacing words matching regular expressions
- ► Removing repeating characters
- ► Spelling correction with Enchant
- ► Replacing synonyms
- ► Replacing negations with antonyms

Introduction

In this chapter, we will go over various word replacement and correction techniques. The recipes cover the gamut of linguistic compression, spelling correction, and text normalization. All of these methods can be very useful for pre-processing text before search indexing, document classification, and text analysis.

Stemming words

Stemming is a technique for removing *affixes* from a word, ending up with the *stem*. For example, the stem of "cooking" is "cook", and a good stemming algorithm knows that the "ing" *suffix* can be removed. Stemming is most commonly used by search engines for indexing words. Instead of storing all forms of a word, a search engine can store only the stems, greatly reducing the size of index while increasing retrieval accuracy.

One of the most common stemming algorithms is the **Porter Stemming Algorithm**, by Martin Porter. It is designed to remove and replace well known suffixes of English words, and its usage in NLTK will be covered next.

 The resulting stem is not always a valid word. For example, the stem of "cookery" is "cookeri". This is a feature, not a bug.

How to do it...

NLTK comes with an implementation of the Porter Stemming Algorithm, which is very easy to use. Simply instantiate the `PorterStemmer` class and call the `stem()` method with the word you want to stem.

```
>>> from nltk.stem import PorterStemmer
>>> stemmer = PorterStemmer()
>>> stemmer.stem('cooking')
'cook'
>>> stemmer.stem('cookery')
'cookeri'
```

How it works...

The `PorterStemmer` knows a number of regular word forms and suffixes, and uses that knowledge to transform your input word to a final stem through a series of steps. The resulting stem is often a shorter word, or at least a common form of the word, that has the same root meaning.

There's more...

There are other stemming algorithms out there besides the Porter Stemming Algorithm, such as the **Lancaster Stemming Algorithm**, developed at Lancaster University. NLTK includes it as the `LancasterStemmer` class. At the time of writing, there is no definitive research demonstrating the superiority of one algorithm over the other. However, Porter Stemming is generally the default choice.

All the stemmers covered next inherit from the `StemmerI` interface, which defines the `stem()` method. The following is an inheritance diagram showing this:

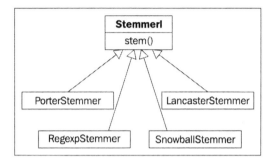

LancasterStemmer

The `LancasterStemmer` functions just like the `PorterStemmer`, but can produce slightly different results. It is known to be slightly more aggressive than the `PorterStemmer`.

```
>>> from nltk.stem import LancasterStemmer
>>> stemmer = LancasterStemmer()
>>> stemmer.stem('cooking')
'cook'
>>> stemmer.stem('cookery')
'cookery'
```

RegexpStemmer

You can also construct your own stemmer using the `RegexpStemmer`. It takes a single regular expression (either compiled or as a string) and will remove any prefix or suffix that matches.

```
>>> from nltk.stem import RegexpStemmer
>>> stemmer = RegexpStemmer('ing')
>>> stemmer.stem('cooking')
'cook'
>>> stemmer.stem('cookery')
'cookery'
>>> stemmer.stem('ingleside')
'leside'
```

A `RegexpStemmer` should only be used in very specific cases that are not covered by the `PorterStemmer` or `LancasterStemmer`.

SnowballStemmer

New in NLTK 2.0b9 is the `SnowballStemmer`, which supports 13 non-English languages. To use it, you create an instance with the name of the language you are using, and then call the `stem()` method. Here is a list of all the supported languages, and an example using the Spanish `SnowballStemmer`:

```
>>> from nltk.stem import SnowballStemmer
>>> SnowballStemmer.languages
('danish', 'dutch', 'finnish', 'french', 'german', 'hungarian',
'italian', 'norwegian', 'portuguese', 'romanian', 'russian',
'spanish', 'swedish')
>>> spanish_stemmer = SnowballStemmer('spanish')
>>> spanish_stemmer.stem('hola')
u'hol'
```

See also

In the next recipe, we will cover lemmatization, which is quite similar to stemming, but subtly different.

Lemmatizing words with WordNet

Lemmatization is very similar to stemming, but is more akin to synonym replacement. A *lemma* is a root word, as opposed to the root *stem*. So unlike stemming, you are always left with a valid word which means the same thing. But the word you end up with can be completely different. A few examples will explain lemmatization...

Getting ready

Be sure you have unzipped the `wordnet` corpus in `nltk_data/corpora/wordnet`. This will allow the `WordNetLemmatizer` to access WordNet. You should also be somewhat familiar with the part-of-speech tags covered in the *Looking up synsets for a word in WordNet* recipe of *Chapter 1, Tokenizing Text and WordNet Basics*.

How to do it...

We will use the `WordNetLemmatizer` to find lemmas:

```
>>> from nltk.stem import WordNetLemmatizer
>>> lemmatizer = WordNetLemmatizer()
>>> lemmatizer.lemmatize('cooking')
'cooking'
```

```
>>> lemmatizer.lemmatize('cooking', pos='v')
'cook'
>>> lemmatizer.lemmatize('cookbooks')
'cookbook'
```

How it works...

The `WordNetLemmatizer` is a thin wrapper around the WordNet corpus, and uses the `morphy()` function of the `WordNetCorpusReader` to find a lemma. If no lemma is found, the word is returned as it is. Unlike with stemming, knowing the part of speech of the word is important. As demonstrated previously, "cooking" does not have a lemma unless you specify that the part of speech (`pos`) is a *verb*. This is because the default part of speech is a *noun*, and since "cooking" is not a noun, no lemma is found. "Cookbooks", on the other hand, is a noun, and its lemma is the singular form, "cookbook".

There's more...

Here's an example that illustrates one of the major differences between stemming and lemmatization:

```
>>> from nltk.stem import PorterStemmer
>>> stemmer = PorterStemmer()
>>> stemmer.stem('believes')
'believ'
>>> lemmatizer.lemmatize('believes')
'belief'
```

Instead of just chopping off the "es" like the `PorterStemmer`, the `WordNetLemmatizer` finds a valid root word. Where a stemmer only looks at the form of the word, the lemmatizer looks at the meaning of the word. And by returning a lemma, you will always get a valid word.

Combining stemming with lemmatization

Stemming and lemmatization can be combined to compress words more than either process can by itself. These cases are somewhat rare, but they do exist:

```
>>> stemmer.stem('buses')
'buse'
>>> lemmatizer.lemmatize('buses')
'bus'
>>> stemmer.stem('bus')
'bu'
```

In this example, stemming saves one character, lemmatizing saves two characters, and stemming the lemma saves a total of three characters out of five characters. That is nearly a 60% compression rate! This level of word compression over many thousands of words, while unlikely to always produce such high gains, can still make a huge difference.

See also

In the previous recipe, we covered stemming basics and WordNet was introduced in the *Looking up synsets for a word in WordNet* and *Looking up lemmas* and *synonyms in WordNet* recipes of *Chapter 1, Tokenizing Text and WordNet Basics*. Looking forward, we will cover the *Using WordNet for Tagging* recipe in *Chapter 4, Part-of-Speech Tagging*.

Translating text with Babelfish

Babelfish is an online language translation API provided by Yahoo. With it, you can translate text in a *source language* to a *target language*. NLTK comes with a simple interface for using it.

Getting ready

Be sure you are connected to the internet first. The `babelfish.translate()` function requires access to Yahoo's online API in order to work.

How to do it...

To translate your text, you first need to know two things:

1. The language of your text or source language.
2. The language you want to translate to or target language.

Language detection is outside the scope of this recipe, so we will assume you already know the source and target languages.

```
>>> from nltk.misc import babelfish
>>> babelfish.translate('cookbook', 'english', 'spanish')
'libro de cocina'
>>> babelfish.translate('libro de cocina', 'spanish', 'english')
'kitchen book'
>>> babelfish.translate('cookbook', 'english', 'german')
'Kochbuch'
>>> babelfish.translate('kochbuch', 'german', 'english')
'cook book'
```

You cannot translate using the same language for both source and target. Attempting to do so will raise a `BabelfishChangedError`.

How it works...

The `translate()` function is a small function that sends a `urllib` request to `http://babelfish.yahoo.com/translate_txt`, and then searches the response for the translated text.

 If Yahoo, for whatever reason, had changed their HTML response to the point that `translate()` cannot identify the translated text, a `BabelfishChangedError` will be raised. This is unlikely to happen, but if it does, you may need to upgrade to a newer version of NLTK and/or report the error.

There's more...

There is also a fun function called `babelize()` that translates back and forth between the source and target language until there are no more changes.

```
>>> for text in babelfish.babelize('cookbook', 'english', 'spanish'):
...     print text
cookbook
libro de cocina
kitchen book
libro de la cocina
book of the kitchen
```

Available languages

You can see all the languages available for translation by examining the `available_languages` attribute.

```
>>> babelfish.available_languages
['Portuguese', 'Chinese', 'German', 'Japanese', 'French', 'Spanish',
'Russian', 'Greek', 'English', 'Korean', 'Italian']
```

The lowercased version of each of these languages can be used as a source or target language for translation.

Replacing words matching regular expressions

Now we are going to get into the process of replacing words. Where stemming and lemmatization are a kind of *linguistic compression*, and word replacement can be thought of as *error correction*, or *text normalization*.

For this recipe, we will be replacing words based on regular expressions, with a focus on *expanding contractions*. Remember when we were tokenizing words in *Chapter 1, Tokenizing Text and WordNet Basics* and it was clear that most tokenizers had trouble with contractions? This recipe aims to fix that by replacing contractions with their expanded forms, such as by replacing "can't" with "cannot", or "would've" with "would have".

Getting ready

Understanding how this recipe works will require a basic knowledge of regular expressions and the re module. The key things to know are *matching patterns* and the re.subn() function.

How to do it...

First, we need to define a number of replacement patterns. This will be a list of tuple pairs, where the first element is the pattern to match on, and the second element is the replacement.

Next, we will create a RegexpReplacer class that will compile the patterns, and provide a replace() method to substitute all found patterns with their replacements.

The following code can be found in the replacers.py module and is meant to be imported, not typed into the console:

```python
import re

replacement_patterns = [
    (r'won\'t', 'will not'),
    (r'can\'t', 'cannot'),
    (r'i\'m', 'i am'),
    (r'ain\'t', 'is not'),
    (r'(\w+)\'ll', '\g<1> will'),
    (r'(\w+)n\'t', '\g<1> not'),
    (r'(\w+)\'ve', '\g<1> have'),
    (r'(\w+)\'s', '\g<1> is'),
    (r'(\w+)\'re', '\g<1> are'),
    (r'(\w+)\'d', '\g<1> would')
]
class RegexpReplacer(object):
```

```
def __init__(self, patterns=replacement_patterns):
  self.patterns = [(re.compile(regex), repl) for (regex, repl) in
    patterns]
def replace(self, text):
  s = text
  for (pattern, repl) in self.patterns:
    (s, count) = re.subn(pattern, repl, s)
  return s
```

How it works...

Here is a simple usage example:

```
>>> from replacers import RegexpReplacer
>>> replacer = RegexpReplacer()
>>> replacer.replace("can't is a contraction")
'cannot is a contraction'
>>> replacer.replace("I should've done that thing I didn't do")
'I should have done that thing I did not do'
```

`RegexpReplacer.replace()` works by replacing every instance of a replacement pattern with its corresponding substitution pattern. In `replacement_patterns`, we have defined tuples such as `(r'(\w+)\'ve', '\g<1> have')`. The first element matches a group of ASCII characters followed by `'ve`. By grouping the characters before the `'ve` in parenthesis, a match group is found and can be used in the substitution pattern with the `\g<1>` reference. So we keep everything before `'ve`, then replace `'ve` with the word `have`. This is how "should've" can become "should have".

There's more...

This replacement technique can work with any kind of regular expression, not just contractions. So you could replace any occurrence of "&" with "and", or eliminate all occurrences of "-" by replacing it with the empty string. The `RegexpReplacer` can take any list of replacement patterns for whatever purpose.

Replacement before tokenization

Let us try using the `RegexpReplacer` as a preliminary step before tokenization:

```
>>> from nltk.tokenize import word_tokenize
>>> from replacers import RegexpReplacer
>>> replacer = RegexpReplacer()
>>> word_tokenize("can't is a contraction")
['ca', "n't", 'is', 'a', 'contraction']
>>> word_tokenize(replacer.replace("can't is a contraction"))
['can', 'not', 'is', 'a', 'contraction']
```

Much better! By eliminating the contractions in the first place, the tokenizer will produce cleaner results. Cleaning up text before processing is a common pattern in natural language processing.

See also

For more information on tokenization, see the first three recipes in *Chapter 1, Tokenizing Text and WordNet Basics*. For more replacement techniques, continue reading the rest of this chapter.

Removing repeating characters

In everyday language, people are often not strictly grammatical. They will write things like "I loooooove it" in order to emphasize the word "love". But computers don't know that "loooooove" is a variation of "love" unless they are told. This recipe presents a method for removing those annoying repeating characters in order to end up with a "proper" English word.

Getting ready

As in the previous recipe, we will be making use of the `re` module, and more specifically, backreferences. A **backreference** is a way to refer to a previously matched group in a regular expression. This is what will allow us to match and remove repeating characters.

How to do it...

We will create a class that has the same form as the `RegexpReplacer` from the previous recipe. It will have a `replace()` method that takes a single word and returns a more correct version of that word, with dubious repeating characters removed. The following code can be found in `replacers.py` and is meant to be imported:

```
import re

class RepeatReplacer(object):
  def __init__(self):
    self.repeat_regexp = re.compile(r'(\w*)(\w)\2(\w*)')
    self.repl = r'\1\2\3'

  def replace(self, word):
    repl_word = self.repeat_regexp.sub(self.repl, word)
    if repl_word != word:
      return self.replace(repl_word)
    else:
      return repl_word
```

And now some example use cases:

```
>>> from replacers import RepeatReplacer
>>> replacer = RepeatReplacer()
>>> replacer.replace('loooove')
'love'
>>> replacer.replace('oooooh')
'oh'
>>> replacer.replace('goose')
'gose'
```

How it works...

`RepeatReplacer` starts by compiling a regular expression for matching and defining a replacement string with backreferences. The `repeat_regexp` matches three groups:

1. Zero or more starting characters (`\w*`).

2. A single character (`\w`), followed by another instance of that character `\2`.

3. Zero or more ending characters (`\w*`).

The *replacement string* is then used to keep all the matched groups, while discarding the backreference to the second group. So the word "loooove" gets split into `(l)(o)o(oove)` and then recombined as "loooove", discarding the second "o". This continues until only one "o" remains, when `repeat_regexp` no longer matches the string, and no more characters are removed.

There's more...

In the preceding examples, you can see that the `RepeatReplacer` is a bit too greedy and ends up changing "goose" into "gose". To correct this issue, we can augment the `replace()` function with a WordNet lookup. If WordNet recognizes the word, then we can stop replacing characters. Here is the WordNet augmented version:

```python
import re
from nltk.corpus import wordnet
class RepeatReplacer(object):
  def __init__(self):
    self.repeat_regexp = re.compile(r'(\w*)(\w)\2(\w*)')
    self.repl = r'\1\2\3'
  def replace(self, word):
    if wordnet.synsets(word):
      return word
    repl_word = self.repeat_regexp.sub(self.repl, word)
    if repl_word != word:
      return self.replace(repl_word)
    else:
      return repl_word
```

Now, "goose" will be found in WordNet, and no character replacement will take place. And "oooooh" will become "ooh" instead of "oh", because "ooh" is actually a word in WordNet, defined as an expression of admiration or pleasure.

See also

Read the next recipe to learn how to correct misspellings. And for more on WordNet, refer to the WordNet recipes in *Chapter 1, Tokenizing Text and WordNet Basics*. We will also be using WordNet for antonym replacement later in this chapter.

Spelling correction with Enchant

Replacing repeating characters is actually an extreme form of spelling correction. In this recipe, we will take on the less extreme case of correcting minor spelling issues using **Enchant**—a spelling correction API.

Getting ready

You will need to install Enchant, and a dictionary for it to use. Enchant is an offshoot of the "Abiword" open source word processor, and more information can be found at `http://www.abisource.com/projects/enchant/`.

For dictionaries, **aspell** is a good open source spellchecker and dictionary that can be found at `http://aspell.net/`.

Finally, you will need the **pyenchant** library, which can be found at `http://www.rfk.id.au/software/pyenchant/`. You should be able to install it with the `easy_install` command that comes with *python-setuptools*, such as by doing `sudo easy_install pyenchant` on Linux or Unix.

How to do it...

We will create a new class called `SpellingReplacer` in `replacers.py`, and this time the `replace()` method will check Enchant to see whether the word is valid or not. If not, we will look up suggested alternatives and return the best match using `nltk.metrics.edit_distance()`:

```
import enchant
from nltk.metrics import edit_distance

class SpellingReplacer(object):
  def __init__(self, dict_name='en', max_dist=2):
    self.spell_dict = enchant.Dict(dict_name)
    self.max_dist = 2
```

```
def replace(self, word):
  if self.spell_dict.check(word):
    return word
  suggestions = self.spell_dict.suggest(word)

  if suggestions and edit_distance(word, suggestions[0]) <=
    self.max_dist:
    return suggestions[0]
  else:
    return word
```

The preceding class can be used to correct English spellings as follows:

```
>>> from replacers import SpellingReplacer
>>> replacer = SpellingReplacer()
>>> replacer.replace('cookbok')
'cookbook'
```

How it works...

`SpellingReplacer` starts by creating a reference to an `enchant` dictionary. Then, in the `replace()` method, it first checks whether the given `word` is present in the dictionary or not. If it is, no spelling correction is necessary, and the word is returned. But if the word is not found, it looks up a list of suggestions and returns the first suggestion, as long as its edit distance is less than or equal to `max_dist`. The **edit distance** is the number of character changes necessary to transform the given word into the suggested word. `max_dist` then acts as a constraint on the Enchant `suggest()` function to ensure that no unlikely replacement words are returned. Here is an example showing all the suggestions for "languege", a misspelling of "language":

```
>>> import enchant
>>> d = enchant.Dict('en')
>>> d.suggest('languege')
['language', 'languisher', 'languish', 'languor', 'languid']
```

Except for the correct suggestion, "language", all the other words have an edit distance of three or greater.

There's more...

You can use language dictionaries other than `'en'`, such as `'en_GB'`, assuming the dictionary has already been installed. To check which other languages are available, use `enchant.list_languages()`:

```
>>> enchant.list_languages()
['en_AU', 'en_GB', 'en_US', 'en_ZA', 'en_CA', 'en']
```

If you try to use a dictionary that doesn't exist, you will get `enchant.DictNotFoundError`. You can first check whether the dictionary exists using `enchant.dict_exists()`, which will return `True` if the named dictionary exists, or `False` otherwise.

en_GB dictionary

Always be sure to use the correct dictionary for whichever language you are doing spelling correction on. `'en_US'` can give you different results than `'en_GB'`, such as for the word "theater". "Theater" is the American English spelling, whereas the British English spelling is "Theatre":

```
>>> import enchant
>>> dUS = enchant.Dict('en_US')
>>> dUS.check('theater')
True
>>> dGB = enchant.Dict('en_GB')
>>> dGB.check('theater')
False
>>> from replacers import SpellingReplacer
>>> us_replacer = SpellingReplacer('en_US')
>>> us_replacer.replace('theater')
'theater'
>>> gb_replacer = SpellingReplacer('en_GB')
>>> gb_replacer.replace('theater')
'theatre'
```

Personal word lists

Enchant also supports personal word lists. These can be combined with an existing dictionary, allowing you to augment the dictionary with your own words. So let us say you had a file named `mywords.txt` that had `nltk` on one line. You could then create a dictionary augmented with your personal word list as follows:

```
>>> d = enchant.Dict('en_US')
>>> d.check('nltk')
False
>>> d = enchant.DictWithPWL('en_US', 'mywords.txt')
>>> d.check('nltk')
True
```

To use an augmented dictionary with our `SpellingReplacer`, we can create a subclass in `replacers.py` that takes an existing spelling dictionary.

```
class CustomSpellingReplacer(SpellingReplacer):
  def __init__(self, spell_dict, max_dist=2):
    self.spell_dict = spell_dict
    self.max_dist = max_dist
```

This `CustomSpellingReplacer` will not replace any words that you put into `mywords.txt`.

```
>>> from replacers import CustomSpellingReplacer
>>> d = enchant.DictWithPWL('en_US', 'mywords.txt')
>>> replacer = CustomSpellingReplacer(d)
>>> replacer.replace('nltk')
'nltk'
```

See also

The previous recipe covered an extreme form of spelling correction by replacing repeating characters. You could also do spelling correction by simple word replacement as discussed in the next recipe.

Replacing synonyms

It is often useful to reduce the vocabulary of a text by replacing words with common synonyms. By compressing the vocabulary without losing meaning, you can save memory in cases such as *frequency analysis* and *text indexing*. Vocabulary reduction can also increase the occurrence of significant collocations, which was covered in the *Discovering word collocations* recipe of *Chapter 1, Tokenizing Text and WordNet Basics*.

Getting ready

You will need to have a defined mapping of a word to its synonym. This is a simple *controlled vocabulary*. We will start by hardcoding the synonyms as a Python dictionary, then explore other options for storing synonym maps.

How to do it...

We'll first create a `WordReplacer` class in `replacers.py` that takes a word replacement mapping:

```
class WordReplacer(object):
  def __init__(self, word_map):
    self.word_map = word_map
  def replace(self, word):
    return self.word_map.get(word, word)
```

Then we can demonstrate its usage for simple word replacement:

```
>>> from replacers import wordReplacer
>>> replacer = WordReplacer({'bday': 'birthday'})
>>> replacer.replace('bday')
'birthday'
>>> replacer.replace('happy')
'happy'
```

How it works...

`WordReplacer` is simply a class wrapper around a Python dictionary. The `replace()` method looks up the given word in its `word_map` and returns the replacement synonym if it exists. Otherwise, the given word is returned as is.

If you were only using the `word_map` dictionary, you would have no need for the `WordReplacer` class, and could instead call `word_map.get()` directly. But `WordReplacer` can act as a base class for other classes that construct the `word_map` from various file formats. Read on for more information.

There's more...

Hardcoding synonyms as a Python dictionary is not a good long-term solution. Two better alternatives are to store the synonyms in a CSV file or in a YAML file. Choose whichever format is easiest for whoever will be maintaining your synonym vocabulary. Both of the classes outlined in the following section inherit the `replace()` method from `WordReplacer`.

CSV synonym replacement

The `CsvWordReplacer` class extends `WordReplacer` in `replacers.py` in order to construct the `word_map` from a CSV file:

```
import csv

class CsvWordReplacer(WordReplacer):
  def __init__(self, fname):
    word_map = {}
    for line in csv.reader(open(fname)):
      word, syn = line
      word_map[word] = syn
    super(CsvWordReplacer, self).__init__(word_map)
```

Your CSV file should be two columns, where the first column is the word, and the second column is the synonym meant to replace it. If this file is called `synonyms.csv` and the first line is `bday, birthday`, then you can do:

```
>>> from replacers import CsvWordReplacer
>>> replacer = CsvWordReplacer('synonyms.csv')
>>> replacer.replace('bday')
'birthday'
>>> replacer.replace('happy')
'happy'
```

YAML synonym replacement

If you have PyYAML installed, you can create a `YamlWordReplacer` in `replacers.py`. Download and installation instructions for PyYAML are located at `http://pyyaml.org/wiki/PyYAML`.

```
import yaml
class YamlWordReplacer(WordReplacer):
  def __init__(self, fname):
    word_map = yaml.load(open(fname))
    super(YamlWordReplacer, self).__init__(word_map)
```

Your YAML file should be a simple mapping of "word: synonym", such as `bday: birthday`. Note that the YAML syntax is very particular, and the space after the colon is required. If the file is named `synonyms.yaml`, you can do:

```
>>> from replacers import YamlWordReplacer
>>> replacer = YamlWordReplacer('synonyms.yaml')
>>> replacer.replace('bday')
'birthday'
>>> replacer.replace('happy')
'happy'
```

See also

You can use the `WordReplacer` to do any kind of word replacement, even spelling correction for more complicated words that can't be automatically corrected, as we did in the previous recipe. In the next recipe, we will cover antonym replacement.

Replacing negations with antonyms

The opposite of synonym replacement is *antonym* replacement. An **antonym** is the opposite meaning of a word. This time, instead of creating custom word mappings, we can use WordNet to replace words with unambiguous antonyms. Refer to the *Looking up lemmas and synonyms in WordNet* recipe in *Chapter 1, Tokenizing Text and WordNet Basics* for more details on antonym lookups.

How to do it...

Let us say you have a sentence such as "let's not uglify our code". With antonym replacement, you can replace "not uglify" with "beautify", resulting in the sentence "let's beautify our code". To do this, we will need to create an `AntonymReplacer` in `replacers.py` as follows:

```
from nltk.corpus import wordnet
class AntonymReplacer(object):
  def replace(self, word, pos=None):
    antonyms = set()
    for syn in wordnet.synsets(word, pos=pos):
      for lemma in syn.lemmas:
        for antonym in lemma.antonyms():
          antonyms.add(antonym.name)
    if len(antonyms) == 1:
      return antonyms.pop()
    else:
      return None

  def replace_negations(self, sent):
    i, l = 0, len(sent)
    words = []
    while i < l:
      word = sent[i]
      if word == 'not' and i+1 < l:
        ant = self.replace(sent[i+1])
        if ant:
          words.append(ant)
          i += 2
          continue
      words.append(word)
      i += 1
    return words
```

Now we can tokenize the original sentence into `["let's", 'not', 'uglify', 'our', 'code']`, and pass this to the `replace_negations()` function. Here are some examples:

```
>>> from replacers import AntonymReplacer
>>> replacer = AntonymReplacer()
>>> replacer.replace('good')
>>> replacer.replace('uglify')
'beautify'
>>> sent = ["let's", 'not', 'uglify', 'our', 'code']
>>> replacer.replace_negations(sent)
["let's", 'beautify', 'our', 'code']
```

How it works...

The `AntonymReplacer` has two methods: `replace()` and `replace_negations()`. The `replace()` method takes a single `word` and an optional part of speech tag, then looks up the synsets for the word in WordNet. Going through all the synsets and every lemma of each synset, it creates a `set` of all antonyms found. If only one antonym is found, then it is an *unambiguous replacement*. If there is more than one antonym found, which can happen quite often, then we don't know for sure which antonym is correct. In the case of multiple antonyms (or no antonyms), `replace()` returns `None` since it cannot make a decision.

In `replace_negations()`, we look through a tokenized sentence for the word "not". If "not" is found, then we try to find an antonym for the next word using `replace()`. If we find an antonym, then it is appended to the list of `words`, replacing "not" and the original word. All other words are appended as it is, resulting in a tokenized sentence with unambiguous negations replaced by their antonyms.

There's more...

Since unambiguous antonyms aren't very common in WordNet, you may want to create a custom antonym mapping the same way we did for synonyms. This `AntonymWordReplacer` could be constructed by inheriting from both `WordReplacer` and `AntonymReplacer`:

```
class AntonymWordReplacer(WordReplacer, AntonymReplacer):
    pass
```

The order of inheritance is very important, as we want the initialization and `replace()` function of `WordReplacer` combined with the `replace_negations()` function from `AntonymReplacer`. The result is a replacer that can do the following:

```
>>> from replacers import AntonymWordReplacer
>>> replacer = AntonymWordReplacer({'evil': 'good'})
>>> replacer.replace_negations(['good', 'is', 'not', 'evil'])
['good', 'is', 'good']
```

Of course, you could also inherit from `CsvWordReplacer` or `YamlWordReplacer` instead of `WordReplacer` if you want to load the antonym word mappings from a file.

See also

The previous recipe covers the `WordReplacer` from the perspective of synonym replacement. And in *Chapter 1, Tokenizing Text and WordNet Basics* Wordnet usage is covered in detail in the *Looking up synsets for a word in Wordnet* and *Looking up lemmas and synonyms in Wordnet* recipes.

3
Creating Custom Corpora

In this chapter, we will cover:

- ▸ Setting up a custom corpus
- ▸ Creating a word list corpus
- ▸ Creating a part-of-speech tagged word corpus
- ▸ Creating a chunked phrase corpus
- ▸ Creating a categorized text corpus
- ▸ Creating a categorized chunk corpus reader
- ▸ Lazy corpus loading
- ▸ Creating a custom corpus view
- ▸ Creating a MongoDB backed corpus reader
- ▸ Corpus editing with file locking

Introduction

In this chapter, we'll cover how to use corpus readers and create custom corpora. At the same time, you'll learn how to use the existing corpus data that comes with NLTK. This information is essential for future chapters when we'll need to access the corpora as training data. We'll also cover creating custom corpus readers, which can be used when your corpus is not in a file format that NLTK already recognizes, or if your corpus is not in files at all, but instead is located in a database such as MongoDB.

Setting up a custom corpus

A **corpus** is a collection of text documents, and **corpora** is the plural of corpus. So a *custom corpus* is really just a bunch of text files in a directory, often alongside many other directories of text files.

Getting ready

You should already have the NLTK data package installed, following the instructions at `http://www.nltk.org/data`. We'll assume that the data is installed to `C:\nltk_data` on Windows, and `/usr/share/nltk_data` on Linux, Unix, or Mac OS X.

How to do it...

NLTK defines a list of data directories, or **paths**, in `nltk.data.path`. Our custom corpora must be within one of these paths so it can be found by NLTK. So as not to conflict with the official data package, we'll create a custom `nltk_data` directory in our home directory. Here's some Python code to create this directory and verify that it is in the list of known paths specified by `nltk.data.path`:

```
>>> import os, os.path
>>> path = os.path.expanduser('~/nltk_data')
>>> if not os.path.exists(path):
...     os.mkdir(path)
>>> os.path.exists(path)
True
>>> import nltk.data
>>> path in nltk.data.path
True
```

If the last line, `path in nltk.data.path`, is `True`, then you should now have a `nltk_data` directory in your home directory. The path should be `%UserProfile%\nltk_data` on Windows, or `~/nltk_data` on Unix, Linux, or Mac OS X. For simplicity, I'll refer to the directory as `~/nltk_data`.

If the last line does not return `True`, try creating the `nltk_data` directory manually in your home directory, then verify that the absolute path is in `nltk.data.path`. It's essential to ensure that this directory exists and is in `nltk.data.path` before continuing. Once you have your `nltk_data` directory, the convention is that corpora reside in a `corpora` subdirectory. Create this `corpora` directory within the `nltk_data` directory, so that the path is `~/nltk_data/corpora`. Finally, we'll create a subdirectory in `corpora` to hold our custom corpus. Let's call it `cookbook`, giving us the full path of `~/nltk_data/corpora/cookbook`.

Now we can create a simple *word list* file and make sure it loads. In *Chapter 2, Replacing and Correcting Words, Spelling correction with Enchant* recipe, we created a word list file called `mywords.txt`. Put this file into `~/nltk_data/corpora/cookbook/`. Now we can use `nltk.data.load()` to load the file.

```
>>> import nltk.data
>>> nltk.data.load('corpora/cookbook/mywords.txt', format='raw')
'nltk\n'
```

 We need to specify `format='raw'` since `nltk.data.load()` doesn't know how to interpret `.txt` files. As we'll see, it does know how to interpret a number of other file formats.

How it works...

The `nltk.data.load()` function recognizes a number of formats, such as `'raw'`, `'pickle'`, and `'yaml'`. If no format is specified, then it tries to guess the format based on the file's extension. In the previous case, we have a `.txt` file, which is not a recognized extension, so we have to specify the `'raw'` format. But if we used a file that ended in `.yaml`, then we would not need to specify the format.

Filenames passed in to `nltk.data.load()` can be *absolute* or *relative* paths. Relative paths must be relative to one of the paths specified in `nltk.data.path`. The file is found using `nltk.data.find(path)`, which searches all known paths combined with the relative path. Absolute paths do not require a search, and are used as is.

There's more...

For most corpora access, you won't actually need to use `nltk.data.load`, as that will be handled by the `CorpusReader` classes covered in the following recipes. But it's a good function to be familiar with for loading `.pickle` files and `.yaml` files, plus it introduces the idea of putting all of your data files into a path known by NLTK.

Loading a YAML file

If you put the `synonyms.yaml` file from the *Chapter 2, Replacing and Correcting Words, Replacing synonyms* recipe, into `~/nltk_data/corpora/cookbook` (next to `mywords.txt`), you can use `nltk.data.load()` to load it without specifying a format.

```
>>> import nltk.data
>>> nltk.data.load('corpora/cookbook/synonyms.yaml')
{'bday': 'birthday'}
```

This assumes that PyYAML is installed. If not, you can find download and installation instructions at `http://pyyaml.org/wiki/PyYAML`.

See also

In the next recipes, we'll cover various corpus readers, and then in the *Lazy corpus loading* recipe, we'll use the `LazyCorpusLoader`, which expects corpus data to be in a `corpora` subdirectory of one of the paths specified by `nltk.data.path`.

Creating a word list corpus

The `WordListCorpusReader` is one of the simplest `CorpusReader` classes. It provides access to a file containing a list of words, one word per line. In fact, you've already used it when we used the `stopwords` corpus in the *Filtering stopwords in a tokenized sentence* and *Discovering word collocations* recipes in *Chapter 1, Tokenizing Text and WordNet Basics*.

Getting ready

We need to start by creating a word list file. This could be a single column CSV file, or just a normal text file with one word per line. Let's create a file named `wordlist` that looks like this:

```
nltk
corpus
corpora
wordnet
```

How to do it...

Now we can instantiate a `WordListCorpusReader` that will produce a list of words from our file. It takes two arguments: the directory path containing the files, and a list of filenames. If you open the Python console in the same directory as the files, then `'.'` can be used as the directory path. Otherwise, you must use a directory path such as: `'nltk_data/corpora/cookbook'`.

```
>>> from nltk.corpus.reader import WordListCorpusReader
>>> reader = WordListCorpusReader('.', ['wordlist'])
>>> reader.words()
['nltk', 'corpus', 'corpora', 'wordnet']
>>> reader.fileids()
['wordlist']
```

How it works...

WordListCorpusReader inherits from CorpusReader, which is a common base class for all corpus readers. CorpusReader does all the work of identifying which files to read, while WordListCorpus reads the files and tokenizes each line to produce a list of words. Here's an inheritance diagram:

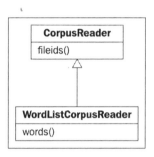

When you call the words() function, it calls nltk.tokenize.line_tokenize() on the raw file data, which you can access using the raw() function.

```
>>> reader.raw()
'nltk\ncorpus\ncorpora\nwordnet\n'
>>> from nltk.tokenize import line_tokenize
>>> line_tokenize(reader.raw())
['nltk', 'corpus', 'corpora', 'wordnet']
```

There's more...

The stopwords corpus is a good example of a multi-file WordListCorpusReader. In *Chapter 1, Tokenizing Text and WordNet Basics*, in the *Filtering stopwords in a tokenized sentence* recipe, we saw that it had one word list file for each language, and you could access the words for that language by calling stopwords.words(fileid). If you want to create your own multi-file word list corpus, this is a great example to follow.

Names corpus

Another word list corpus that comes with NLTK is the names corpus. It contains two files: female.txt and male.txt, each containing a list of a few thousand common first names organized by gender.

```
>>> from nltk.corpus import names
>>> names.fileids()
['female.txt', 'male.txt']
>>> len(names.words('female.txt'))
5001
```

```
>>> len(names.words('male.txt'))
2943
```

English words

NLTK also comes with a large list of English words. There's one file with 850 `basic` words, and another list with over 200,000 known English words.

```
>>> from nltk.corpus import words
>>> words.fileids()
['en', 'en-basic']
>>> len(words.words('en-basic'))
850
>>> len(words.words('en'))
234936
```

See also

In *Chapter 1, Tokenizing Text and WordNet Basics*, the *Filtering stopwords in a tokenized sentence* recipe, has more details on using the `stopwords` corpus. In the following recipes, we'll cover more advanced corpus file formats and corpus reader classes.

Creating a part-of-speech tagged word corpus

Part-of-speech tagging is the process of identifying the part-of-speech tag for a word. Most of the time, a *tagger* must first be trained on a *training corpus*. How to train and use a tagger is covered in detail in *Chapter 4, Part-of-Speech Tagging*, but first we must know how to create and use a training corpus of part-of-speech tagged words.

Getting ready

The simplest format for a tagged corpus is of the form "word/tag". Following is an excerpt from the `brown` corpus:

```
The/at-tl expense/nn and/cc time/nn involved/vbn are/ber astronomical/
jj ./.
```

Each word has a *tag* denoting its part-of-speech. For example, nn refers to a noun, while a tag that starts with vb is a verb.

How to do it...

If you were to put the previous excerpt into a file called `brown.pos`, you could then create a `TaggedCorpusReader` and do the following:

```
>>> from nltk.corpus.reader import TaggedCorpusReader
>>> reader = TaggedCorpusReader('.', r'.*\.pos')
>>> reader.words()
['The', 'expense', 'and', 'time', 'involved', 'are', ...]
>>> reader.tagged_words()
[('The', 'AT-TL'), ('expense', 'NN'), ('and', 'CC'), ...]
>>> reader.sents()
[['The', 'expense', 'and', 'time', 'involved', 'are', 'astronomical',
'.']]
>>> reader.tagged_sents()
[[('The', 'AT-TL'), ('expense', 'NN'), ('and', 'CC'), ('time', 'NN'),
('involved', 'VBN'), ('are', 'BER'), ('astronomical', 'JJ'), ('.',
'.')]]
>>> reader.paras()
[[['The', 'expense', 'and', 'time', 'involved', 'are', 'astronomical',
'.']]]
>>> reader.tagged_paras()
[[[('The', 'AT-TL'), ('expense', 'NN'), ('and', 'CC'), ('time', 'NN'),
('involved', 'VBN'), ('are', 'BER'), ('astronomical', 'JJ'), ('.',
'.')]]]
```

How it works...

This time, instead of naming the file explicitly, we use a regular expression, `r'.*\.pos'`, to match all files whose name ends with `.pos`. We could have done the same thing as we did with the `WordListCorpusReader`, and pass `['brown.pos']` as the second argument, but this way you can see how to include multiple files in a corpus without naming each one explicitly.

`TaggedCorpusReader` provides a number of methods for extracting text from a corpus. First, you can get a list of all words, or a list of tagged tokens. A **tagged token** is simply a tuple of `(word, tag)`. Next, you can get a list of every sentence, and also every tagged sentence, where the sentence is itself a list of words or tagged tokens. Finally, you can get a list of paragraphs, where each paragraph is a list of sentences, and each sentence is a list of words or tagged tokens. Here's an inheritance diagram listing all the major methods:

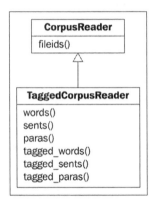

There's more...

The functions demonstrated in the previous diagram all depend on *tokenizers* for splitting the text. `TaggedCorpusReader` tries to have good defaults, but you can customize them by passing in your own tokenizers at initialization time.

Customizing the word tokenizer

The default word tokenizer is an instance of `nltk.tokenize.WhitespaceTokenizer`. If you want to use a different tokenizer, you can pass that in as `word_tokenizer`.

```
>>> from nltk.tokenize import SpaceTokenizer
>>> reader = TaggedCorpusReader('.', r'.*\.pos', word_
tokenizer=SpaceTokenizer())
>>> reader.words()
['The', 'expense', 'and', 'time', 'involved', 'are', ...]
```

Customizing the sentence tokenizer

The default sentence tokenizer is an instance of `nltk.tokenize.RegexpTokenize` with `'\n'` to identify the gaps. It assumes that each sentence is on a line all by itself, and individual sentences do not have line breaks. To customize this, you can pass in your own tokenizer as `sent_tokenizer`.

```
>>> from nltk.tokenize import LineTokenizer
>>> reader = TaggedCorpusReader('.', r'.*\.pos', sent_
tokenizer=LineTokenizer())
>>> reader.sents()
[['The', 'expense', 'and', 'time', 'involved', 'are', 'astronomical',
'.']]
```

Customizing the paragraph block reader

Paragraphs are assumed to be split by blank lines. This is done with the default `para_block_reader`, which is `nltk.corpus.reader.util.read_blankline_block`. There are a number of other block reader functions in `nltk.corpus.reader.util`, whose purpose is to read blocks of text from a *stream*. Their usage will be covered in more detail in the later recipe, *Creating a custom corpus view*, where we'll create a custom corpus reader.

Customizing the tag separator

If you don't want to use `'/'` as the word/tag separator, you can pass an alternative string to `TaggedCorpusReader` for sep. The default is `sep='/'`, but if you want to split words and tags with `'|'`, such as 'word|tag', then you should pass in `sep='|'`.

Simplifying tags with a tag mapping function

If you'd like to somehow transform the part-of-speech tags, you can pass in a `tag_mapping_function` at initialization, then call one of the `tagged_*` functions with `simplify_tags=True`. Here's an example where we lowercase each tag:

```
>>> reader = TaggedCorpusReader('.', r'.*\.pos', tag_mapping_
function=lambda t: t.lower())
>>> reader.tagged_words(simplify_tags=True)
[('The', 'at-tl'), ('expense', 'nn'), ('and', 'cc'), ...]
```

Calling `tagged_words()` without `simplify_tags=True` would produce the same result as if you did not pass in a `tag_mapping_function`.

There are also a number of tag simplification functions defined in `nltk.tag.simplify`. These can be useful for reducing the number of different part-of-speech tags.

```
>>> from nltk.tag import simplify
>>> reader = TaggedCorpusReader('.', r'.*\.pos', tag_mapping_
function=simplify.simplify_brown_tag)
>>> reader.tagged_words(simplify_tags=True)
```

```
[('The', 'DET'), ('expense', 'N'), ('and', 'CNJ'), ...]
>>> reader = TaggedCorpusReader('.', r'.*\.pos', tag_mapping_
function=simplify.simplify_tag)
>>> reader.tagged_words(simplify_tags=True)
[('The', 'A'), ('expense', 'N'), ('and', 'C'), ...]
```

See also

Chapter 4, Part-of-Speech Tagging will cover part-of-speech tags and tagging in much more detail. And for more on tokenizers, see the first three recipes of *Chapter 1, Tokenizing Text and WordNet Basics*.

In the next recipe, we'll create a *chunked phrase* corpus, where each phrase is also part-of-speech tagged.

Creating a chunked phrase corpus

A **chunk** is a short phrase within a sentence. If you remember sentence diagrams from grade school, they were a tree-like representation of phrases within a sentence. This is exactly what chunks are: *sub-trees within a sentence tree*, and they will be covered in much more detail in *Chapter 5, Extracting Chunks*. Following is a sample sentence tree with three noun phrase (**NP**) chunks shown as sub-trees.

This recipe will cover how to create a corpus with sentences that contain chunks.

Getting ready

Here is an excerpt from the tagged `treebank` corpus. It has part-of-speech tags, as in the previous recipe, but it also has square brackets for denoting chunks. This is the same sentence as in the previous tree diagram, but in text form:

```
[Earlier/JJR staff-reduction/NN moves/NNS] have/VBP trimmed/VBN about/
IN [300/CD jobs/NNS] ,/, [the/DT spokesman/NN] said/VBD ./.
```

In this format, every chunk is a *noun phrase*. Words that are not within brackets are part of the sentence tree, but are not part of any noun phrase sub-tree.

How to do it...

Put this excerpt into a file called `treebank.chunk`, and then do the following:

```
>>> from nltk.corpus.reader import ChunkedCorpusReader
>>> reader = ChunkedCorpusReader('.', r'.*\.chunk')
>>> reader.chunked_words()
[Tree('NP', [('Earlier', 'JJR'), ('staff-reduction', 'NN'), ('moves',
'NNS')]), ('have', 'VBP'), ...]
>>> reader.chunked_sents()
[Tree('S', [Tree('NP', [('Earlier', 'JJR'), ('staff-reduction', 'NN'),
('moves', 'NNS')]), ('have', 'VBP'), ('trimmed', 'VBN'), ('about',
'IN'), Tree('NP', [('300', 'CD'), ('jobs', 'NNS')]), (',', ','),
Tree('NP', [('the', 'DT'), ('spokesman', 'NN')]), ('said', 'VBD'),
('.', '.')])]
>>> reader.chunked_paras()
[[Tree('S', [Tree('NP', [('Earlier', 'JJR'), ('staff-reduction',
'NN'), ('moves', 'NNS')]), ('have', 'VBP'), ('trimmed', 'VBN'),
('about', 'IN'), Tree('NP', [('300', 'CD'), ('jobs', 'NNS')]), (',',
','), Tree('NP', [('the', 'DT'), ('spokesman', 'NN')]), ('said',
'VBD'), ('.', '.')])]]
```

The `ChunkedCorpusReader` provides the same methods as the `TaggedCorpusReader`
for getting tagged tokens, along with three new methods for getting chunks. Each chunk is
represented as an instance of `nltk.tree.Tree`. Sentence level trees look like `Tree('S',
[...])` while noun phrase trees look like `Tree('NP', [...])`. In `chunked_sents()`,
you get a list of sentence trees, with each noun-phrase as a sub-tree of the sentence. In
`chunked_words()`, you get a list of noun phrase trees alongside tagged tokens of words that
were not in a chunk. Here's an inheritance diagram listing the major methods:

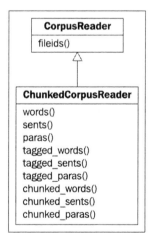

You can draw a `Tree` by calling the `draw()` method. Using the corpus reader defined earlier, you could do `reader.chunked_sents()[0].draw()` to get the same sentence tree diagram shown at the beginning of this recipe.

How it works...

`ChunkedCorpusReader` is similar to the `TaggedCorpusReader` from the last recipe. It has the same default `sent_tokenizer` and `para_block_reader`, but instead of a `word_tokenizer`, it uses a `str2chunktree()` function. The default is `nltk.chunk. util.tagstr2tree()`, which parses a sentence string containing bracketed chunks into a sentence tree, with each chunk as a noun phrase sub-tree. Words are split by whitespace, and the default word/tag separator is `'/'`. If you want to customize the chunk parsing, then you can pass in your own function for `str2chunktree()`.

There's more...

An alternative format for denoting chunks is called IOB tags. **IOB** tags are similar to part-of-speech tags, but provide a way to denote the inside, outside, and beginning of a chunk. They also have the benefit of allowing multiple different chunk phrase types, not just noun phrases. Here is an excerpt from the `conll2000` corpus. Each word is on its own line with a part-of-speech tag followed by an IOB tag.

```
Mr. NNP B-NP
Meador NNP I-NP
had VBD B-VP
been VBN I-VP
executive JJ B-NP
vice NN I-NP
president NN I-NP
of IN B-PP
Balcor NNP B-NP
. . O
```

`B-NP` denotes the beginning of a noun phrase, while `I-NP` denotes that the word is inside of the current noun phrase. `B-VP` and `I-VP` denote the beginning and inside of a verb phrase. `O` ends the sentence.

To read a corpus using the IOB format, you must use the `ConllChunkCorpusReader`. Each sentence is separated by a blank line, but there is no separation for paragraphs. This means that the `para_*` methods are not available. If you put the previous IOB example text into a file named `conll.iob`, you can create and use a `ConllChunkCorpusReader` with the code we are about to see. The third argument to `ConllChunkCorpusReader` should be a tuple or list specifying the types of chunks in the file, which in this case is (`'NP'`, `'VP'`, `'PP'`).

```
>>> from nltk.corpus.reader import ConllChunkCorpusReader
>>> conllreader = ConllChunkCorpusReader('.', r'.*\.iob', ('NP',
'VP', 'PP'))
>>> conllreader.chunked_words()
[Tree('NP', [('Mr.', 'NNP'), ('Meador', 'NNP')]), Tree('VP',
[('had', 'VBD'), ('been', 'VBN')]), ...]
>>> conllreader.chunked_sents()
[Tree('S', [Tree('NP', [('Mr.', 'NNP'), ('Meador', 'NNP')]),
Tree('VP', [('had', 'VBD'), ('been', 'VBN')]), Tree('NP',
[('executive', 'JJ'), ('vice', 'NN'), ('president', 'NN')]),
Tree('PP', [('of', 'IN')]), Tree('NP', [('Balcor', 'NNP')]), ('.',
'.')])]
>>> conllreader.iob_words()
[('Mr.', 'NNP', 'B-NP'), ('Meador', 'NNP', 'I-NP'), ...]
>>> conllreader.iob_sents()
[[('Mr.', 'NNP', 'B-NP'), ('Meador', 'NNP', 'I-NP'), ('had',
'VBD', 'B-VP'), ('been', 'VBN', 'I-VP'), ('executive', 'JJ', 'B-
NP'), ('vice', 'NN', 'I-NP'), ('president', 'NN', 'I-NP'), ('of',
'IN', 'B-PP'), ('Balcor', 'NNP', 'B-NP'), ('.', '.', 'O')]]
```

The previous code also shows the iob_words() and iob_sents() methods, which
return lists of three tuples of (word, pos, iob). The inheritance diagram for
ConllChunkCorpusReader looks like the following, with most of the methods implemented
by its superclass, ConllCorpusReader:

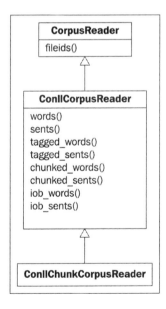

Tree leaves

When it comes to chunk trees, the leaves of a tree are the tagged tokens. So if you want to get a list of all the tagged tokens in a tree, call the `leaves()` method.

```
>>> reader.chunked_words()[0].leaves()
[('Earlier', 'JJR'), ('staff-reduction', 'NN'), ('moves', 'NNS')]
>>> reader.chunked_sents()[0].leaves()
[('Earlier', 'JJR'), ('staff-reduction', 'NN'), ('moves', 'NNS'),
('have', 'VBP'), ('trimmed', 'VBN'), ('about', 'IN'), ('300',
'CD'), ('jobs', 'NNS'), (',', ','), ('the', 'DT'), ('spokesman',
'NN'), ('said', 'VBD'), ('.', '.')]
>>> reader.chunked_paras()[0][0].leaves()
[('Earlier', 'JJR'), ('staff-reduction', 'NN'), ('moves', 'NNS'),
('have', 'VBP'), ('trimmed', 'VBN'), ('about', 'IN'), ('300',
'CD'), ('jobs', 'NNS'), (',', ','), ('the', 'DT'), ('spokesman',
'NN'), ('said', 'VBD'), ('.', '.')]
```

Treebank chunk corpus

The `nltk.corpus.treebank_chunk` corpus uses `ChunkedCorpusReader` to provide part-of-speech tagged words and noun phrase chunks of Wall Street Journal headlines. NLTK comes with a 5% sample from the Penn Treebank Project. You can find out more at `http://www.cis.upenn.edu/~treebank/home.html`.

CoNLL2000 corpus

CoNLL stands for the **Conference on Computational Natural Language Learning**. For the year 2000 conference, a shared task was undertaken to produce a corpus of chunks based on the Wall Street Journal corpus. In addition to noun phrases (NP), it also contains verb phrases (VP) and prepositional phrases (PP). This chunked corpus is available as `nltk.corpus.conll2000`, which is an instance of `ConllChunkCorpusReader`. You can read more at `http://www.cnts.ua.ac.be/conll2000/chunking/`.

See also

Chapter 5, Extracting Chunks will cover chunk extraction in detail. Also see the previous recipe for details on getting tagged tokens from a corpus reader.

Creating a categorized text corpus

If you have a large corpus of text, you may want to categorize it into separate sections. The brown corpus, for example, has a number of different categories.

```
>>> from nltk.corpus import brown
>>> brown.categories()
```

```
['adventure', 'belles_lettres', 'editorial', 'fiction',
'government', 'hobbies', 'humor', 'learned', 'lore', 'mystery',
'news', 'religion', 'reviews', 'romance', 'science_fiction']
```

In this recipe, we'll learn how to create our own categorized text corpus.

Getting ready

The easiest way to categorize a corpus is to have one file for each category. Following are two excerpts from the `movie_reviews` corpus:

`movie_pos.txt`

the thin red line is flawed but it provokes .

`movie_neg.txt`

a big-budget and glossy production can not make up for a lack of spontaneity that permeates their tv show .

With these two files, we'll have two categories: `pos` and `neg`.

How to do it...

We'll use the `CategorizedPlaintextCorpusReader`, which inherits from both `PlaintextCorpusReader` and `CategorizedCorpusReader`. These two superclasses require three arguments: the root directory, the `fileids`, and a category specification.

```
>>> from nltk.corpus.reader import
CategorizedPlaintextCorpusReader
>>> reader = CategorizedPlaintextCorpusReader('.', r'movie_.*\.
txt', cat_pattern=r'movie_(\w+)\.txt')
>>> reader.categories()
['neg', 'pos']
>>> reader.fileids(categories=['neg'])
['movie_neg.txt']
>>> reader.fileids(categories=['pos'])
['movie_pos.txt']
```

How it works...

The first two arguments to `CategorizedPlaintextCorpusReader` are the root directory and `fileids`, which are passed on to the `PlaintextCorpusReader` to read in the files. The `cat_pattern` keyword argument is a regular expression for extracting the category names from the `fileids`. In our case, the category is the part of the `fileid` after `movie_` and before `.txt`. **The category must be surrounded by grouping parenthesis**.

`cat_pattern` is passed to `CategorizedCorpusReader`, which overrides the common corpus reader functions such as `fileids()`, `words()`, `sents()`, and `paras()` to accept a `categories` keyword argument. This way, you could get all the pos sentences by calling `reader.sents(categories=['pos'])`. `CategorizedCorpusReader` also provides the `categories()` function, which returns a list of all known categories in the corpus.

`CategorizedPlaintextCorpusReader` is an example of using multiple-inheritance to join methods from multiple superclasses, as shown in the following diagram:

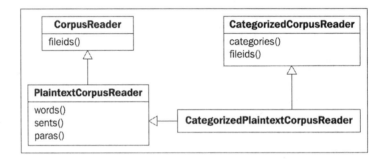

There's more...

Instead of `cat_pattern`, you could pass in a `cat_map`, which is a dictionary mapping a `fileid` to a list of category labels.

```
>>> reader = CategorizedPlaintextCorpusReader('.', r'movie_.*\.
txt', cat_map={'movie_pos.txt': ['pos'], 'movie_neg.txt':
['neg']})
>>> reader.categories()
['neg', 'pos']
```

Category file

A third way of specifying categories is to use the `cat_file` keyword argument to specify a filename containing a mapping of `fileid` to category. For example, the `brown` corpus has a file called `cats.txt` that looks like this:

```
ca44 news
cb01 editorial
```

The `reuters` corpus has files in multiple categories, and its `cats.txt` looks like this:

```
test/14840 rubber coffee lumber palm-oil veg-oil
test/14841 wheat grain
```

Categorized tagged corpus reader

The `brown` corpus reader is actually an instance of `CategorizedTaggedCorpusReader`, which inherits from `CategorizedCorpusReader` and `TaggedCorpusReader`. Just like in `CategorizedPlaintextCorpusReader`, it overrides all the methods of `TaggedCorpusReader` to allow a `categories` argument, so you can call `brown.tagged_sents(categories=['news'])` to get all the tagged sentences from the news category. You can use the `CategorizedTaggedCorpusReader` just like `CategorizedPlaintextCorpusReader` for your own categorized and tagged text corpora.

Categorized corpora

The `movie_reviews` corpus reader is an instance of `CategorizedPlaintextCorpusReader`, as is the `reuters` corpus reader. But where the `movie_reviews` corpus only has two categories (neg and pos), `reuters` has 90 categories. These corpora are often used for training and evaluating classifiers, which will be covered in *Chapter 7, Text Classification*.

See also

In the next recipe, we'll create a subclass of `CategorizedCorpusReader` and `ChunkedCorpusReader` for reading a categorized chunk corpus. Also see *Chapter 7, Text Classification* in which we use categorized text for classification.

Creating a categorized chunk corpus reader

NLTK provides a `CategorizedPlaintextCorpusReader` and `CategorizedTaggedCorpusReader`, but there's no categorized corpus reader for chunked corpora. So in this recipe, we're going to make one.

Getting ready

Refer to the earlier recipe, *Creating a chunked phrase corpus*, for an explanation of `ChunkedCorpusReader`, and to the previous recipe for details on `CategorizedPlaintextCorpusReader` and `CategorizedTaggedCorpusReader`, both of which inherit from `CategorizedCorpusReader`.

How to do it...

We'll create a class called `CategorizedChunkedCorpusReader` that inherits from both `CategorizedCorpusReader` and `ChunkedCorpusReader`. It is heavily based on the `CategorizedTaggedCorpusReader`, and also provides three additional methods for getting categorized chunks. The following code is found in `catchunked.py`:

```
from nltk.corpus.reader import CategorizedCorpusReader,
ChunkedCorpusReader

class CategorizedChunkedCorpusReader(CategorizedCorpusReader,
ChunkedCorpusReader):
  def __init__(self, *args, **kwargs):
    CategorizedCorpusReader.__init__(self, kwargs)
    ChunkedCorpusReader.__init__(self, *args, **kwargs)

  def _resolve(self, fileids, categories):
    if fileids is not None and categories is not None:
      raise ValueError('Specify fileids or categories, not both')
    if categories is not None:
      return self.fileids(categories)
    else:
      return fileids
```

All of the following methods call the corresponding function in `ChunkedCorpusReader` with the value returned from `_resolve()`. We'll start with the plain text methods.

```
  def raw(self, fileids=None, categories=None):
    return ChunkedCorpusReader.raw(self, self._resolve(fileids,
categories))

  def words(self, fileids=None, categories=None):
    return ChunkedCorpusReader.words(self, self._resolve(fileids,
categories))

  def sents(self, fileids=None, categories=None):
    return ChunkedCorpusReader.sents(self, self._resolve(fileids,
categories))

  def paras(self, fileids=None, categories=None):
```

```
    return ChunkedCorpusReader.paras(self, self._resolve(fileids,
categories))
```

Next comes the tagged text methods.

```
    def tagged_words(self, fileids=None, categories=None, simplify_
tags=False):
        return ChunkedCorpusReader.tagged_words(
            self, self._resolve(fileids, categories), simplify_tags)

    def tagged_sents(self, fileids=None, categories=None, simplify_
tags=False):
        return ChunkedCorpusReader.tagged_sents(
            self, self._resolve(fileids, categories), simplify_tags)

    def tagged_paras(self, fileids=None, categories=None, simplify_
tags=False):
        return ChunkedCorpusReader.tagged_paras(
            self, self._resolve(fileids, categories), simplify_tags)
```

And finally, the chunked methods, which is what we've really been after.

```
    def chunked_words(self, fileids=None, categories=None):
        return ChunkedCorpusReader.chunked_words(
            self, self._resolve(fileids, categories))

    def chunked_sents(self, fileids=None, categories=None):
        return ChunkedCorpusReader.chunked_sents(
            self, self._resolve(fileids, categories))

    def chunked_paras(self, fileids=None, categories=None):
        return ChunkedCorpusReader.chunked_paras(
            self, self._resolve(fileids, categories))
```

All these methods together give us a complete CategorizedChunkedCorpusReader.

How it works...

`CategorizedChunkedCorpusReader` overrides all the `ChunkedCorpusReader` methods to take a `categories` argument for locating `fileids`. These `fileids` are found with the internal `_resolve()` function. This `_resolve()` function makes use of `CategorizedCorpusReader.fileids()` to return `fileids` for a given list of `categories`. If no `categories` are given, `_resolve()` just returns the given `fileids`, which could be `None`, in which case all files are read. The initialization of both `CategorizedCorpusReader` and `ChunkedCorpusReader` is what makes this all possible. If you look at the code for `CategorizedTaggedCorpusReader`, you'll see it's very similar. The inheritance diagram looks like this:

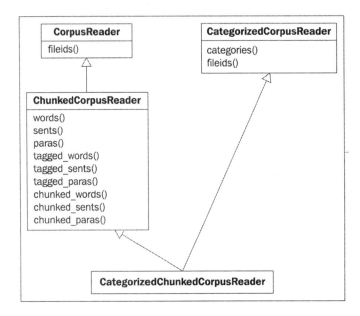

Here's some example code for using the `treebank` corpus. All we're doing is making categories out of the `fileids`, but the point is that you could use the same techniques to create your own categorized chunk corpus.

```
>>> import nltk.data
>>> from catchunked import CategorizedChunkedCorpusReader
>>> path = nltk.data.find('corpora/treebank/tagged')
>>> reader = CategorizedChunkedCorpusReader(path, r'wsj_.*\.pos',
cat_pattern=r'wsj_(.*)\.pos')
>>> len(reader.categories()) == len(reader.fileids())
True
>>> len(reader.chunked_sents(categories=['0001']))
16
```

We use `nltk.data.find()` to search the data directories to get a `FileSystemPathPointer` to the `treebank` corpus. All the `treebank` tagged files start with `wsj_` followed by a number, and end with `.pos`. The previous code turns that file number into a category.

There's more...

As covered in the *Creating a chunked phrase corpus* recipe, there's an alternative format and reader for a chunk corpus using IOB tags. To have a categorized corpus of IOB chunks, we have to make a new corpus reader.

Categorized Conll chunk corpus reader

Here's a subclass of `CategorizedCorpusReader` and `ConllChunkReader` called `CategorizedConllChunkCorpusReader`. It overrides all methods of `ConllCorpusReader` that take a `fileids` argument, so the methods can also take a `categories` argument. The `ConllChunkCorpusReader` is just a small subclass of `ConllCorpusReader` that handles initialization; most of the work is done in `ConllCorpusReader`. This code can also be found in `catchunked.py`.

```
from nltk.corpus.reader import CategorizedCorpusReader,
ConllCorpusReader, ConllChunkCorpusReader

class CategorizedConllChunkCorpusReader(CategorizedCorpusReader,
ConllChunkCorpusReader):
  def __init__(self, *args, **kwargs):
    CategorizedCorpusReader.__init__(self, kwargs)
    ConllChunkCorpusReader.__init__(self, *args, **kwargs)

  def _resolve(self, fileids, categories):
    if fileids is not None and categories is not None:
      raise ValueError('Specify fileids or categories, not both')
    if categories is not None:
      return self.fileids(categories)
    else:
      return fileids
```

All the following methods call the corresponding method of `ConllCorpusReader` with the value returned from `_resolve()`. We'll start with the plain text methods.

```
  def raw(self, fileids=None, categories=None):
    return ConllCorpusReader.raw(self, self._resolve(fileids,
categories))

  def words(self, fileids=None, categories=None):
```

```
        return ConllCorpusReader.words(self, self._resolve(fileids,
categories))

    def sents(self, fileids=None, categories=None):
        return ConllCorpusReader.sents(self, self._resolve(fileids,
categories))
```

The `ConllCorpusReader` does not recognize paragraphs, so there are no `*_paras()` methods. Next are the tagged and chunked methods.

```
    def tagged_words(self, fileids=None, categories=None):
        return ConllCorpusReader.tagged_words(self, self.
resolve(fileids, categories))

    def tagged_sents(self, fileids=None, categories=None):
        return ConllCorpusReader.tagged_sents(self, self.
resolve(fileids, categories))

    def chunked_words(self, fileids=None, categories=None, chunk_
types=None):
        return ConllCorpusReader.chunked_words(
          self, self._resolve(fileids, categories), chunk_types)

    def chunked_sents(self, fileids=None, categories=None, chunk_
types=None):
        return ConllCorpusReader.chunked_sents(
          self, self._resolve(fileids, categories), chunk_types)
```

For completeness, we must override the following methods of the `ConllCorpusReader`:

```
    def parsed_sents(self, fileids=None, categories=None, pos_in_
tree=None):
        return ConllCorpusReader.parsed_sents(
          self, self._resolve(fileids, categories), pos_in_tree)

    def srl_spans(self, fileids=None, categories=None):
        return ConllCorpusReader.srl_spans(self, self.
resolve(fileids, categories))

    def srl_instances(self, fileids=None, categories=None, pos_in_
tree=None, flatten=True):
        return ConllCorpusReader.srl_instances(
          self, self._resolve(fileids, categories), pos_in_tree,
flatten)
```

```
    def iob_words(self, fileids=None, categories=None):
        return ConllCorpusReader.iob_words(self, self._
resolve(fileids, categories))

    def iob_sents(self, fileids=None, categories=None):
        return ConllCorpusReader.iob_sents(self, self._
resolve(fileids, categories))
```

The inheritance diagram for this class is as follows:

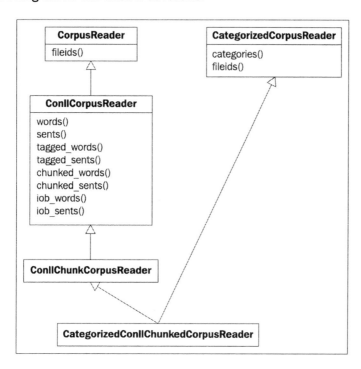

Following is some example code using the conll2000 corpus. Like with treebank, we're using the fileids for categories. The ConllChunkCorpusReader requires a third argument to specify the chunk_types. These chunk_types are used to parse the IOB tags. As you learned in the *Creating a chunked phrase corpus* recipe, the conll2000 corpus recognizes three chunk types:

- ▸ NP for noun phrases
- ▸ VP for verb phrases
- ▸ PP for prepositional phrases

```
>>> import nltk.data
>>> from catchunked import CategorizedConllChunkCorpusReader
```

```
>>> path = nltk.data.find('corpora/conll2000')
>>> reader = CategorizedConllChunkCorpusReader(path, r'.*\.txt',
('NP','VP','PP'), cat_pattern=r'(.*)\.txt')
>>> reader.categories()
['test', 'train']
>>> reader.fileids()
['test.txt', 'train.txt']
>>> len(reader.chunked_sents(categories=['test']))
2012
```

See also

In the *Creating a chunked phrase corpus* recipe in this chapter, we covered both the `ChunkedCorpusReader` and `ConllChunkCorpusReader`. And in the previous recipe, we covered `CategorizedPlaintextCorpusReader` and `CategorizedTaggedCorpusReader`, which share the same superclass used by `CategorizedChunkedCorpusReader` and `CategorizedConllChunkReader`—`CategorizedCorpusReader`.

Lazy corpus loading

Loading a corpus reader can be an expensive operation due to the number of files, file sizes, and various initialization tasks. And while you'll often want to specify a corpus reader in a common module, you don't always need to access it right away. To speed up module import time when a corpus reader is defined, NLTK provides a `LazyCorpusLoader` class that can transform itself into your actual corpus reader as soon as you need it. This way, you can define a corpus reader in a common module without it slowing down module loading.

How to do it...

`LazyCorpusLoader` requires two arguments: the `name` of the corpus and the corpus reader class, plus any other arguments needed to initialize the corpus reader class.

The `name` argument specifies the root directory name of the corpus, which must be within a `corpora` subdirectory of one of the paths in `nltk.data.path`. See the first recipe of this chapter, *Setting up a custom corpus*, for more details on `nltk.data.path`.

For example, if you have a custom corpora named `cookbook` in your local `nltk_data` directory, its path would be `~/nltk_data/corpora/cookbook`. You'd then pass `'cookbook'` to `LazyCorpusLoader` as the `name`, and `LazyCorpusLoader` will look in `~/nltk_data/corpora` for a directory named `'cookbook'`.

The second argument to `LazyCorpusLoader` is `reader_cls`, which should be the name of a subclass of `CorpusReader`, such as `WordListCorpusReader`. You will also need to pass in any other arguments required by the `reader_cls` for initialization. This will be demonstrated as follows, using the same `wordlist` file we created in the earlier recipe, *Creating a word list corpus*. The third argument to `LazyCorpusLoader` is the list of filenames and `fileids` that will be passed in to `WordListCorpusReader` at initialization.

```
>>> from nltk.corpus.util import LazyCorpusLoader
>>> from nltk.corpus.reader import WordListCorpusReader
>>> reader = LazyCorpusLoader('cookbook', WordListCorpusReader,
['wordlist'])
>>> isinstance(reader, LazyCorpusLoader)
True
>>> reader.fileids()
['wordlist']
>>> isinstance(reader, LazyCorpusLoader)
False
>>> isinstance(reader, WordListCorpusReader)
True
```

How it works...

`LazyCorpusLoader` stores all the arguments given, but otherwise does nothing until you try to access an attribute or method. This way initialization is very fast, eliminating the overhead of loading the corpus reader immediately. As soon as you do access an attribute or method, it does the following:

1. Calls `nltk.data.find('corpora/%s' % name)` to find the corpus data root directory.
2. Instantiate the corpus reader class with the root directory and any other arguments.
3. Transforms itself into the corpus reader class.

So in the previous example code, before we call `reader.fileids()`, `reader` is an instance of `LazyCorpusLoader`, but after the call, `reader` is an instance of `WordListCorpusReader`.

There's more...

All of the corpora included with NLTK and defined in `nltk.corpus` are initially an instance of `LazyCorpusLoader`. Here's some code from `nltk.corpus` defining the `treebank` corpora.

```
treebank = LazyCorpusLoader(
    'treebank/combined', BracketParseCorpusReader, r'wsj_.*\.mrg',
```

```
        tag_mapping_function=simplify_wsj_tag)
    treebank_chunk = LazyCorpusLoader(
        'treebank/tagged', ChunkedCorpusReader, r'wsj_.*\.pos',
        sent_tokenizer=RegexpTokenizer(r'(?<=/\.)\s*(?![^\[]*\])',
    gaps=True),
        para_block_reader=tagged_treebank_para_block_reader)
    treebank_raw = LazyCorpusLoader(
        'treebank/raw', PlaintextCorpusReader, r'wsj_.*')
```

As you can see, any number of additional arguments can be passed through by
LazyCorpusLoader to its reader_cls.

Creating a custom corpus view

A **corpus view** is a class wrapper around a corpus file that reads in blocks of tokens as
needed. Its purpose is to provide a *view* into a file without reading the whole file at once (since
corpus files can often be quite large). If the corpus readers included by NLTK already meet
all your needs, then you do not have to know anything about corpus views. But, if you have a
custom file format that needs special handling, this recipe will show you how to create and
use a custom corpus view. The main corpus view class is StreamBackedCorpusView, which
opens a single file as a *stream*, and maintains an internal cache of blocks it has read.

Blocks of tokens are read in with a *block reader* function. A **block** can be any piece of text,
such as a paragraph or a line, and **tokens** are parts of a block, such as individual words.
In the *Creating a part-of-speech tagged word corpus* recipe, we discussed the default
para_block_reader function of the TaggedCorpusReader, which reads lines from
a file until it finds a blank line, then returns those lines as a single paragraph token. The
actual block reader function is: nltk.corpus.reader.util.read_blankline_block.
TaggedCorpusReader passes this block reader function into a TaggedCorpusView
whenever it needs to read blocks from a file. TaggedCorpusView is a subclass of
StreamBackedCorpusView that knows to split paragraphs of "word/tag" into (word,
tag) tuples.

How to do it...

We'll start with the simple case of a plain text file with a heading that should be ignored by the
corpus reader. Let's make a file called heading_text.txt that looks like this:

```
A simple heading
Here is the actual text for the corpus.
Paragraphs are split by blanklines.
This is the 3rd paragraph.
```

Normally we'd use the `PlaintextCorpusReader` but, by default, it will treat `A simple heading` as the first paragraph. To ignore this heading, we need to subclass the `PlaintextCorpusReader` so we can override its `CorpusView` class variable with our own `StreamBackedCorpusView` subclass. This code is found in `corpus.py`.

```
from nltk.corpus.reader import PlaintextCorpusReader
from nltk.corpus.reader.util import StreamBackedCorpusView

class IgnoreHeadingCorpusView(StreamBackedCorpusView):
  def __init__(self, *args, **kwargs):
    StreamBackedCorpusView.__init__(self, *args, **kwargs)
    # open self._stream
    self._open()
    # skip the heading block
    self.read_block(self._stream)
    # reset the start position to the current position in the
stream
    self._filepos = [self._stream.tell()]

class IgnoreHeadingCorpusReader(PlaintextCorpusReader):
  CorpusView = IgnoreHeadingCorpusView
```

To demonstrate that this works as expected, here's the code showing that the default `PlaintextCorpusReader` finds four paragraphs, while our `IgnoreHeadingCorpusReader` only has three paragraphs.

```
>>> from nltk.corpus.reader import PlaintextCorpusReader
>>> plain = PlaintextCorpusReader('.', ['heading_text.txt'])
>>> len(plain.paras())
4
>>> from corpus import IgnoreHeadingCorpusReader
>>> reader = IgnoreHeadingCorpusReader('.', ['heading_text.txt'])
>>> len(reader.paras())
3
```

How it works...

The `PlaintextCorpusReader` by design has a `CorpusView` class variable that can be overridden by subclasses. So we do just that, and make our `IgnoreHeadingCorpusView` the `CorpusView`.

Most corpus readers do not have a `CorpusView` class variable because they require very specific corpus views.

The `IgnoreHeadingCorpusView` is a subclass of `StreamBackedCorpusView` that does the following on initialization:

1. Open the file using `self._open()`. This function is defined by `StreamBackedCorpusView`, and sets the internal instance variable `self._stream` to the opened file.

2. Read one block with `read_blankline_block()`, which will read the heading as a paragraph, and move the stream's file position forward to the next block.

3. Reset the start file position to the current position of `self._stream`. `self._filepos` is an internal index of where each block is in the file.

Here's a diagram illustrating the relationships between the classes:

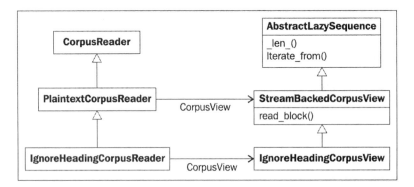

There's more...

Corpus views can get a lot fancier and more complicated, but the core concept is the same: read *blocks* from a `stream` to return a list of *tokens*. There are a number of block readers provided in `nltk.corpus.reader.util`, but you can always create your own. If you do want to define your own block reader function, then you have two choices on how to implement it:

1. Define it as a separate function and pass it in to `StreamBackedCorpusView` as `block_reader`. This is a good option if your block reader is fairly simple, reusable, and doesn't require any outside variables or configuration.

2. Subclass `StreamBackedCorpusView` and override the `read_block()` method. This is what many custom corpus views do because the block reading is highly specialized and requires additional functions and configuration, usually provided by the corpus reader when the corpus view is initialized.

Block reader functions

Following is a survey of most of the included block readers in `nltk.corpus.reader.util`. Unless otherwise noted, each block reader function takes a single argument: the `stream` to read from.

- `read_whitespace_block()` will read 20 lines from the stream, splitting each line into tokens by whitespace.

- `read_wordpunct_block()` reads 20 lines from the stream, splitting each line using `nltk.tokenize.wordpunct_tokenize()`.

- `read_line_block()` reads 20 lines from the stream and returns them as a list, with each line as a token.

- `read_blankline_block()` will read lines from the stream until it finds a blank line. It will then return a single token of all lines found combined into a single string.

- `read_regexp_block()` takes two additional arguments, which must be regular expressions that can be passed to `re.match()`: a `start_re` and `end_re`. `start_re` matches the starting line of a block, and `end_re` matches the ending line of the block. `end_re` defaults to `None`, in which case the block will end as soon as a new `start_re` match is found. The return value is a single token of all lines in the block joined into a single string.

Pickle corpus view

If you want to have a corpus of pickled objects, you can use the `PickleCorpusView`, a subclass of `StreamBackedCorpusView` found in `nltk.corpus.reader.util`. A file consists of blocks of pickled objects, and can be created with the `PickleCorpusView.write()` class method, which takes a sequence of objects and an output file, then pickles each object using `pickle.dump()` and writes it to the file. It overrides the `read_block()` method to return a list of unpickled objects from the stream, using `pickle.load()`.

Concatenated corpus view

Also found in `nltk.corpus.reader.util` is the `ConcatenatedCorpusView`. This class is useful if you have multiple files that you want a corpus reader to treat as a single file. A `ConcatenatedCorpusView` is created by giving it a list of `corpus_views`, which are then iterated over as if they were a single view.

See also

The concept of block readers was introduced in the *Creating a part-of-speech tagged word corpus* recipe in this chapter.

Creating a MongoDB backed corpus reader

All the corpus readers we've dealt with so far have been file-based. That is in part due to the design of the `CorpusReader` base class, and also the assumption that most corpus data will be in text files. But sometimes you'll have a bunch of data stored in a database that you want to access and use just like a text file corpus. In this recipe, we'll cover the case where you have documents in MongoDB, and you want to use a particular field of each document as your block of text.

Getting ready

MongoDB is a document-oriented database that has become a popular alternative to relational databases such as MySQL. The installation and setup of MongoDB is outside the scope of this book, but you can find instructions at `http://www.mongodb.org/display/DOCS/Quickstart`.

You'll also need to install PyMongo, a Python driver for MongoDB. You should be able to do this with either `easy_install` or `pip`, by doing `sudo easy_install pymongo` or `sudo pip install pymongo`.

The code in the *How to do it...* section assumes that your database is on `localhost` port `27017`, which is the MongoDB default configuration, and that you'll be using the `test` database with a collection named `corpus` that contains documents with a `text` field. Explanations for these arguments are available in the PyMongo documentation at `http://api.mongodb.org/python/`.

How to do it...

Since the `CorpusReader` class assumes you have a file-based corpus, we can't directly subclass it. Instead, we're going to emulate both the `StreamBackedCorpusView` and `PlaintextCorpusReader`. `StreamBackedCorpusView` is a subclass of `nltk.util.AbstractLazySequence`, so we'll subclass `AbstractLazySequence` to create a MongoDB view, and then create a new class that will use the view to provide functionality similar to the `PlaintextCorpusReader`. This code is found in `mongoreader.py`.

```
import pymongo
from nltk.data import LazyLoader
from nltk.tokenize import TreebankWordTokenizer
from nltk.util import AbstractLazySequence, LazyMap,
LazyConcatenation
class MongoDBLazySequence(AbstractLazySequence):
  def __init__(self, host='localhost', port=27017, db='test',
collection='corpus', field='text'):
    self.conn = pymongo.Connection(host, port)
    self.collection = self.conn[db][collection]
    self.field = field
  def __len__(self):
    return self.collection.count()
  def iterate_from(self, start):
    f = lambda d: d.get(self.field, '')
    return iter(LazyMap(f, self.collection.find(fields=[self.
field], skip=start)))
class MongoDBCorpusReader(object):
  def __init__(self, word_tokenizer=TreebankWordTokenizer(),
        sent_tokenizer=LazyLoader('tokenizers/punkt/english.
pickle'),
        **kwargs):
    self._seq = MongoDBLazySequence(**kwargs)
    self._word_tokenize = word_tokenizer.tokenize
    self._sent_tokenize = sent_tokenizer.tokenize
  def text(self):
    return self._seq
  def words(self):
    return LazyConcatenation(LazyMap(self._word_tokenize, self.
text()))
  def sents(self):
    return LazyConcatenation(LazyMap(self._sent_tokenize, self.
text()))
```

How it works...

`AbstractLazySequence` is an abstract class that provides read-only, on-demand iteration. Subclasses must implement the `__len__()` and `iterate_from(start)` methods, while it provides the rest of the list and iterator emulation methods. By creating the `MongoDBLazySequence` subclass as our view, we can iterate over documents in the MongoDB collection on-demand, without keeping all the documents in memory. `LazyMap` is a lazy version of Python's built-in `map()` function, and is used in `iterate_from()` to transform the document into the specific field that we're interested in. It's also a subclass of `AbstractLazySequence`.

The `MongoDBCorpusReader` creates an internal instance of `MongoDBLazySequence` for iteration, then defines the word and sentence tokenization methods. The `text()` method simply returns the instance of `MongoDBLazySequence`, which results in a lazily evaluated list of each text field. The `words()` method uses `LazyMap` and `LazyConcatenation` to return a lazily evaluated list of all words, while the `sents()` method does the same for sentences. The `sent_tokenizer` is loaded on demand with `LazyLoader`, which is a wrapper around `nltk.data.load()`, analogous to `LazyCorpusLoader`. `LazyConcatentation` is a subclass of `AbstractLazySequence` too, and produces a flat list from a given list of lists (each list may also be lazy). In our case, we're concatenating the results of `LazyMap` to ensure we don't return nested lists.

There's more...

All of the parameters are configurable. For example, if you had a `db` named `website`, with a `collection` named `comments`, whose documents had a `field` called `comment`, you could create a `MongoDBCorpusReader` as follows:

```
>>> reader = MongoDBCorpusReader(db='website',
collection='comments', field='comment')
```

You can also pass in custom instances for `word_tokenizer` and `sent_tokenizer`, as long as the objects implement the `nltk.tokenize.TokenizerI` interface by providing a `tokenize(text)` method.

See also

Corpus views were covered in the previous recipe, and tokenization was covered in *Chapter 1, Tokenizing Text and WordNet Basics*.

Corpus editing with file locking

Corpus readers and views are all read-only, but there may be times when you want to add to or edit the corpus files. However, modifying a corpus file while other processes are using it, such as through a corpus reader, can lead to dangerous undefined behavior. This is where file locking comes in handy.

Getting ready

You must install the `lockfile` library using `sudo easy_install lockfile` or `sudo pip install lockfile`. This library provides cross-platform file locking, and so will work on Windows, Unix/Linux, Mac OX, and more. You can find detailed documentation on `lockfile` at `http://packages.python.org/lockfile/`.

For the following code to work, you must also have Python 2.6. Versions 2.4 and earlier do not support the `with` keyword.

How to do it...

Here are two file editing functions: `append_line()` and `remove_line()`. Both try to acquire an *exclusive lock* on the file before updating it. An **exclusive lock** means that these functions will wait until no other process is reading from or writing to the file. Once the lock is acquired, any other process that tries to access the file will have to wait until the lock is released. This way, modifying the file will be safe and not cause any undefined behavior in other processes. These functions can be found in `corpus.py`.

```
import lockfile, tempfile, shutil

def append_line(fname, line):
  with lockfile.FileLock(fname):
    fp = open(fname, 'a+')
    fp.write(line)
    fp.write('\n')
    fp.close()

def remove_line(fname, line):
  with lockfile.FileLock(fname):
    tmp = tempfile.TemporaryFile()
    fp = open(fname, 'r+')
    # write all lines from orig file, except if matches given line
    for l in fp:
      if l.strip() != line:
        tmp.write(l)
```

```
# reset file pointers so entire files are copied
fp.seek(0)
tmp.seek(0)
# copy tmp into fp, then truncate to remove trailing line(s)
shutil.copyfileobj(tmp, fp)
fp.truncate()
fp.close()
tmp.close()
```

The lock acquiring and releasing happens transparently when you do `with lockfile.FileLock(fname)`.

Instead of using `with lockfile.FileLock(fname)`, you can also get a lock by calling `lock = lockfile.FileLock(fname)`, then call `lock.acquire()` to acquire the lock, and `lock.release()` to release the lock. This alternative usage is compatible with Python 2.4.

How it works...

You can use these functions as follows:

```
>>> from corpus import append_line, remove_line
>>> append_line('test.txt', 'foo')
>>> remove_line('test.txt', 'foo')
```

In `append_line()`, a lock is acquired, the file is opened in *append mode*, the text is written along with an end-of-line character, and then the file is closed, releasing the lock.

A lock acquired by `lockfile` only protects the file from other processes that also use `lockfile`. In other words, just because your Python process has a lock with `lockfile`, doesn't mean a non-Python process can't modify the file. For this reason, it's best to only use `lockfile` with files that will not be edited by any non-Python processes, or Python processes that do not use `lockfile`.

The `remove_line()` function is a bit more complicated. Because we're removing a line and not a specific section of the file, we need to iterate over the file to find each instance of the line to remove. The easiest way to do this while writing the changes back to the file, is to use a `TemporaryFile` to hold the changes, then copy that file back into the original file using `shutil.copyfileobj()`.

These functions are best suited for a word list corpus, or some other corpus type with presumably unique lines, that may be edited by multiple people at about the same time, such as through a web interface. Using these functions with a more document-oriented corpus such as `brown`, `treebank`, or `conll2000`, is probably a bad idea.

4
Part-of-Speech Tagging

In this chapter, we will cover:

- ▸ Default tagging
- ▸ Training a unigram part-of-speech tagger
- ▸ Combining taggers with backoff tagging
- ▸ Training and combining Ngram taggers
- ▸ Creating a model of likely word tags
- ▸ Tagging with regular expressions
- ▸ Affix tagging
- ▸ Training a Brill tagger
- ▸ Training the TnT tagger
- ▸ Using WordNet for tagging
- ▸ Tagging proper names
- ▸ Classifier-based tagging

Introduction

Part-of-speech tagging is the process of converting a sentence, in the form of a list of words, into a list of tuples, where each tuple is of the form (word, tag). The **tag** is a part-of-speech tag and signifies whether the word is a noun, adjective, verb, and so on.

Most of the taggers we will cover are *trainable*. They use a list of tagged sentences as their training data, such as what you get from the tagged_sents() function of a TaggedCorpusReader (see the *Creating a part-of-speech tagged word corpus* recipe in *Chapter 3, Creating Custom Corpora* for more details). With these training sentences, the tagger generates an internal model that will tell them how to tag a word. Other taggers use external data sources or match word patterns to choose a tag for a word.

All taggers in NLTK are in the nltk.tag package and inherit from the TaggerI base class. TaggerI requires all subclasses to implement a tag() method, which takes a list of words as input, and returns a list of tagged words as output. TaggerI also provides an evaluate() method for evaluating the accuracy of the tagger (covered at the end of the *Default tagging* recipe). Many taggers can also be combined into a backoff chain, so that if one tagger cannot tag a word, the next tagger is used, and so on.

Part-of-speech tagging is a necessary step before *chunking*, which is covered in *Chapter 5, Extracting Chunks*. Without the part-of-speech tags, a chunker cannot know how to extract phrases from a sentence. But with part-of-speech tags, you can tell a chunker how to identify phrases based on tag patterns.

Default tagging

Default tagging provides a baseline for part-of-speech tagging. It simply assigns the same part-of-speech tag to every token. We do this using the DefaultTagger.

Getting ready

We are going to use the treebank corpus for most of this chapter because it's a common standard and is quick to load and test. But everything we do should apply equally well to brown, conll2000, and any other part-of-speech tagged corpus.

How to do it...

The DefaultTagger takes a single argument—the tag you want to apply. We will give it 'NN', which is the tag for a singular noun.

```
>>> from nltk.tag import DefaultTagger
>>> tagger = DefaultTagger('NN')
```

```
>>> tagger.tag(['Hello', 'World'])
[('Hello', 'NN'), ('World', 'NN')]
```

Every tagger has a `tag()` method that takes a list of tokens, where each token is a single word. This list of tokens is usually a list of words produced by a word tokenizer (see *Chapter 1, Tokenizing Text and WordNet Basics* for more on tokenization). As you can see, `tag()` returns a list of tagged tokens, where a **tagged token** is a tuple of `(word, tag)`.

How it works...

`DefaultTagger` is a subclass of `SequentialBackoffTagger`. Every subclass of `SequentialBackoffTagger` must implement the `choose_tag()` method, which takes three arguments:

1. The list of `tokens`.
2. The `index` of the current token whose tag we want to choose.
3. The `history`, which is a list of the previous tags.

`SequentialBackoffTagger` implements the `tag()` method, which calls the `choose_tag()` of the subclass for each index in the tokens list, while accumulating a history of the previously tagged tokens. This history is the reason for the *Sequential* in `SequentialBackoffTagger`. We will get to the *Backoff* portion of the name in the *Combining taggers with backoff tagging* recipe. The following is a diagram showing the inheritance tree:

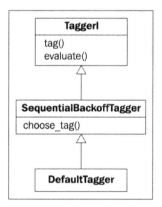

The `choose_tag()` method of `DefaultTagger` is very simple—it returns the tag we gave it at initialization time. It does not care about the current token or the history.

There's more...

There are a lot of different tags you could give to the `DefaultTagger`. You can find a complete list of possible tags for the `treebank` corpus at `http://www.ling.upenn.edu/courses/Fall_2003/ling001/penn_treebank_pos.html`. These tags are also documented in *Appendix, Penn Treebank Part-of-Speech Tags*.

Evaluating accuracy

To know how accurate a tagger is, you can use the `evaluate()` method, which takes a list of tagged tokens as a gold standard to evaluate the tagger. Using our default tagger created earlier, we can evaluate it against a subset of the `treebank` corpus tagged sentences.

```
>>> from nltk.corpus import treebank
>>> test_sents = treebank.tagged_sents()[3000:]
>>> tagger.evaluate(test_sents)
0.14331966328512843
```

So by just choosing `'NN'` for every tag, we can achieve 14% accuracy testing on ¼th of the `treebank` corpus. We will be reusing these same `test_sents` for evaluating more taggers in upcoming recipes.

Batch tagging sentences

`TaggerI` also implements a `batch_tag()` method that can be used to tag a list of sentences, instead of a single sentence. Here's an example of tagging two simple sentences:

```
>>> tagger.batch_tag([['Hello', 'world', '.'], ['How', 'are', 'you',
'?']])
[[('Hello', 'NN'), ('world', 'NN'), ('.', 'NN')], [('How', 'NN'),
('are', 'NN'), ('you', 'NN'), ('?', 'NN')]]
```

The result is a list of two tagged sentences, and of course every tag is NN because we are using the `DefaultTagger`. The `batch_tag()` method can be quite useful if you have many sentences you wish to tag all at once.

Untagging a tagged sentence

Tagged sentences can be untagged using `nltk.tag.untag()`. Calling this function with a tagged sentence will return a list of words without the tags.

```
>>> from nltk.tag import untag
>>> untag([('Hello', 'NN'), ('World', 'NN')])
['Hello', 'World']
```

See also

For more on tokenization, see *Chapter 1, Tokenizing Text and WordNet Basics*. And to learn more about tagged sentences, see the *Creating a part-of-speech tagged word corpus* recipe in *Chapter 3, Creating Custom Corpora*. For a complete list of part-of-speech tags found in the treebank corpus, see *Appendix, Penn Treebank Part-of-Speech Tags*.

Training a unigram part-of-speech tagger

A **unigram** generally refers to a single token. Therefore, a *unigram tagger* only uses a single word as its *context* for determining the part-of-speech tag.

The UnigramTagger inherits from NgramTagger, which is a subclass of ContextTagger, which inherits from SequentialBackoffTagger. In other words, the UnigramTagger is a *context-based tagger* whose context is a single word, or unigram.

How to do it...

UnigramTagger can be trained by giving it a list of tagged sentences at initialization.

```
>>> from nltk.tag import UnigramTagger
>>> from nltk.corpus import treebank
>>> train_sents = treebank.tagged_sents()[:3000]
>>> tagger = UnigramTagger(train_sents)
>>> treebank.sents()[0]
['Pierre', 'Vinken', ',', '61', 'years', 'old', ',', 'will', 'join',
'the', 'board', 'as', 'a', 'nonexecutive', 'director', 'Nov.', '29',
'.']
>>> tagger.tag(treebank.sents()[0])
[('Pierre', 'NNP'), ('Vinken', 'NNP'), (',', ','), ('61', 'CD'),
('years', 'NNS'), ('old', 'JJ'), (',', ','), ('will', 'MD'), ('join',
'VB'), ('the', 'DT'), ('board', 'NN'), ('as', 'IN'), ('a', 'DT'),
('nonexecutive', 'JJ'), ('director', 'NN'), ('Nov.', 'NNP'), ('29',
'CD'), ('.', '.')]
```

We use the first 3,000 tagged sentences of the treebank corpus as the training set to initialize the UnigramTagger. Then we see the first sentence as a list of words, and can see how it is transformed by the tag() function into a list of tagged tokens.

How it works...

The `UnigramTagger` builds a *context model* from the list of tagged sentences. Because `UnigramTagger` inherits from `ContextTagger`, instead of providing a `choose_tag()` method, it must implement a `context()` method, which takes the same three arguments as `choose_tag()`. The result of `context()` is, in this case, the word token. The context token is used to create the model, and also to look up the best tag once the model is created. Here's an inheritance diagram showing each class, starting at `SequentialBackoffTagger`:

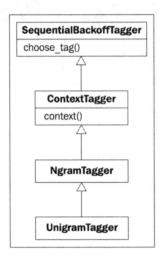

Let's see how accurate the `UnigramTagger` is on the test sentences (see the previous recipe for how `test_sents` is created).

```
>>> tagger.evaluate(test_sents)
0.85763004532700193
```

It has almost 86% accuracy for a tagger that only uses single word lookup to determine the part-of-speech tag. All accuracy gains from here on will be much smaller.

There's more...

The model building is actually implemented in `ContextTagger`. Given the list of tagged sentences, it calculates the frequency that a tag has occurred for each context. The tag with the highest frequency for a context is stored in the model.

Overriding the context model

All taggers that inherit from ContextTagger can take a pre-built model instead of training their own. This model is simply a Python dict mapping a context key to a tag. The context keys will depend on what the ContextTagger subclass returns from its context() method. For UnigramTagger, context keys are individual words. But for other NgramTagger subclasses, the context keys will be tuples.

Here's an example where we pass a very simple model to the UnigramTagger instead of a training set:

```
>>> tagger = UnigramTagger(model={'Pierre': 'NN'})
>>> tagger.tag(treebank.sents()[0])
[('Pierre', 'NN'), ('Vinken', None), (',', None), ('61', None),
('years', None), ('old', None), (',', None), ('will', None), ('join',
None), ('the', None), ('board', None), ('as', None), ('a', None),
('nonexecutive', None),('director', None), ('Nov.', None), ('29',
None), ('.', None)]
```

Since the model only contained the context key, 'Pierre', only the first word got a tag. Every other word got None as the tag since the context word was not in the model. So unless you know exactly what you are doing, let the tagger train its own model instead of passing in your own.

One good case for passing a self-created model to the UnigramTagger is for when you have a dictionary of words and tags, and you know that every word should always map to its tag. Then, you can put this UnigramTagger as your first backoff tagger (covered in the next recipe), to look up tags for unambiguous words.

Minimum frequency cutoff

The ContextTagger uses frequency of occurrence to decide which tag is most likely for a given context. By default, it will do this even if the context word and tag occurs only once. If you would like to set a minimum frequency threshold, then you can pass a cutoff value to the UnigramTagger.

```
>>> tagger = UnigramTagger(train_sents, cutoff=3)
>>> tagger.evaluate(test_sents)
0.775350744657889
```

In this case, using cutoff=3 has decreased accuracy, but there may be times when a cutoff is a good idea.

In the next recipe, we will cover backoff tagging to combine taggers. And in the *Creating a model of likely word tags* recipe, we will learn how to statistically determine tags for very common words.

Combining taggers with backoff tagging

Backoff tagging is one of the core features of SequentialBackoffTagger. It allows you to chain taggers together so that if one tagger doesn't know how to tag a word, it can pass the word on to the next backoff tagger. If that one can't do it, it can pass the word on to the next backoff tagger, and so on until there are no backoff taggers left to check.

How to do it...

Every subclass of SequentialBackoffTagger can take a backoff keyword argument whose value is another instance of a SequentialBackoffTagger. So we will use the DefaultTagger from the *Default tagging* recipe as the backoff to the UnigramTagger from the *Training a unigram part-of-speech tagger* recipe. Refer to both recipes for details on train_sents and test_sents.

```
>>> tagger1 = DefaultTagger('NN')
>>> tagger2 = UnigramTagger(train_sents, backoff=tagger1)
>>> tagger2.evaluate(test_sents)
0.87459529462551266
```

By using a default tag of NN whenever the UnigramTagger is unable to tag a word, we have increased the accuracy by almost 2%!

How it works...

When a SequentialBackoffTagger is initialized, it creates an internal list of backoff taggers with itself as the first element. If a backoff tagger is given, then the backoff tagger's internal list of taggers is appended. Here's some code to illustrate this:

```
>>> tagger1._taggers == [tagger1]
True
>>> tagger2._taggers == [tagger2, tagger1]
True
```

The _taggers is the internal list of backoff taggers that the Sequentia̶l̶
uses when the tag() method is called. It goes through its list of taggers, cal̶
tag() on each one. As soon as a tag is found, it stops and returns that tag. Thi̶s̶
if the primary tagger can tag the word, then that's the tag that will be returned. But̶
None, then the next tagger is tried, and so on until a tag is found, or else None is retur̶
course, None will never be returned if your final backoff tagger is a DefaultTagger.

There's more...

While most of the taggers included in NLTK are subclasses of SequentialBackoffTagger, not all of them are. There's a few taggers that we will cover in later recipes that cannot be used as part of a backoff tagging chain, such as the BrillTagger. However, these taggers generally take another tagger to use as a baseline, and a SequentialBackoffTagger is often a good choice for that baseline.

Pickling and unpickling a trained tagger

Since training a tagger can take a while, and you generally only need to do the training once, pickling a trained tagger is a useful way to save it for later usage. If your trained tagger is called tagger, then here's how to dump and load it with pickle:

```
>>> import pickle
>>> f = open('tagger.pickle', 'w')
>>> pickle.dump(tagger, f)
>>> f.close()
>>> f = open('tagger.pickle', 'r')
>>> tagger = pickle.load(f)
```

If your tagger pickle file is located in a NLTK data directory, you could also use nltk.data. load('tagger.pickle') to load the tagger.

See also

In the next recipe, we will combine more taggers with backoff tagging. Also see the previous two recipes for details on the DefaultTagger and UnigramTagger.

Training and combining Ngram taggers

In addition to UnigramTagger, there are two more NgramTagger subclasses: BigramTagger and TrigramTagger. BigramTagger uses the previous tag as part of its context, while TrigramTagger uses the previous two tags. An **ngram** is a subsequence of *n* items, so the BigramTagger looks at two items (the previous tag and word), and the TrigramTagger looks at three items.

ndling words whose part-of-speech tag is context dependent.
of-speech depending on how they are used. For example,
rs that "tag" words. In this case, "tag" is used as a verb. But
peech tag, so "tag" can also be a noun. The idea with the
t by looking at the previous words and part-of-speech tags,
speech tag for the current word.

this chapter for details on constructing `train_sents` and

By themselves, `BigramTagger` and `TrigramTagger` perform quite poorly. This is partly because they cannot learn context from the first word(s) in a sentence.

```
>>> from nltk.tag import BigramTagger, TrigramTagger
>>> bitagger = BigramTagger(train_sents)
>>> bitagger.evaluate(test_sents)
0.11336067342974315
>>> tritagger = TrigramTagger(train_sents)
>>> tritagger.evaluate(test_sents)
0.0688107058061731
```

Where they can make a contribution is when we combine them with backoff tagging. This time, instead of creating each tagger individually, we will create a function that will take `train_sents`, a list of `SequentialBackoffTagger` classes, and an optional final backoff tagger, and then train each tagger with the previous tagger as a backoff. Here's code from `tag_util.py`:

```
def backoff_tagger(train_sents, tagger_classes, backoff=None):
    for cls in tagger_classes:
        backoff = cls(train_sents, backoff=backoff)
    return backoff
```

And to use it, we can do the following:

```
>>> from tag_util import backoff_tagger
>>> backoff = DefaultTagger('NN')
>>> tagger = backoff_tagger(train_sents, [UnigramTagger, BigramTagger, TrigramTagger], backoff=backoff)
>>> tagger.evaluate(test_sents)
0.88163177206993304
```

So we have gained almost 1% accuracy by including the `BigramTagger` and `TrigramTagger` in the backoff chain. For corpora other than `treebank`, the accuracy gain may be more significant.

How it works...

The `backoff_tagger` function creates an instance of each tagger class in the list, giving it the `train_sents` and the previous tagger as a backoff. The order of the list of tagger classes is quite important—the first class in the list will be trained first, and be given the initial backoff tagger. This tagger will then become the backoff tagger for the next tagger class in the list. The final tagger returned will be an instance of the last tagger class in the list. Here's some code to clarify this chain:

```
>>> tagger._taggers[-1] == backoff
True
>>> isinstance(tagger._taggers[0], TrigramTagger)
True
>>> isinstance(tagger._taggers[1], BigramTagger)
True
```

So we end up with a `TrigramTagger`, whose first backoff is a `BigramTagger`. Then the next backoff will be a `UnigramTagger`, whose backoff is the `DefaultTagger`.

There's more...

The `backoff_tagger` function doesn't just work with `NgramTagger` classes. It can be used for constructing a chain containing any subclasses of `SequentialBackoffTagger`.

`BigramTagger` and `TrigramTagger`, because they are subclasses of `NgramTagger` and `ContextTagger`, can also take a model and cutoff argument, just like the `UnigramTagger`. But unlike for `UnigramTagger`, the context keys of the model must be 2-tuples, where the first element is a section of the history, and the second element is the current token. For the `BigramTagger`, an appropriate context key looks like `((prevtag,), word)`, and for `TrigramTagger` it looks like `((prevtag1, prevtag2), word)`.

Quadgram Tagger

The `NgramTagger` class can be used by itself to create a tagger that uses Ngrams longer than three for its context key.

```
>>> from nltk.tag import NgramTagger
>>> quadtagger = NgramTagger(4, train_sents)
>>> quadtagger.evaluate(test_sents)
0.058191236779624435
```

It's even worse than the `TrigramTagger`! Here's an alternative implementation of a `QuadgramTagger` that we can include in a list to `backoff_tagger`. This code can be found in `taggers.py`:

```
from nltk.tag import NgramTagger

class QuadgramTagger(NgramTagger):
    def __init__(self, *args, **kwargs):
        NgramTagger.__init__(self, 4, *args, **kwargs)
```

This is essentially how `BigramTagger` and `TrigramTagger` are implemented; simple subclasses of `NgramTagger` that pass in the number of *ngrams* to look at in the `history` argument of the `context()` method.

Now let's see how it does as part of a backoff chain:

```
>>> from taggers import QuadgramTagger
>>> quadtagger = backoff_tagger(train_sents, [UnigramTagger,
BigramTagger, TrigramTagger, QuadgramTagger], backoff=backoff)
>>> quadtagger.evaluate(test_sents)
0.88111374919058927
```

It's actually slightly worse than before when we stopped with the `TrigramTagger`. So the lesson is that too much context can have a negative effect on accuracy.

See also

The previous two recipes cover the `UnigramTagger` and backoff tagging.

Creating a model of likely word tags

As mentioned earlier in this chapter in the *Training a unigram part-of-speech tagger* recipe, using a custom model with a `UnigramTagger` should only be done if you know exactly what you are doing. In this recipe, we are going to create a model for the most common words, most of which always have the same tag no matter what.

How to do it...

To find the most common words, we can use `nltk.probability.FreqDist` to count word frequencies in the `treebank` corpus. Then, we can create a `ConditionalFreqDist` for tagged words, where we count the frequency of every tag for every word. Using these counts, we can construct a model of the 200 most frequent words as keys, with the most frequent tag for each word as a value. Here's the model creation function defined in `tag_util.py`:

```
from nltk.probability import FreqDist, ConditionalFreqDist

def word_tag_model(words, tagged_words, limit=200):
    fd = FreqDist(words)
    most_freq = fd.keys()[:limit]
    cfd = ConditionalFreqDist(tagged_words)
    return dict((word, cfd[word].max()) for word in most_freq)
```

And to use it with a `UnigramTagger`, we can do the following:

```
>>> from tag_util import word_tag_model
>>> from nltk.corpus import treebank
>>> model = word_tag_model(treebank.words(), treebank.tagged_words())
>>> tagger = UnigramTagger(model=model)
>>> tagger.evaluate(test_sents)
0.55972372113101665
```

An accuracy of almost 56% is ok, but nowhere near as good as the trained `UnigramTagger`. Let's try adding it to our backoff chain:

```
>>> default_tagger = DefaultTagger('NN')
>>> likely_tagger = UnigramTagger(model=model, backoff=default_tagger)
>>> tagger = backoff_tagger(train_sents, [UnigramTagger, BigramTagger,
TrigramTagger], backoff=likely_tagger)
>>> tagger.evaluate(test_sents)
0.88163177206993304
```

The final accuracy is exactly the same as without the `likely_tagger`. This is because the frequency calculations we did to create the model are almost exactly what happens when we train a `UnigramTagger`.

How it works...

The `word_tag_model()` function takes a list of all words, a list of all tagged words, and the maximum number of words we want to use for our model. We give the list of words to a `FreqDist`, which counts the frequency of each word. Then we get the top 200 words from the `FreqDist` by calling `fd.keys()`, which returns all words ordered by highest frequency to lowest. We give the list of tagged words to a `ConditionalFreqDist`, which creates a `FreqDist` of tags for each word, with the word as the *condition*. Finally, we return a `dict` of the top 200 words mapped to their most likely tag.

There's more...

It may seem useless to include this tagger as it does not change the accuracy. But the point of this recipe is to demonstrate how to construct a useful model for a `UnigramTagger`. Custom model construction is a way to create a manual override of trained taggers that are otherwise black boxes. And by putting the likely tagger in the front of the chain, we can actually improve accuracy a little bit:

```
>>> tagger = backoff_tagger(train_sents, [UnigramTagger, BigramTagger,
TrigramTagger], backoff=default_tagger)
>>> likely_tagger = UnigramTagger(model=model, backoff=tagger)
>>> likely_tagger.evaluate(test_sents)
0.88245197496222749
```

Putting custom model taggers at the front of the backoff chain gives you complete control over how specific words are tagged, while letting the trained taggers handle everything else.

See also

The *Training a unigram part-of-speech tagger* recipe has details on the `UnigramTagger` and a simple custom model example. See the earlier recipes *Combining taggers with backoff tagging* and *Training and combining Ngram taggers* for details on backoff tagging.

Tagging with regular expressions

You can use regular expression matching to tag words. For example, you can match numbers with \d to assign the tag **CD** (which refers to a **Cardinal number**). Or you could match on known word patterns, such as the suffix "ing". There's lot of flexibility here, but be careful of over-specifying since language is naturally inexact, and there are always exceptions to the rule.

Getting ready

For this recipe to make sense, you should be familiar with regular expression syntax and Python's `re` module.

How to do it...

The `RegexpTagger` expects a list of 2-tuples, where the first element in the tuple is a regular expression, and the second element is the tag. The following patterns can be found in `tag_util.py`:

```
patterns = [
    (r'^\d+$', 'CD'),
    (r'.*ing$', 'VBG'), # gerunds, i.e. wondering
    (r'.*ment$', 'NN'), # i.e. wonderment
    (r'.*ful$', 'JJ') # i.e. wonderful
]
```

Once you have constructed this list of patterns, you can pass it into `RegexpTagger`.

```
>>> from tag_util import patterns
>>> from nltk.tag import RegexpTagger
>>> tagger = RegexpTagger(patterns)
>>> tagger.evaluate(test_sents)
0.037470321605870924
```

So it's not too great with just a few patterns, but since `RegexpTagger` is a subclass of `SequentialBackoffTagger`, it can be useful as part of a backoff chain, especially if you are able to come up with more word patterns.

How it works...

The `RegexpTagger` saves the `patterns` given at initialization, then on each call to `choose_tag()`, it iterates over the patterns and returns the tag for the first expression that matches the current word using `re.match()`. This means that if you have two expressions that could match, the tag of the first one will always be returned, and the second expression won't even be tried.

There's more...

The `RegexpTagger` can replace the `DefaultTagger` if you give it a pattern such as `(r'.*', 'NN')`. This pattern should, of course, be last in the list of patterns, otherwise no other patterns will match.

See also

In the next recipe, we will cover the `AffixTagger`, which learns how to tag based on prefixes and suffixes of words. And see the *Default tagging* recipe for details on the `DefaultTagger`.

Affix tagging

The `AffixTagger` is another `ContextTagger` subclass, but this time the *context* is either the *prefix* or the *suffix* of a word. This means the `AffixTagger` is able to learn tags based on fixed-length substrings of the beginning or ending of a word.

How to do it...

The default arguments for an `AffixTagger` specify three-character suffixes, and that words must be at least five characters long. If a word is less than five characters long, then `None` is returned as the tag.

```
>>> from nltk.tag import AffixTagger
>>> tagger = AffixTagger(train_sents)
>>> tagger.evaluate(test_sents)
0.27528599179797109
```

So it does ok by itself with the default arguments. Let's try it by specifying three-character prefixes:

```
>>> prefix_tagger = AffixTagger(train_sents, affix_length=3)
>>> prefix_tagger.evaluate(test_sents)
0.23682279300669112
```

To learn on two-character suffixes, the code looks like this:

```
>>> suffix_tagger = AffixTagger(train_sents, affix_length=-2)
>>> suffix_tagger.evaluate(test_sents)
0.31953377940859057
```

How it works...

A positive value for `affix_length` means that the `AffixTagger` will learn word prefixes, essentially `word[:affix_length]`. If the `affix_length` is negative, then suffixes are learned using `word[affix_length:]`.

There's more...

You can combine multiple affix taggers in a backoff chain if you want to learn about multiple character length affixes. Here's an example of four `AffixTagger` classes learning about two and three-character prefixes and suffixes:

```
>>> pre3_tagger = AffixTagger(train_sents, affix_length=3)
>>> pre3_tagger.evaluate(test_sents)
0.23682279300669112
>>> pre2_tagger = AffixTagger(train_sents, affix_length=2,
backoff=pre3_tagger)
>>> pre2_tagger.evaluate(test_sents)
0.29816533563565722
>>> suf2_tagger = AffixTagger(train_sents, affix_length=-2,
backoff=pre2_tagger)
>>> suf2_tagger.evaluate(test_sents)
0.32523203108137277
>>> suf3_tagger = AffixTagger(train_sents, affix_length=-3,
backoff=suf2_tagger)
>>> suf3_tagger.evaluate(test_sents)
0.35924886682495144
```

As you can see, the accuracy goes up each time.

 The preceding ordering is not the best, nor is it the worst. I will leave it to you to explore the possibilities and discover the best backoff chain of `AffixTagger` and `affix_length` values.

Min stem length

`AffixTagger` also takes a `min_stem_length` keyword argument with a default value of `2`. If the word length is less than `min_stem_length` plus the absolute value of `affix_length`, then `None` is returned by the `context()` method. Increasing `min_stem_length` forces the `AffixTagger` to only learn on longer words, while decreasing `min_stem_length` will allow it to learn on shorter words. Of course, for shorter words, the `affix_length` could be equal to or greater than the word length, and `AffixTagger` would essentially be acting like a `UnigramTagger`.

See also

You can manually specify prefixes and suffixes using regular expressions, as shown in the previous recipe. The *Training a unigram part-of-speech tagger* and *Training and combining Ngram taggers* recipes have details on `NgramTagger` subclasses, which are also subclasses of `ContextTagger`.

Training a Brill tagger

The `BrillTagger` is a transformation-based tagger. It is the first tagger that is not a subclass of `SequentialBackoffTagger`. Instead, the `BrillTagger` uses a series of rules to correct the results of an *initial tagger*. These rules are scored based on how many errors they correct minus the number of new errors they produce.

How to do it...

Here's a function from `tag_util.py` that trains a `BrillTagger` using `FastBrillTaggerTrainer`. It requires an `initial_tagger` and `train_sents`.

```
from nltk.tag import brill

def train_brill_tagger(initial_tagger, train_sents, **kwargs):
  sym_bounds = [(1,1), (2,2), (1,2), (1,3)]
  asym_bounds = [(-1,-1), (1,1)]
  templates = [
  brill.SymmetricProximateTokensTemplate(brill.ProximateTagsRule,
*sym_bounds),
    brill.SymmetricProximateTokensTemplate(brill.ProximateWordsRule,
*sym_bounds),
    brill.ProximateTokensTemplate(brill.ProximateTagsRule, *asym_
bounds),
    brill.ProximateTokensTemplate(brill.ProximateWordsRule, *asym_
bounds)
  ]
  trainer = brill.FastBrillTaggerTrainer(initial_tagger, templates,
deterministic=True)
  return trainer.train(train_sents, **kwargs)
```

To use it, we can create our `initial_tagger` from a backoff chain of `NgramTagger` classes, then pass that into the `train_brill_tagger()` function to get a `BrillTagger` back.

```
>>> default_tagger = DefaultTagger('NN')
>>> initial_tagger = backoff_tagger(train_sents, [UnigramTagger,
BigramTagger, TrigramTagger], backoff=default_tagger)
>>> initial_tagger.evaluate(test_sents)
0.88163177206993304
>>> from tag_util import train_brill_tagger
>>> brill_tagger = train_brill_tagger(initial_tagger, train_sents)
>>> brill_tagger.evaluate(test_sents)
0.88327217785452194
```

So the `BrillTagger` has slightly increased accuracy over the `initial_tagger`.

How it works...

The `FastBrillTaggerTrainer` takes an `initial_tagger` and a list of `templates`. These templates must implement the `BrillTemplateI` interface. The two template implementations included with NLTK are `ProximateTokensTemplate` and `SymmetricProximateTokensTemplate`. Each template is used to generate a list of `BrillRule` subclasses. The actual class of the rules produced is passed in to the template at initialization. The basic workflow looks like this:

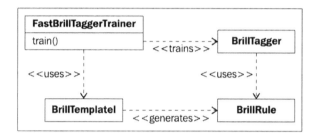

The two `BrillRule` subclasses used are `ProximateTagsRule` and `ProximateWordsRule`, which are both subclasses of `ProximateTokensRule`. `ProximateTagsRule` looks at surrounding tags to do error correction, and `ProximateWordsRule` looks at the surrounding words.

The *bounds* that we pass in to each template are lists of (`start`, `end`) tuples that get passed in to each rule as *conditions*. The conditions tell the rule which tokens it can look at. For example, if the condition is (`1`, `1`), then the rule will only look at the next token. But if the condition is (`1`, `2`), then the rule will look at both the next token and the token after it. For (`-1`, `-1`) the rule will look only at the previous token.

`ProximateTokensTemplate` produces `ProximateTokensRule` that look at each token for its given conditions to do error correction. Positive and negative conditions must be explicitly specified. `SymmetricProximateTokensTemplate`, on the other hand, produces pairs of `ProximateTokensRule`, where one rule uses the given conditions, and the other rule uses the negative of the conditions. So when we pass a list of positive (`start`, `end`) tuples to a `SymmetricProximateTokensTemplate`, it will also produce a `ProximateTokensRule` that uses (`-start`, `-end`). This is why it's *symmetric*—it produces rules that look on both sides of the token.

> Unlike with `ProximateTokensTemplate`, you should not give negative bounds to `SymmetricProximateTokensTemplate`, since it will produce those itself. Only use positive number bounds with `SymmetricProximateTokensTemplate`.

There's more...

You can control the number of rules generated using the `max_rules` keyword argument to the `FastBrillTaggerTrainer.train()` method. The default value is `200`. You can also control the quality of rules used with the `min_score` keyword argument. The default value is `2`, though `3` can be a good choice as well.

 Increasing `max_rules` or `min_score` will greatly increase training time, without necessarily increasing accuracy. Change these values with care.

Tracing

You can watch the `FastBrillTaggerTrainer` do its work by passing `trace=1` into the constructor. This can give you output such as:

```
Training Brill tagger on 3000 sentences...
    Finding initial useful rules...
        Found 10709 useful rules.
    Selecting rules...
```

This means it found `10709` rules with a score of at least `min_score`, and then it selects the best rules, keeping no more than `max_rules`.

The default is `trace=0`, which means the trainer will work silently without printing its status.

See also

The *Training and combining Ngram taggers* recipe details the construction of the `initial_tagger` used previously, and the *Default tagging* recipe explains the `default_tagger`.

Training the TnT tagger

TnT stands for **Trigrams'n'Tags**. It is a statistical tagger based on second order Markov models. You can read the original paper that lead to the implementation at `http://acl.ldc.upenn.edu/A/A00/A00-1031.pdf`.

How to do it...

The `TnT` tagger has a slightly different API than previous taggers we have encountered. You must explicitly call the `train()` method after you have created it. Here's a basic example:

```
>>> from nltk.tag import tnt
>>> tnt_tagger = tnt.TnT()
```

```
>>> tnt_tagger.train(train_sents)
>>> tnt_tagger.evaluate(test_sents)
0.87580401467731495
```

It's quite a good tagger all by itself, only slightly less accurate than the `BrillTagger` from the previous recipe. But if you do not call `train()` before `evaluate()`, you will get an accuracy of 0%.

How it works...

TnT maintains a number of internal `FreqDist` and `ConditionalFreqDist` instances based on the training data. These frequency distributions count unigrams, bigrams, and trigrams. Then, during tagging, the frequencies are used to calculate the probabilities of possible tags for each word. So instead of constructing a backoff chain of `NgramTagger` subclasses, the `TnT` tagger uses all the ngram models together to choose the best tag. It also tries to guess the tags for the whole sentence at once, by choosing the most likely model for the entire sentence, based on the probabilities of each possible tag.

 Training is fairly quick, but tagging is significantly slower than the other taggers we have covered. This is due to all the floating point math that must be done to calculate the tag probabilities of each word.

There's more...

TnT accepts a few optional keyword arguments. You can pass in a tagger for unknown words as `unk`. If this tagger is already trained, then you must also pass in `Trained=True`. Otherwise it will call `unk.train(data)` with the same data you pass in to the `train()` method. Since none of the previous taggers have a public `train()` method, we recommend always passing `Trained=True` if you also pass an `unk` tagger. Here's an example using a `DefaultTagger`, which does not require any training:

```
>>> from nltk.tag import DefaultTagger
>>> unk = DefaultTagger('NN')
>>> tnt_tagger = tnt.TnT(unk=unk, Trained=True)
>>> tnt_tagger.train(train_sents)
>>> tnt_tagger.evaluate(test_sents)
0.89272609540254699
```

So we got an almost 2% increase in accuracy! You must use a tagger that can tag a single word without having seen that word before. This is because the unknown tagger's `tag()` method is only called with a single word sentence. Other good candidates for an unknown tagger are `RegexpTagger` or `AffixTagger`. Passing in a `UnigramTagger` that's been trained on the same data is pretty much useless, as it will have seen the exact same words, and therefore have the same unknown word blind spots.

Controlling the beam search

Another parameter you can modify for `TnT` is N, which controls the number of possible solutions the tagger maintains while trying to guess the tags for a sentence. N defaults to 1,000. Increasing it will greatly increase the amount of memory used during tagging, without necessarily increasing accuracy. Decreasing N will decrease memory usage, but could also decrease accuracy. Here's what happens when you set N=100:

```
>>> tnt_tagger = tnt.TnT(N=100)
>>> tnt_tagger.train(train_sents)
>>> tnt_tagger.evaluate(test_sents)
0.87580401467731495
```

So the accuracy is exactly the same, but we use significantly less memory to achieve it. However, don't assume that accuracy will not change if you decrease N; experiment with your own data to be sure.

Capitalization significance

You can pass C=True if you want capitalization of words to be significant. The default is C=False, which means all words are lowercased. The documentation on C says that treating capitalization as significant probably will not increase accuracy. In my own testing, there was a very slight (< 0.01%) increase in accuracy with C=True, probably because case-sensitivity can help identify proper nouns.

See also

We covered the `DefaultTagger` in the *Default tagging* recipe, backoff tagging in the *Combining taggers with backoff tagging* recipe, `NgramTagger` subclasses in the *Training a unigram part-of-speech tagger* and *Training combining Ngram taggers* recipes, `RegexpTagger` in the *Tagging with regular expressions* recipe, and the `AffixTagger` in the *Affix tagging* recipe.

Using WordNet for tagging

If you remember from the *Looking up synsets for a word in Wordnet* recipe in *Chapter 1, Tokenizing Text and WordNet Basics*, WordNet synsets specify a part-of-speech tag. It's a very restricted set of possible tags, and many words have multiple synsets with different part-of-speech tags, but this information can be useful for tagging unknown words. WordNet is essentially a giant dictionary, and it's likely to contain many words that are not in your training data.

Getting ready

First, we need to decide how to map WordNet part-of-speech tags to the Penn Treebank part-of-speech tags we have been using. The following is a table mapping one to the other. See the *Looking up synsets for a word in Wordnet* recipe in *Chapter 1, Tokenizing Text and WordNet Basics* for more details. The "s", which was not shown before, is just another kind of adjective, at least for tagging purposes.

WordNet Tag	Treebank Tag
n	NN
a	JJ
s	JJ
r	RB
v	VB

How to do it...

Now we can create a class that will look up words in WordNet, then chose the most common tag from the synsets it finds. The `WordNetTagger` defined next can be found in `taggers.py`:

```
from nltk.tag import SequentialBackoffTagger
from nltk.corpus import wordnet
from nltk.probability import FreqDist

class WordNetTagger(SequentialBackoffTagger):
  '''
  >>> wt = WordNetTagger()
  >>> wt.tag(['food', 'is', 'great'])
  [('food', 'NN'), ('is', 'VB'), ('great', 'JJ')]
  '''
  def __init__(self, *args, **kwargs):
    SequentialBackoffTagger.__init__(self, *args, **kwargs)
    self.wordnet_tag_map = {
```

```
            'n': 'NN',
            's': 'JJ',
            'a': 'JJ',
            'r': 'RB',
            'v': 'VB'
        }
    def choose_tag(self, tokens, index, history):
        word = tokens[index]
        fd = FreqDist()
        for synset in wordnet.synsets(word):
            fd.inc(synset.pos)
        return self.wordnet_tag_map.get(fd.max())
```

How it works...

The `WordNetTagger` simply counts the number of each part-of-speech tag found in the synsets for a word. The most common tag is then mapped to a `treebank` tag using an internal mapping. Here's some sample usage code:

```
>>> from taggers import WordNetTagger
>>> wn_tagger = WordNetTagger()
>>> wn_tagger.evaluate(train_sents)
0.18451574615215904
```

So it's not too accurate, but that's to be expected. We only have enough information to produce four different kinds of tags, while there are 36 possible tags in `treebank`. And many words can have different part-of-speech tags depending on their context. But if we put the `WordNetTagger` at the end of an `NgramTagger` backoff chain, then we can improve accuracy over the `DefaultTagger`.

```
>>> from tag_util import backoff_tagger
>>> from nltk.tag import UnigramTagger, BigramTagger, TrigramTagger
>>> tagger = backoff_tagger(train_sents, [UnigramTagger, BigramTagger,
TrigramTagger], backoff=wn_tagger)
>>> tagger.evaluate(test_sents)
0.88564644938484782
```

See also

The *Looking up synsets for a word in Wordnet* recipe in *Chapter 1, Tokenizing Text and WordNet Basics* details how to use the `wordnet` corpus and what kinds of part-of-speech tags it knows about. And in the *Combining taggers with backoff tagging* and *Training and combining Ngram taggers* recipes, we went over backoff tagging with ngram taggers.

Tagging proper names

Using the included `names` corpus, we can create a simple tagger for tagging names as *proper nouns*.

How to do it...

The `NamesTagger` is a subclass of `SequentialBackoffTagger` as it's probably only useful near the end of a backoff chain. At initialization, we create a set of all names in the `names` corpus, lowercasing each name to make lookup easier. Then we implement the `choose_tag()` method, which simply checks if the current word is in the `names_set`. If it is, we return the tag *NNP* (which is the tag for *proper nouns*). If it isn't, we return `None` so the next tagger in the chain can tag the word. The following code can be found in `taggers.py`:

```
from nltk.tag import SequentialBackoffTagger
from nltk.corpus import names

class NamesTagger(SequentialBackoffTagger):
  def __init__(self, *args, **kwargs):
    SequentialBackoffTagger.__init__(self, *args, **kwargs)
    self.name_set = set([n.lower() for n in names.words()])
  def choose_tag(self, tokens, index, history):
    word = tokens[index]
    if word.lower() in self.name_set:
      return 'NNP'
    else:
      return None
```

How it works...

`NamesTagger` should be pretty self-explanatory. Its usage is also simple:

```
>>> from taggers import NamesTagger
>>> nt = NamesTagger()
>>> nt.tag(['Jacob'])
[('Jacob', 'NNP')]
```

It's probably best to use the `NamesTagger` right before a `DefaultTagger`, so it's at the end of a backoff chain. But it could probably go anywhere in the chain since it's unlikely to mistag a word.

See also

The *Combining taggers with backoff tagging* recipe goes over the details of using
`SequentialBackoffTagger` subclasses.

Classifier based tagging

The `ClassifierBasedPOSTagger` uses *classification* to do part-of-speech tagging.
Features are extracted from words, then passed to an internal classifier. The classifier
classifies the features and returns a label; in this case, a part-of-speech tag. Classification
will be covered in detail in *Chapter 7, Text Classification*.

`ClassifierBasedPOSTagger` is a subclass of `ClassifierBasedTagger` that
implements a **feature detector** that combines many of the techniques of previous taggers into
a single **feature set**. The feature detector finds multiple length suffixes, does some regular
expression matching, and looks at the unigram, bigram, and trigram history to produce a fairly
complete set of features for each word. The feature sets it produces are used to train the
internal classifier, and are used for classifying words into part-of-speech tags.

How to do it...

Basic usage of the `ClassifierBasedPOSTagger` is much like any other
`SequentialBackoffTaggger`. You pass in training sentences, it trains an internal classifier,
and you get a very accurate tagger.

```
>>> from nltk.tag.sequential import ClassifierBasedPOSTagger
>>> tagger = ClassifierBasedPOSTagger(train=train_sents)
>>> tagger.evaluate(test_sents)
0.93097345132743359
```

 Notice a slight modification to initialization—`train_sents` must be passed
in as the `train` keyword argument.

How it works...

`ClassifierBasedPOSTagger` inherits from `ClassifierBasedTagger` and only
implements a `feature_detector()` method. All the training and tagging is done in
`ClassifierBasedTagger`. It defaults to training a `NaiveBayesClassifier` with the
given training data. Once this classifier is trained, it is used to classify word features produced
by the `feature_detector()` method.

The `ClassifierBasedTagger` is often the most accurate tagger, but it's also one of the slowest taggers. If speed is an issue, you should stick with a `BrillTagger` based on a backoff chain of `NgramTagger` subclasses and other simple taggers.

The `ClassifierBasedTagger` also inherits from `FeatursetTaggerI` (which is just an empty class), creating an inheritance tree that looks like this:

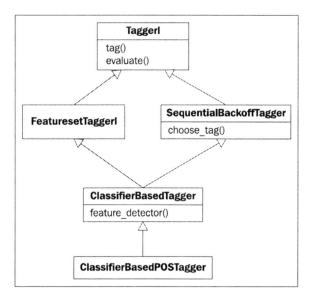

There's more...

You can use a different classifier instead of `NaiveBayesClassifier` by passing in your own `classifier_builder` function. For example, to use a `MaxentClassifier`, you would do the following:

```
>>> from nltk.classify import MaxentClassifier
>>> me_tagger = ClassifierBasedPOSTagger(train=train_sents,
classifier_builder=MaxentClassifier.train)
>>> me_tagger.evaluate(test_sents)
0.93093028275415501
```

 The `MaxentClassifier` takes even longer to train than `NaiveBayesClassifier`. If you have `scipy` and `numpy` installed, training will be faster than normal, but still slower than `NaiveBayesClassifier`.

Custom feature detector

If you want to do your own feature detection, there are two ways to do it.

1. Subclass `ClassifierBasedTagger` and implement a `feature_detector()` method.

2. Pass a method as the `feature_detector` keyword argument into `ClassifierBasedTagger` at initialization.

Either way, you need a feature detection method that can take the same arguments as `choose_tag()`: `tokens`, `index`, and `history`. But instead of returning a tag, you return a `dict` of key-value features, where the key is the feature name, and the value is the feature value. A very simple example would be a unigram feature detector (found in `tag_util.py`).

```
def unigram_feature_detector(tokens, index, history):
    return {'word': tokens[index]}
```

Then using the second method, you would pass the following into `ClassifierBasedTagger` as `feature_detector`:

```
>>> from nltk.tag.sequential import ClassifierBasedTagger
>>> from tag_util import unigram_feature_detector
>>> tagger = ClassifierBasedTagger(train=train_sents, feature_
detector=unigram_feature_detector)
>>> tagger.evaluate(test_sents)
0.87338657457371038
```

Cutoff probability

Because a classifier will always return the best result it can, passing in a backoff tagger is useless unless you also pass in a `cutoff_prob` to specify the probability threshold for classification. Then, if the probability of the chosen tag is less than `cutoff_prob`, the backoff tagger will be used. Here's an example using the `DefaultTagger` as the `backoff`, and setting `cutoff_prob` to `0.3`:

```
>>> default = DefaultTagger('NN')
>>> tagger = ClassifierBasedPOSTagger(train=train_sents,
backoff=default, cutoff_prob=0.3)
>>> tagger.evaluate(test_sents)
0.93110295704726964
```

So we get a slight increase in accuracy if the `ClassifierBasedPOSTagger` uses the `DefaultTagger` whenever its tag probability is less than 30%.

Pre-trained classifier

If you want to use a classifier that's already been trained, then you can pass that in to `ClassifierBasedTagger` or `ClassifierBasedPOSTagger` as `classifier`. In this case, the `classifier_builder` argument is ignored and no training takes place. However, you must ensure that the classifier has been trained on and can classify feature sets produced by whatever `feature_detector()` method you use.

See also

Chapter 7, Text Classification will cover classification in depth.

5
Extracting Chunks

In this chapter, we will cover:

- ▶ Chunking and chinking with regular expressions
- ▶ Merging and splitting chunks with regular expressions
- ▶ Expanding and removing chunks with regular expressions
- ▶ Partial parsing with regular expressions
- ▶ Training a tagger-based chunker
- ▶ Classification-based chunking
- ▶ Extracting named entities
- ▶ Extracting proper noun chunks
- ▶ Extracting location chunks
- ▶ Training a named entity chunker

Introduction

Chunk extraction or **partial parsing** is the process of extracting short phrases from a part-of-speech tagged sentence. This is different than full parsing, in that we are interested in standalone **chunks** or **phrases** instead of full parse trees. The idea is that meaningful phrases can be extracted from a sentence by simply looking for particular patterns of part-of-speech tags.

As in *Chapter 4, Part-of-Speech Tagging*, we will be using the **Penn Treebank corpus** for basic training and testing chunk extraction. We will also be using the CoNLL 2000 corpus as it has a simpler and more flexible format that supports multiple chunk types (refer to the *Creating a chunked phrase corpus* recipe in *Chapter 3, Creating Custom Corpora* for more details on the `conll2000` corpus and IOB tags).

Chunking and chinking with regular expressions

Using modified regular expressions, we can define **chunk patterns**. These are patterns of part-of-speech tags that define what kinds of words make up a chunk. We can also define patterns for what kinds of words should not be in a chunk. These unchunked words are known as **chinks**.

A `ChunkRule` specifies what to include in a chunk, while a `ChinkRule` specifies what to exclude from a chunk. In other words, **chunking** creates chunks, while **chinking** breaks up those chunks.

Getting ready

We first need to know how to define chunk patterns. These are modified regular expressions designed to match sequences of part-of-speech tags. An individual tag is specified by surrounding angle brackets, such as <NN> to match a noun tag. Multiple tags can then be combined, as in <DT><NN> to match a determiner followed by a noun. Regular expression syntax can be used within the angle brackets to match individual tag patterns, so you can do <NN.*> to match all nouns including NN and NNS. You can also use regular expression syntax outside of the angle brackets to match patterns of tags. <DT>?<NN.*>+ will match an optional determiner followed by one or more nouns. The chunk patterns are converted internally to regular expressions using the `tag_pattern2re_pattern()` function:

```
>>> from nltk.chunk import tag_pattern2re_pattern
>>> tag_pattern2re_pattern('<DT>?<NN.*>+')
'(<(DT)>)?(<(NN[^\\{\\}<>]*)>)+'
```

You don't have to use this function to do chunking, but it might be useful or interesting to see how your chunk patterns convert to regular expressions.

How to do it...

The pattern for specifying a chunk is to use surrounding curly braces, such as {<DT><NN>}. To specify a chink, you flip the braces, as in }<VB>{. These rules can be combined into a **grammar** for a particular phrase type. Here's a grammar for noun-phrases that combines both a chunk and a chink pattern, along with the result of parsing the sentence "The book has many chapters":

```
>>> from nltk.chunk import RegexpParser
>>> chunker = RegexpParser(r'''
... NP:
...     {<DT><NN.*><.*>*<NN.*>}
...     }<VB.*>{
```

```
...  ''')
>>> chunker.parse([('the', 'DT'), ('book', 'NN'),
('has', 'VBZ'), ('many', 'JJ'), ('chapters', 'NNS')])
Tree('S', [Tree('NP', [('the', 'DT'), ('book', 'NN')]),
('has', 'VBZ'), Tree('NP', [('many', 'JJ'), ('chapters',
'NNS')])])
```

The grammar tells the `RegexpParser` that there are two rules for parsing `NP` chunks. The first chunk pattern says that a chunk starts with a *determiner* followed by any kind of *noun*. Then any number of other words is allowed, until a final noun is found. The second pattern says that verbs should be *chinked*, thus separating any large chunks that contain a verb. The result is a tree with two noun-phrase chunks: "the book" and "many chapters".

> Tagged sentences are always parsed into a `Tree` (found in the `nltk.tree` module). The top node of the `Tree` is `'S'`, which stands for *sentence*. Any chunks found will be subtrees whose nodes will refer to the chunk type. In this case, the chunk type is `'NP'` for *noun-phrase*. Trees can be drawn calling the `draw()` method, as in `t.draw()`.

How it works...

Here's what happens, step-by-step:

1. The sentence is converted into a flat `Tree`, as shown in the following figure:

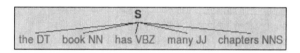

2. The `Tree` is used to create a `ChunkString`.

3. `RegexpParser` parses the grammar to create a `NP RegexpChunkParser` with the given rules.

4. A `ChunkRule` is created and applied to the `ChunkString`, which matches the entire sentence into a chunk, as shown in the following figure:

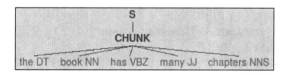

5. A `ChinkRule` is created and applied to the same `ChunkString`, which splits the big chunk into two smaller chunks with a verb between them, as shown in the following figure:

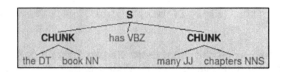

6. The `ChunkString` is converted back to a `Tree`, now with two **NP** chunk subtrees, as shown in the following figure:

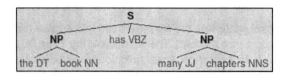

You can do this yourself using the classes in `nltk.chunk.regexp`. `ChunkRule` and `ChinkRule` are both subclasses of `RegexpChunkRule` and require two arguments: the pattern, and a description of the rule. `ChunkString` is an object that starts with a flat tree, which is then modified by each rule when it is passed in to the rule's `apply()` method. A `ChunkString` is converted back to a `Tree` with the `to_chunkstruct()` method. Here's the code to demonstrate it:

```
>>> from nltk.chunk.regexp import ChunkString, ChunkRule, ChinkRule
>>> from nltk.tree import Tree
>>> t = Tree('S', [('the', 'DT'), ('book', 'NN'), ('has', 'VBZ'),
('many', 'JJ'), ('chapters', 'NNS')])
>>> cs = ChunkString(t)
>>> cs
<ChunkString: '<DT><NN><VBZ><JJ><NNS>'>
>>> ur = ChunkRule('<DT><NN.*><.*>*<NN.*>', 'chunk determiners and
nouns')
>>> ur.apply(cs)
>>> cs
<ChunkString: '{<DT><NN><VBZ><JJ><NNS>}'>
>>> ir = ChinkRule('<VB.*>', 'chink verbs')
>>> ir.apply(cs)
>>> cs
<ChunkString: '{<DT><NN>}<VBZ>{<JJ><NNS>}'>
>>> cs.to_chunkstruct()
Tree('S', [Tree('CHUNK', [('the', 'DT'), ('book', 'NN')]), ('has',
'VBZ'), Tree('CHUNK', [('many', 'JJ'), ('chapters', 'NNS')])])
```

The preceding tree diagrams can be drawn at each step by calling `cs.to_chunkstruct().draw()`.

There's more...

You will notice that the subtrees from the `ChunkString` are tagged as `'CHUNK'` and not `'NP'`. That's because the previous rules are phrase agnostic; they create chunks without needing to know what kind of chunks they are.

Internally, the `RegexpParser` creates a `RegexpChunkParser` for each chunk phrase type. So if you are only chunking NP phrases, there will only be one `RegexpChunkParser`. The `RegexpChunkParser` gets all the rules for the specific chunk type, and handles applying the rules in order and converting the `'CHUNK'` trees to the specific chunk type, such as `'NP'`.

Here's some code to illustrate the usage of `RegexpChunkParser`. We pass the previous two rules into the `RegexpChunkParser`, and then parse the same sentence tree we created before. The resulting tree is just like what we got from applying both rules in order, except `'CHUNK'` has been replaced with `'NP'` in the two subtrees. This is because `RegexpChunkParser` defaults to `chunk_node='NP'`.

```
>>> from nltk.chunk import RegexpChunkParser
>>> chunker = RegexpChunkParser([ur, ir])
>>> chunker.parse(t)
Tree('S', [Tree('NP', [('the', 'DT'), ('book', 'NN')]), ('has',
'VBZ'), Tree('NP', [('many', 'JJ'), ('chapters', 'NNS')])])
```

Different chunk types

If you wanted to parse a different chunk type, then you could pass that in as `chunk_node` to `RegexpChunkParser`. Here's the same code we have just seen, but instead of `'NP'` subtrees, we will call them `'CP'` for *custom phrase*.

```
>>> from nltk.chunk import RegexpChunkParser
>>> chunker = RegexpChunkParser([ur, ir], chunk_node='CP')
>>> chunker.parse(t)
Tree('S', [Tree('CP', [('the', 'DT'), ('book', 'NN')]),
('has', 'VBZ'), Tree('CP', [('many', 'JJ'), ('chapters',
'NNS')])])
```

`RegexpParser` does this internally when you specify multiple phrase types. This will be covered in *Partial parsing with regular expressions*.

Alternative patterns

The same parsing results can be obtained by using two chunk patterns in the grammar, and discarding the chink pattern:

```
>>> chunker = RegexpParser(r'''
... NP:
...     {<DT><NN.*>}
...     {<JJ><NN.*>}
```

```
... ''')
>>> chunker.parse(t)
Tree('S', [Tree('NP', [('the', 'DT'), ('book', 'NN')]), ('has',
'VBZ'), Tree('NP', [('many', 'JJ'), ('chapters', 'NNS')])])
```

In fact, you could reduce the two chunk patterns into a single pattern.

```
>>> chunker = RegexpParser(r'''
... NP:
...     {(<DT>|<JJ>)<NN.*>}
... ''')
>>> chunker.parse(t)
Tree('S', [Tree('NP', [('the', 'DT'), ('book', 'NN')]), ('has',
'VBZ'), Tree('NP', [('many', 'JJ'), ('chapters', 'NNS')])])
```

How you create and combine patterns is really up to you. Pattern creation is a process of trial and error, and entirely depends on what your data looks like and which patterns are easiest to express.

Chunk rule with context

You can also create chunk rules with a surrounding tag context. For example, if your pattern is <DT>{<NN>}, which will be parsed into a ChunkRuleWithContext. Any time there's a tag on either side of the curly braces, you will get a ChunkRuleWithContext instead of a ChunkRule. This can allow you to be more specific about when to parse particular kinds of chunks.

Here's an example of using ChunkWithContext directly. It takes four arguments: the left context, the pattern to chunk, the right context, and a description:

```
>>> from nltk.chunk.regexp import ChunkRuleWithContext
>>> ctx = ChunkRuleWithContext('<DT>', '<NN.*>', '<.*>', 'chunk nouns
only after determiners')
>>> cs = ChunkString(t)
>>> cs
<ChunkString: '<DT><NN><VBZ><JJ><NNS>'>
>>> ctx.apply(cs)
>>> cs
<ChunkString: '<DT>{<NN>}<VBZ><JJ><NNS>'>
>>> cs.to_chunkstruct()
Tree('S', [('the', 'DT'), Tree('CHUNK', [('book', 'NN')]), ('has',
'VBZ'), ('many', 'JJ'), ('chapters', 'NNS')])
```

This example only chunks nouns that follow a determiner, therefore ignoring the noun that follows an adjective. Here's how it would look using the `RegexpParser`:

```
>>> chunker = RegexpParser(r'''
... NP:
...     <DT>{<NN.*>}
... ''')
>>> chunker.parse(t)
Tree('S', [('the', 'DT'), Tree('NP', [('book', 'NN')]), ('has',
'VBZ'), ('many', 'JJ'), ('chapters', 'NNS')])
```

See also

In the next recipe, we will cover merging and splitting chunks.

Merging and splitting chunks with regular expressions

In this recipe, we will cover two more rules for chunking. A `MergeRule` can merge two chunks together based on the end of the first chunk and the beginning of the second chunk. A `SplitRule` will split a chunk into two based on the specified split pattern.

How to do it...

A `SplitRule` is specified with two opposing curly braces surrounded by a pattern on either side. To split a chunk after a noun, you would do `<NN.*>}{<.*>`. A `MergeRule` is specified by flipping the curly braces, and will join chunks where the end of the first chunk matches the left pattern, and the beginning of the next chunk matches the right pattern. To merge two chunks where the first ends with a noun and the second begins with a noun, you would use `<NN.*>{}<NN.*>`.

The order of rules is very important and re-ordering can affect the results. The `RegexpParser` applies the rules one at a time from top to bottom, so each rule will be applied to the `ChunkString` resulting from the previous rule.

Here's an example of splitting and merging, starting with the sentence tree as shown next:

1. The whole sentence is chunked, as shown in the following diagram:

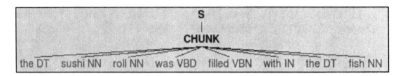

2. The chunk is split into multiple chunks after every noun, as shown in the following tree:

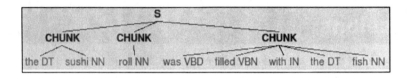

3. Each chunk with a determiner is split into separate chunks, creating four chunks where there were three:

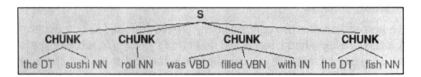

4. Chunks ending with a noun are merged with the next chunk if it begins with a noun, reducing the four chunks back down to three, as shown in the following diagram:

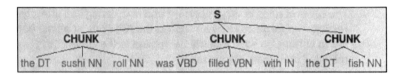

Using the `RegexpParser`, the code looks like this:

```
>>> chunker = RegexpParser(r'''
... NP:
...       {<DT><.*>*<NN.*>}
...       <NN.*>}{<.*>
```

```
...        <.*>}{<DT>
...        <NN.*>{}<NN.*>
... ''')
>>> sent = [('the', 'DT'), ('sushi', 'NN'), ('roll', 'NN'),
('was', 'VBD'), ('filled', 'VBN'), ('with', 'IN'), ('the',
'DT'), ('fish', 'NN')]
>>> chunker.parse(sent)
Tree('S', [Tree('NP', [('the', 'DT'), ('sushi', 'NN'),
('roll', 'NN')]), Tree('NP', [('was', 'VBD'), ('filled',
'VBN'), ('with', 'IN')]), Tree('NP', [('the', 'DT'),
('fish', 'NN')])])
```

And the final tree of NP chunks is shown in the following diagram:

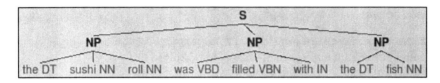

How it works...

The `MergeRule` and `SplitRule` classes take three arguments: the left pattern, right pattern, and a description. The `RegexpParser` takes care of splitting the original patterns on the curly braces to get the left and right sides, but you can also create these manually. Here's a step-by-step walkthrough of how the original sentence is modified by applying each rule:

```
>>> from nltk.chunk.regexp import MergeRule, SplitRule
>>> cs = ChunkString(Tree('S', sent))
>>> cs
<ChunkString: '<DT><NN><NN><VBD><VBN><IN><DT><NN>'>
>>> ur = ChunkRule('<DT><.*>*<NN.*>', 'chunk determiner to noun')
>>> ur.apply(cs)
>>> cs
<ChunkString: '{<DT><NN><NN><VBD><VBN><IN><DT><NN>}'>
>>> sr1 = SplitRule('<NN.*>', '<.*>', 'split after noun')
>>> sr1.apply(cs)
>>> cs
<ChunkString: '{<DT><NN>}{<NN>}{<VBD><VBN><IN><DT><NN>}'>
>>> sr2 = SplitRule('<.*>', '<DT>', 'split before determiner')
>>> sr2.apply(cs)
>>> cs
<ChunkString: '{<DT><NN>}{<NN>}{<VBD><VBN><IN>}{<DT><NN>}'>
>>> mr = MergeRule('<NN.*>', '<NN.*>', 'merge nouns')
>>> mr.apply(cs)
```

```
>>> cs
<ChunkString: '{<DT><NN><NN>}{<VBD><VBN><IN>}{<DT><NN>}'>
>>> cs.to_chunkstruct()
Tree('S', [Tree('CHUNK', [('the', 'DT'), ('sushi', 'NN'),
('roll', 'NN')]), Tree('CHUNK', [('was', 'VBD'),
('filled', 'VBN'), ('with', 'IN')]), Tree('CHUNK',
[('the', 'DT'), ('fish', 'NN')])])
```

There's more...

The parsing of the rules and splitting of left and right patterns is done in the static `parse()` method of the `RegexpChunkRule` superclass. This is called by the `RegexpParser` to get the list of rules to pass in to the `RegexpChunkParser`. Here are some examples of parsing the patterns used before:

```
>>> from nltk.chunk.regex import RegexpChunkRule
>>> RegexpChunkRule.parse('{<DT><.*>*<NN.*>}')
<ChunkRule: '<DT><.*>*<NN.*>'>
>>> RegexpChunkRule.parse('<.*>}{<DT>')
<SplitRule: '<.*>', '<DT>'>
>>> RegexpChunkRule.parse('<NN.*>{}<NN.*>')
<MergeRule: '<NN.*>', '<NN.*>'>
```

Rule descriptions

Descriptions for each rule can be specified with a comment string after the rule (a comment string must start with #). If no comment string is found, the rule's description will be empty. Here's an example:

```
>>> RegexpChunkRule.parse('{<DT><.*>*<NN.*>} # chunk everything').
descr()
'chunk everything'
>>> RegexpChunkRule.parse('{<DT><.*>*<NN.*>}').descr()
''
```

Comment string descriptions can also be used within grammar strings that are passed to `RegexpParser`.

See also

The previous recipe goes over how to use `ChunkRule` and how rules are passed in to `RegexpChunkParser`.

Expanding and removing chunks with regular expressions

There are three `RegexpChunkRule` subclasses that are not supported by `RegexpChunkRule.parse()` and therefore must be created manually if you want to use them. These rules are:

1. `ExpandLeftRule`: Adds unchunked (chink) words to the left of a chunk to the chunk.

2. `ExpandRightRule`: Adds unchunked (chink) words to the right of a chunk to the chunk.

3. `UnChunkRule`: Unchunk any matching chunk.

How to do it...

`ExpandLeftRule` and `ExpandRightRule` both take two patterns along with a description as arguments. For `ExpandLeftRule`, the first pattern is the chink we want to add to the beginning of the chunk, while the right pattern will match the beginning of the chunk we want to expand. With `ExpandRightRule`, the left pattern should match the end of the chunk we want to expand, and the right pattern matches the chink we want to add to the end of the chunk. The idea is similar to the `MergeRule`, but in this case we are merging chink words instead of other chunks.

`UnChunkRule` is the opposite of `ChunkRule`. Any chunk that exactly matches the `UnChunkRule` pattern will be unchunked, and become a chink. Here's some code demonstrating usage with the `RegexpChunkParser`:

```
>>> from nltk.chunk.regexp import ChunkRule, ExpandLeftRule,
ExpandRightRule, UnChunkRule
>>> from nltk.chunk import RegexpChunkParser
>>> ur = ChunkRule('<NN>', 'single noun')
>>> el = ExpandLeftRule('<DT>', '<NN>', 'get left determiner')
>>> er = ExpandRightRule('<NN>', '<NNS>', 'get right plural noun')
>>> un = UnChunkRule('<DT><NN.*>*', 'unchunk everything')
>>> chunker = RegexpChunkParser([ur, el, er, un])
>>> sent = [('the', 'DT'), ('sushi', 'NN'), ('rolls', 'NNS')]
>>> chunker.parse(sent)
Tree('S', [('the', 'DT'), ('sushi', 'NN'), ('rolls', 'NNS')])
```

You will notice the end result is a flat sentence, which is exactly what we started with. That's because the final `UnChunkRule` undid the chunk created by the previous rules. Read on to see the step-by-step procedure of what happened.

How it works...

The preceding rules were applied in the following order, starting with the sentence tree shown below:

1. Make single nouns into a chunk, as shown in the following diagram:

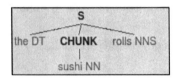

2. Expand left determiners into chunks that begin with a noun, as shown in the following diagram:

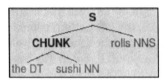

3. Expand right plural nouns into chunks that end with a noun, chunking the whole sentence as shown in the following diagram:

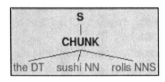

4. Unchunk every chunk that is a determiner + noun + plural noun, resulting in the original sentence tree, as shown in the following diagram:

Here's the code showing each step:

```
>>> from nltk.chunk.regexp import ChunkString
>>> from nltk.tree import Tree
>>> cs = ChunkString(Tree('S', sent))
>>> cs
<ChunkString: '<DT><NN><NNS>'>
>>> ur.apply(cs)
>>> cs
<ChunkString: '<DT>{<NN>}<NNS>'>
>>> el.apply(cs)
>>> cs
<ChunkString: '{<DT><NN>}<NNS>'>
>>> er.apply(cs)
>>> cs
<ChunkString: '{<DT><NN><NNS>}'>
>>> un.apply(cs)
>>> cs
<ChunkString: '<DT><NN><NNS>'>
```

There's more...

In practice, you can probably get away with only using the previous four rules: `ChunkRule`, `ChinkRule`, `MergeRule`, and `SplitRule`. But if you do need very fine-grained control over chunk parsing and removing, now you know how to do it with the expansion and unchunk rules.

See also

The previous two recipes covered the more common chunk rules that are supported by `RegexpChunkRule.parse()` and `RegexpParser`.

Partial parsing with regular expressions

So far, we have only been parsing noun-phrases. But `RegexpParser` supports grammar with multiple phrase types, such as *verb-phrases* and *prepositional-phrases*. We can put the rules we have learned to use and define a grammar that can be evaluated against the `conll2000` corpus, which has NP, VP, and PP phrases.

How to do it...

We will define a grammar to parse three phrase types. For noun-phrases, we have a `ChunkRule` that looks for an optional determiner followed by one or more nouns. We then have a `MergeRule` for adding an adjective to the front of a noun chunk. For prepositional-phrases, we simply chunk any `IN` word, such as "in" or "on". For verb-phrases, we chunk an optional modal word (such as "should") followed by a verb.

 Each grammar rule is followed by a # comment. This comment is passed in to each rule as the description. Comments are optional, but they can be helpful notes for understanding what the rule does, and will be included in trace output.

```
>>> chunker = RegexpParser(r'''
... NP:
... {<DT>?<NN.*>+}  # chunk optional determiner with nouns
... <JJ>{}<NN.*>  # merge adjective with noun chunk
... PP:
... {<IN>}  # chunk preposition
... VP:
... {<MD>?<VB.*>}  # chunk optional modal with verb
... ''')
>>> from nltk.corpus import conll2000
>>> score = chunker.evaluate(conll2000.chunked_sents())
>>> score.accuracy()
0.61485735457576884
```

When we call `evaluate()` on the `chunker`, we give it a list of chunked sentences and get back a `ChunkScore` object, which can give us the accuracy of the `chunker`, along with a number of other metrics.

How it works...

The `RegexpParser` parses the grammar string into sets of rules, one set of rules for each phrase type. These rules are used to create a `RegexpChunkParser`. The rules are parsed using `RegexpChunkRule.parse()`, which returns one of the five subclasses: `ChunkRule`, `ChinkRule`, `MergeRule`, `SplitRule`, or `ChunkRuleWithContext`.

Now that the grammar has been translated into sets of rules, these rules are used to parse a tagged sentence into a `Tree` structure. `RegexpParser` inherits from `ChunkParserI`, which provides a `parse()` method to parse the tagged words. Whenever a part of the tagged tokens match a chunk rule, a subtree is constructed so that the tagged tokens become the leaves of a `Tree` whose node string is the chunk tag. `ChunkParserI` also provides the `evaluate()` method, which compares the given chunked sentences to the output of the `parse()` method to construct and return a `ChunkScore` object.

There's more...

You can also evaluate this `chunker` on the `treebank_chunk` corpus.

```
>>> from nltk.corpus import treebank_chunk
>>> treebank_score = chunker.evaluate(treebank_chunk.chunked_sents())
>>> treebank_score.accuracy()
0.49033970276008493
```

The `treebank_chunk` corpus is a special version of the `treebank` corpus that provides a `chunked_sents()` method. The regular `treebank` corpus cannot provide that method due to its file format.

ChunkScore metrics

`ChunkScore` provides a few other metrics besides accuracy. Of the chunks the `chunker` was able to guess, precision tells you how many were correct. Recall tells you how well the `chunker` did at finding correct chunks, compared to how many total chunks there were.

```
>>> score.precision()
0.60201948127375005
>>> score.recall()
0.60607250250584699
```

You can also get lists of chunks that were missed by the `chunker`, chunks that were incorrectly found, correct chunks, and guessed chunks. These can be useful to figure out how to improve your chunk grammar.

```
>>> len(score.missed())
47161
>>> len(score.incorrect())
47967
>>> len(score.correct())
119720
>>> len(score.guessed())
120526
```

As you can see by the number of incorrect chunks, and by comparing `guessed()` and `correct()`, our chunker guessed that there were more chunks that actually existed. And it also missed a good number of correct chunks.

Looping and tracing

If you want to apply the chunk rules in your grammar more than once, you pass `loop=2` into `RegexpParser` at initialization. The default is `loop=1`.

To watch an internal trace of the chunking process, pass `trace=1` into `RegexpParser`. To get even more output, pass in `trace=2`. This will give you a printout of what the chunker is doing as it is doing it. Rule comments/descriptions will be included in the trace output, giving you a good idea of which rule is applied when.

See also

If coming up with regular expression chunk patterns seems like too much work, then read the next recipes where we will cover how to train a chunker based on a corpus of chunked sentences.

Training a tagger-based chunker

Training a chunker can be a great alternative to manually specifying regular expression chunk patterns. Instead of a painstaking process of trial and error to get the exact right patterns, we can use existing corpus data to train chunkers much like we did in *Chapter 4, Part-of-Speech Tagging*.

How to do it...

As with the part-of-speech tagging, we will use the treebank corpus data for training. But this time we will use the `treebank_chunk` corpus, which is specifically formatted to produce chunked sentences in the form of trees. These `chunked_sents()` will be used by a `TagChunker` class to train a tagger-based chunker. The `TagChunker` uses a helper function `conll_tag_chunks()` to extract a list of (`pos`, `iob`) tuples from a list of `Tree`. These (`pos`, `iob`) tuples are then used to train a tagger in the same way (`word`, `pos`) tuples were used in *Chapter 4, Part-of-Speech Tagging* to train part-of-speech taggers. But instead of learning part-of-speech tags for words, we are learning IOB tags for part-of-speech tags. Here's the code from `chunkers.py`:

```
import nltk.chunk, itertools
from nltk.tag import UnigramTagger, BigramTagger
from tag_util import backoff_tagger

def conll_tag_chunks(chunk_sents):
  tagged_sents = [nltk.chunk.tree2conlltags(tree) for tree in
chunk_sents]
  return [[(t, c) for (w, t, c) in sent] for sent in tagged_sents]

class TagChunker(nltk.chunk.ChunkParserI):
  def __init__(self, train_chunks, tagger_classes=[UnigramTagger,
BigramTagger]):
    train_sents = conll_tag_chunks(train_chunks)
    self.tagger = backoff_tagger(train_sents, tagger_classes)
```

```
def parse(self, tagged_sent):
    if not tagged_sent: return None
    (words, tags) = zip(*tagged_sent)
    chunks = self.tagger.tag(tags)
    wtc = itertools.izip(words, chunks)
    return nltk.chunk.conlltags2tree([(w,t,c) for (w,(t,c)) in wtc])
```

Once we have our trained `TagChunker`, we can then evaluate the `ChunkScore` the same way we did for the `RegexpParser` in the previous recipes.

```
>>> from chunkers import TagChunker
>>> from nltk.corpus import treebank_chunk
>>> train_chunks = treebank_chunk.chunked_sents()[:3000]
>>> test_chunks = treebank_chunk.chunked_sents()[3000:]
>>> chunker = TagChunker(train_chunks)
>>> score = chunker.evaluate(test_chunks)
>>> score.accuracy()
0.97320393352514278
>>> score.precision()
0.91665343705350055
>>> score.recall()
0.9465573770491803
```

Pretty darn accurate! Training a chunker is clearly a great alternative to manually specified grammars and regular expressions.

How it works...

Recall from the *Creating a chunked phrase corpus* recipe in *Chapter 3, Creating Custom Corpora* that the `conll2000` corpus defines chunks using IOB tags, which specify the type of chunk and where it begins and ends. We can train a part-of-speech tagger on these IOB tag patterns, and then use that to power a `ChunkerI` subclass. But first we need to transform a `Tree` that you would get from the `chunked_sents()` method of a corpus into a format usable by a part-of-speech tagger. This is what `conll_tag_chunks()` does. It uses `nltk.chunk.tree2conlltags()` to convert a sentence `Tree` into a list of 3-tuples of the form `(word, pos, iob)` where `pos` is the part-of-speech tag and `iob` is an IOB tag, such as `B-NP` to mark the beginning of a noun-phrase, or `I-NP` to mark that the word is inside the noun-phrase. The reverse of this method is `nltk.chunk.conlltags2tree()`. Here's some code to demonstrate these `nltk.chunk` functions:

```
>>> import nltk.chunk
>>> from nltk.tree import Tree
>>> t = Tree('S', [Tree('NP', [('the', 'DT'), ('book', 'NN')])])
>>> nltk.chunk.tree2conlltags(t)
[('the', 'DT', 'B-NP'), ('book', 'NN', 'I-NP')]
>>> nltk.chunk.conlltags2tree([('the', 'DT', 'B-NP'), ('book', 'NN',
'I-NP')])
Tree('S', [Tree('NP', [('the', 'DT'), ('book', 'NN')])])
```

The next step is to convert these 3-tuples into 2-tuples that the tagger can recognize. Because the `RegexpParser` uses part-of-speech tags for chunk patterns, we will do that here too and use part-of-speech tags as if they were words to tag. By simply dropping the `word` from 3-tuple `(word, pos, iob)`, the `conll_tag_chunks()` function returns a list of 2-tuples of the form `(pos, iob)`. When given the preceding example `Tree` in a list, the results are in a format we can feed to a tagger.

```
>>> conll_tag_chunks([t])
[[('DT', 'B-NP'), ('NN', 'I-NP')]]
```

The final step is a subclass of `ChunkParserI` called `TagChunker`. It trains on a list of chunk trees using an internal tagger. This internal tagger is composed of a `UnigramTagger` and a `BigramTagger` in a backoff chain, using the `backoff_tagger()` method created in the *Training and combining Ngram taggers* recipe in *Chapter 4, Part-of-Speech Tagging*.

Finally, `ChunkerI` subclasses must implement a `parse()` method that expects a part-of-speech tagged sentence. We unzip that sentence into a list of words and part-of-speech tags. The tags are then tagged by the tagger to get IOB tags, which are then re-combined with the words and part-of-speech tags to create 3-tuples we can pass to `nltk.chunk.conlltags2tree()` to return a final `Tree`.

There's more...

Since we have been talking about the `conll` IOB tags, let us see how the `TagChunker` does on the `conll2000` corpus:

```
>>> from nltk.corpus import conll2000
>>> conll_train = conll2000.chunked_sents('train.txt')
>>> conll_test = conll2000.chunked_sents('test.txt')
>>> chunker = TagChunker(conll_train)
>>> score = chunker.evaluate(conll_test)
>>> score.accuracy()
0.89505456234037617
>>> score.precision()
0.81148419743556754
>>> score.recall()
0.86441916769448635
```

Not quite as good as on `treebank_chunk`, but `conll2000` is a much larger corpus, so it's not too surprising.

Using different taggers

If you want to use different tagger classes with the `TagChunker`, you can pass them in as `tagger_classes`. For example, here's the `TagChunker` using just a `UnigramTagger`:

```
>>> from nltk.tag import UnigramTagger
>>> uni_chunker = TagChunker(train_chunks, tagger_
classes=[UnigramTagger])
>>> score = uni_chunker.evaluate(test_chunks)
>>> score.accuracy()
0.96749259243354657
```

The `tagger_classes` will be passed directly into the `backoff_tagger()` function, which means they must be subclasses of `SequentialBackoffTagger`. In testing, the default of `tagger_classes=[UnigramTagger, BigramTagger]` produces the best results.

See also

The *Training and combining Ngram taggers* recipe in *Chapter 4, Part-of-Speech Tagging* covers backoff tagging with a `UnigramTagger` and `BigramTagger`. `ChunkScore` metrics returned by the `evaluate()` method of a chunker were explained in the previous recipe.

Classification-based chunking

Unlike most part-of-speech taggers, the `ClassifierBasedTagger` learns from features. That means we can create a `ClassifierChunker` that can learn from both the words and part-of-speech tags, instead of only the part-of-speech tags as the `TagChunker` does.

How to do it...

For the `ClassifierChunker`, we don't want to discard the words from the training sentences, as we did in the previous recipe. Instead, to remain compatible with the 2-tuple `(word, pos)` format required for training a `ClassiferBasedTagger`, we convert the `(word, pos, iob)` 3-tuples from `nltk.chunk.tree2conlltags()` into `((word, pos), iob)` 2-tuples using the `chunk_trees2train_chunks()` function. This code can be found in `chunkers.py`:

```
import nltk.chunk
from nltk.tag import ClassifierBasedTagger

def chunk_trees2train_chunks(chunk_sents):
  tag_sents = [nltk.chunk.tree2conlltags(sent) for sent in chunk_
sents]
  return [[((w,t),c) for (w,t,c) in sent] for sent in tag_sents]
```

Next, we need a feature detector function to pass into `ClassifierBasedTagger`. Our default feature detector function, `prev_next_pos_iob()`, knows that the list of `tokens` is really a list of `(word, pos)` tuples, and can use that to return a feature set suitable for a classifier. To give the classifier as much information as we can, this feature set contains the current, previous and next word, and part-of-speech tag, along with the previous IOB tag.

```
def prev_next_pos_iob(tokens, index, history):
  word, pos = tokens[index]

  if index == 0:
    prevword, prevpos, previob = ('<START>',)*3
  else:
    prevword, prevpos = tokens[index-1]
    previob = history[index-1]

  if index == len(tokens) - 1:
    nextword, nextpos = ('<END>',)*2
  else:
    nextword, nextpos = tokens[index+1]

  feats = {
    'word': word,
    'pos': pos,
    'nextword': nextword,
    'nextpos': nextpos,
    'prevword': prevword,
    'prevpos': prevpos,
    'previob': previob
  }
  return feats
```

Now we can define the `ClassifierChunker`, which uses an internal `ClassifierBasedTagger` with features extracted using `prev_next_pos_iob()`, and training sentences from `chunk_trees2train_chunks()`. As a subclass of `ChunkerParserI`, it implements the `parse()` method, which converts the `((w, t), c)` tuples produced by the internal tagger into a `Tree` using `nltk.chunk.conlltags2tree()`.

```
class ClassifierChunker(nltk.chunk.ChunkParserI):
  def __init__(self, train_sents, feature_detector=prev_next_pos_iob,
**kwargs):
    if not feature_detector:
      feature_detector = self.feature_detector

    train_chunks = chunk_trees2train_chunks(train_sents)
    self.tagger = ClassifierBasedTagger(train=train_chunks,
      feature_detector=feature_detector, **kwargs)
```

```
def parse(self, tagged_sent):
    if not tagged_sent: return None
    chunks = self.tagger.tag(tagged_sent)
    return nltk.chunk.conlltags2tree([(w,t,c) for ((w,t),c) in
chunks])
```

Using the same `train_chunks` and `test_chunks` from the `treebank_chunk` corpus in the previous recipe, we can evaluate this code from `chunkers.py`:

```
>>> from chunkers import ClassifierChunker
>>> chunker = ClassifierChunker(train_chunks)
>>> score = chunker.evaluate(test_chunks)
>>> score.accuracy()
0.97217331558380216
>>> score.precision()
0.92588387933830685
>>> score.recall()
0.93590163934426229
```

Compared to the `TagChunker`, all the scores have gone up a bit. Let us see how it does on `conll2000`:

```
>>> chunker = ClassifierChunker(conll_train)
>>> score = chunker.evaluate(conll_test)
>>> score.accuracy()
0.92646220740021534
>>> score.precision()
0.87379243109102189
>>> score.recall()
0.90073546206203459
```

This is much improved over the `TagChunker`.

How it works...

Like the `TagChunker` in the previous recipe, we are training a part-of-speech tagger for IOB tagging. But in this case, we want to include the word as a feature to power a classifier. By creating nested 2-tuples of the form `((word, pos), iob)`, we can pass the word through the tagger into our feature detector function. `chunk_trees2train_chunks()` produces these nested 2-tuples, and `prev_next_pos_iob()` is aware of them and uses each element as a feature. The following features are extracted:

- The current word and part-of-speech tag
- The previous word, part-of-speech tag, and IOB tag
- The next word and part-of-speech tag

The arguments to `prev_next_pos_iob()` look the same as the `feature_detector()` method of the `ClassifierBasedTagger`: `tokens`, `index`, and `history`. But this time, `tokens` will be a list of `(word, pos)` 2-tuples, and `history` will be a list of IOB tags. The special feature values `'<START>'` and `'<END>'` are used if there are no previous or next tokens.

The `ClassifierChunker` uses an internal `ClassifierBasedTagger` and `prev_next_pos_iob()` as its default `feature_detector`. The results from the tagger, which are in the same nested 2-tuple form, are then reformatted into 3-tuples to return a final `Tree` using `nltk.chunk.conlltags2tree()`.

There's more...

You can use your own feature detector function by passing it in to the `ClassifierChunker` as `feature_detector`. The `tokens` will contain a list of `(word, tag)` tuples, and `history` will be a list of the previous IOB tags found.

Using a different classifier builder

The `ClassifierBasedTagger` defaults to using `NaiveBayesClassifier.train` as its `classifier_builder`. But you can use any classifier you want by overriding the `classifier_builder` keyword argument. Here's an example using `MaxentClassifier.train`:

```
>>> from nltk.classify import MaxentClassifier
>>> builder = lambda toks: MaxentClassifier.train(toks, trace=0, max_
iter=10, min_lldelta=0.01)
>>> me_chunker = ClassifierChunker(train_chunks, classifier_
builder=builder)
>>> score = me_chunker.evaluate(test_chunks)
>>> score.accuracy()
0.9748357452655988
>>> score.precision()
0.93794355504208615
>>> score.recall()
0.93163934426229511
```

Instead of using `MaxentClassifier.train` directly, it has been wrapped in a `lambda` so that its output is quiet (`trace=0`) and it finishes in a reasonable amount of time. As you can see, the scores are slightly different compared to using the `NaiveBayesClassifier`.

The previous recipe, *Training a tagger-based chunker*, introduced the idea of using a part-of-speech tagger for training a chunker. The *Classifier-based tagging* recipe in *Chapter 4, Part-of-Speech Tagging* describes `ClassifierBasedPOSTagger`, which is a subclass of `ClassifierBasedTagger`. In *Chapter 7, Text Classification*, we will cover classification in detail.

Extracting named entities

Named entity recognition is a specific kind of chunk extraction that uses **entity tags** instead of, or in addition to, chunk tags. Common entity tags include PERSON, ORGANIZATION, and LOCATION. Part-of-speech tagged sentences are parsed into chunk trees as with normal chunking, but the nodes of the trees can be entity tags instead of chunk phrase tags.

How to do it...

NLTK comes with a pre-trained named entity chunker. This chunker has been trained on data from the ACE program, a **NIST (National Institute of Standards and Technology)** sponsored program for **Automatic Content Extraction**, which you can read more about here: `http://www.itl.nist.gov/iad/894.01/tests/ace/`. Unfortunately, this data is not included in the NLTK corpora, but the trained chunker is. This chunker can be used through the `ne_chunk()` method in the `nltk.chunk` module. `ne_chunk()` will chunk a single sentence into a `Tree`. The following is an example using `ne_chunk()` on the first tagged sentence of the `treebank_chunk` corpus:

```
>>> from nltk.chunk import ne_chunk
>>> ne_chunk(treebank_chunk.tagged_sents()[0])
Tree('S', [Tree('PERSON', [('Pierre', 'NNP')]), Tree('ORGANIZATION',
[('Vinken', 'NNP')]), (',', ','), ('61', 'CD'), ('years', 'NNS'),
('old', 'JJ'), (',', ','), ('will', 'MD'), ('join', 'VB'), ('the',
'DT'), ('board', 'NN'), ('as', 'IN'), ('a', 'DT'), ('nonexecutive',
'JJ'), ('director', 'NN'), ('Nov.', 'NNP'), ('29', 'CD'), ('.',
'.')])
```

You can see two entity tags are found: PERSON and ORGANIZATION. Each of these subtrees contain a list of the words that are recognized as a PERSON or ORGANIZATION. To extract these named entities, we can write a simple helper method that will get the leaves of all the subtrees we are interested in.

```
def sub_leaves(tree, node):
  return [t.leaves() for t in tree.subtrees
    (lambda s: s.node == node)]
```

Then we can call this method to get all the PERSON or ORGANIZATION leaves from a tree.

```
>>> tree = ne_chunk(treebank_chunk.tagged_sents()[0])
>>> from chunkers import sub_leaves
>>> sub_leaves(tree, 'PERSON')
[[('Pierre', 'NNP')]]
>>> sub_leaves(tree, 'ORGANIZATION')
[[('Vinken', 'NNP')]]
```

You may notice that the chunker has mistakenly separated "Vinken" into its own ORGANIZATION Tree instead of including it with the PERSON Tree containing "Pierre". Such is the case with statistical natural language processing—you can't always expect perfection.

How it works...

The pre-trained named entity chunker is much like any other chunker, and in fact uses a MaxentClassifier powered ClassifierBasedTagger to determine IOB tags. But instead of B-NP and I-NP IOB tags, it uses B-PERSON, I-PERSON, B-ORGANIZATION, I-ORGANIZATION, and more. It also uses the O tag to mark words that are not part of a named entity (and thus outside the named entity subtrees).

There's more...

To process multiple sentences at a time, you can use batch_ne_chunk(). Here's an example where we process the first 10 sentences from treebank_chunk.tagged_sents() and get the ORGANIZATION sub_leaves():

```
>>> from nltk.chunk import batch_ne_chunk
>>> trees = batch_ne_chunk(treebank_chunk.tagged_sents()[:10])
>>> [sub_leaves(t, 'ORGANIZATION') for t in trees]
[[[('Vinken', 'NNP')]], [[('Elsevier', 'NNP')]],
[[('Consolidated', 'NNP'), ('Gold', 'NNP'), ('Fields',
'NNP')]], [], [], [[('Inc.', 'NNP')]], [[('Micronite',
'NN')]], [[('New', 'NNP'), ('England', 'NNP'), ('Journal',
'NNP')]], [[('Lorillard', 'NNP')]], [], []]
```

You can see there are a couple of multi-word ORGANIZATION chunks, such as "New England Journal". There are also a few sentences that have no ORGANIZATION chunks, as indicated by the empty lists [].

Binary named entity extraction

If you don't care about the particular kind of named entity to extract, you can pass `binary=True` into `ne_chunk()` or `batch_ne_chunk()`. Now, all named entities will be tagged with NE:

```
>>> ne_chunk(treebank_chunk.tagged_sents()[0], binary=True)
Tree('S', [Tree('NE', [('Pierre', 'NNP'), ('Vinken', 'NNP')]),
(',', ','), ('61', 'CD'), ('years', 'NNS'), ('old', 'JJ'),
(',', ','), ('will', 'MD'), ('join', 'VB'), ('the', 'DT'),
('board', 'NN'), ('as', 'IN'), ('a', 'DT'), ('nonexecutive',
'JJ'), ('director', 'NN'), ('Nov.', 'NNP'), ('29', 'CD'),
('.', '.')])
```

If we get the `sub_leaves()`, we can see that "Pierre Vinken" is correctly combined into a single named entity.

```
>>> sub_leaves(ne_chunk(treebank_chunk.tagged_sents()[0],
binary=True), 'NE')
[[('Pierre', 'NNP'), ('Vinken', 'NNP')]]
```

See also

In the next recipe, we will create our own simple named entity chunker.

Extracting proper noun chunks

A simple way to do named entity extraction is to chunk all proper nouns (tagged with NNP). We can tag these chunks as NAME, since the definition of a proper noun is the name of a person, place, or thing.

How to do it...

Using the `RegexpParser`, we can create a very simple grammar that combines all proper nouns into a NAME chunk. Then we can test this on the first tagged sentence of `treebank_chunk` to compare the results to the previous recipe.

```
>>> chunker = RegexpParser(r'''
... NAME:
...     {<NNP>+}
... ''')
>>> sub_leaves(chunker.parse(treebank_chunk.tagged_sents()[0]),
'NAME')
[[('Pierre', 'NNP'), ('Vinken', 'NNP')], [('Nov.', 'NNP')]]
```

Although we get "Nov." as a NAME chunk, this isn't a wrong result, as "Nov." is the name of a month.

How it works...

The NAME chunker is a simple usage of the RegexpParser, covered in *Chunking and chinking with regular expressions, Merging and splitting chunks with regular expressions,* and *Partial parsing with regular expressions* recipes of this chapter. All sequences of NNP tagged words are combined into NAME chunks.

There's more...

If we wanted to be sure to only chunk the names of people, then we can build a PersonChunker that uses the names corpus for chunking. This class can be found in chunkers.py:

```python
import nltk.chunk
from nltk.corpus import names

class PersonChunker(nltk.chunk.ChunkParserI):
  def __init__(self):
    self.name_set = set(names.words())

  def parse(self, tagged_sent):
    iobs = []
    in_person = False

    for word, tag in tagged_sent:
      if word in self.name_set and in_person:
        iobs.append((word, tag, 'I-PERSON'))
      elif word in self.name_set:
        iobs.append((word, tag, 'B-PERSON'))
        in_person = True
      else:
        iobs.append((word, tag, 'O'))
        in_person = False

    return nltk.chunk.conlltags2tree(iobs)
```

The PersonChunker iterates over the tagged sentence, checking if each word is in its names_set (constructed from the names corpus). If the current word is in the names_set, then it uses either the B-PERSON or I-PERSON IOB tags, depending on whether the previous word was also in the names_set. Any word that's not in the names_set gets the O IOB tag. When complete, the list of IOB tags is converted to a Tree using nltk.chunk.conlltags2tree(). Using it on the same tagged sentence as before, we get the following result:

```python
>>> from chunkers import PersonChunker
>>> chunker = PersonChunker()
>>> sub_leaves(chunker.parse(treebank_chunk.tagged_sents()[0]),
'PERSON')
[[('Pierre', 'NNP')]]
```

We no longer get "Nov.", but we have also lost "Vinken", as it is not found in the `names` corpus. This recipe highlights some of the difficulties of chunk extraction and natural language processing in general:

- If you use general patterns, you will get general results
- If you are looking for specific results, you must use specific data
- If your specific data is incomplete, your results will be incomplete too

See also

The previous recipe defines the `sub_leaves()` method used to show the found chunks. In the next recipe, we will cover how to find `LOCATION` chunks based on the `gazetteers` corpus.

Extracting location chunks

To identify location chunks, we can make a different kind of `ChunkParserI` subclass that uses the `gazetteers` corpus to identify location words. `gazetteers` is a `WordListCorpusReader` that contains the following location words:

- Country names
- U.S. states and abbreviations
- Major U.S. cities
- Canadian provinces
- Mexican states

How to do it...

The `LocationChunker`, found in `chunkers.py`, iterates over a tagged sentence looking for words that are found in the `gazetteers` corpus. When it finds one or more location words, it creates a `LOCATION` chunk using IOB tags. The helper method `iob_locations()` is where the IOB `LOCATION` tags are produced, and the `parse()` method converts these IOB tags to a `Tree`.

```
import nltk.chunk
from nltk.corpus import gazetteers

class LocationChunker(nltk.chunk.ChunkParserI):
  def __init__(self):
    self.locations = set(gazetteers.words())
    self.lookahead = 0
```

```
      for loc in self.locations:
        nwords = loc.count(' ')

        if nwords > self.lookahead:
          self.lookahead = nwords

  def iob_locations(self, tagged_sent):
    i = 0
    l = len(tagged_sent)
    inside = False

    while i < l:
      word, tag = tagged_sent[i]
      j = i + 1
      k = j + self.lookahead
      nextwords, nexttags = [], []
      loc = False

      while j < k:
        if ' '.join([word] + nextwords) in self.locations:
          if inside:
            yield word, tag, 'I-LOCATION'
          else:
            yield word, tag, 'B-LOCATION'

          for nword, ntag in zip(nextwords, nexttags):
            yield nword, ntag, 'I-LOCATION'

          loc, inside = True, True
          i = j
          break

        if j < l:
          nextword, nexttag = tagged_sent[j]
          nextwords.append(nextword)
          nexttags.append(nexttag)
          j += 1
        else:
          break

      if not loc:
        inside = False
        i += 1
        yield word, tag, 'O'
```

```
def parse(self, tagged_sent):
    iobs = self.iob_locations(tagged_sent)
    return nltk.chunk.conlltags2tree(iobs)
```

We can use the `LocationChunker` to parse the following sentence into two locations, "San Francisco, CA is cold compared to San Jose, CA":

```
>>> from chunkers import LocationChunker
>>> t = loc.parse([('San', 'NNP'), ('Francisco', 'NNP'),
('CA', 'NNP'), ('is', 'BE'), ('cold', 'JJ'), ('compared',
'VBD'), ('to', 'TO'), ('San', 'NNP'), ('Jose', 'NNP'),
('CA', 'NNP')])
>>> sub_leaves(t, 'LOCATION')
[[('San', 'NNP'), ('Francisco', 'NNP'), ('CA', 'NNP')],
[('San', 'NNP'), ('Jose', 'NNP'), ('CA', 'NNP')]]
```

And the result is that we get two LOCATION chunks, just as expected.

How it works...

The `LocationChunker` starts by constructing a `set` of all locations in the `gazetteers` corpus. Then it finds the maximum number of words in a single location string, so it knows how many words it must look ahead when parsing a tagged sentence.

The `parse()` method calls a helper method `iob_locations()`, which generates 3-tuples of the form `(word, pos, iob)` where iob is either O if the word is not a location, or B-LOCATION or I-LOCATION for LOCATION chunks. `iob_locations()` finds location chunks by looking at the current word and the next words to check if the combined word is in the locations `set`. Multiple location words that are next to each other are then put into the same LOCATION chunk, such as in the preceding example with "San Francisco" and "CA".

Like in the previous recipe, it's simpler and more convenient to construct a list of `(word, pos, iob)` tuples to pass in to `nltk.chunk.conlltags2tree()` to return a `Tree`. The alternative is to construct a `Tree` manually, but that requires keeping track of children, subtrees, and where you currently are in the `Tree`.

There's more...

One of the nice aspects of this `LocationChunker` is that it doesn't care about the part-of-speech tags. As long as the location words are found in the locations set, any part-of-speech tag will do.

In the next recipe, we will cover how to train a named entity chunker using the `ieer` corpus.

Training a named entity chunker

You can train your own named entity chunker using the `ieer` corpus, which stands for **Information Extraction—Entity Recognition (ieer)**. It takes a bit of extra work though, because the `ieer` corpus has chunk trees, but no part-of-speech tags for words.

How to do it...

Using the `ieertree2conlltags()` and `ieer_chunked_sents()` functions in `chunkers.py`, we can create named entity chunk trees from the `ieer` corpus to train the `ClassifierChunker` created in *Classification-based chunking* recipe of this chapter.

```
import nltk.tag, nltk.chunk, itertools
from nltk.corpus import ieer

def ieertree2conlltags(tree, tag=nltk.tag.pos_tag):
  words, ents = zip(*tree.pos())
  iobs = []
  prev = None

  for ent in ents:
    if ent == tree.node:
      iobs.append('O')
      prev = None
    elif prev == ent:
      iobs.append('I-%s' % ent)
    else:
      iobs.append('B-%s' % ent)
      prev = ent

  words, tags = zip(*tag(words))
  return itertools.izip(words, tags, iobs)

def ieer_chunked_sents(tag=nltk.tag.pos_tag):
  for doc in ieer.parsed_docs():
    tagged = ieertree2conlltags(doc.text, tag)
    yield nltk.chunk.conlltags2tree(tagged)
```

We will use 80 out of 94 sentences for training, and the rest for testing. Then we can see how it does on the first sentence of the `treebank_chunk` corpus.

```
>>> from chunkers import ieer_chunked_sents, ClassifierChunker
>>> from nltk.corpus import treebank_chunk
>>> ieer_chunks = list(ieer_chunked_sents())
>>> len(ieer_chunks)
94
>>> chunker = ClassifierChunker(ieer_chunks[:80])
>>> chunker.parse(treebank_chunk.tagged_sents()[0])
Tree('S', [Tree('LOCATION', [('Pierre', 'NNP'), ('Vinken', 'NNP')]),
(',', ','), Tree('DURATION', [('61', 'CD'), ('years', 'NNS')]),
Tree('MEASURE', [('old', 'JJ')]), (',', ','), ('will', 'MD'),
('join', 'VB'), ('the', 'DT'), ('board', 'NN'), ('as', 'IN'), ('a',
'DT'), ('nonexecutive', 'JJ'), ('director', 'NN'), Tree('DATE',
[('Nov.', 'NNP'), ('29', 'CD')]), ('.', '.')])
```

So it found a correct DURATION and DATE, but tagged "Pierre Vinken" as a LOCATION. Let us see how it scores against the rest of `ieer` chunk trees:

```
>>> score = chunker.evaluate(ieer_chunks[80:])
>>> score.accuracy()
0.88290183880706252
>>> score.precision()
0.40887174541947929
>>> score.recall()
0.50536352800953521
```

Accuracy is pretty good, but precision and recall are very low. That means lots of false negatives and false positives.

How it works...

The truth is, we are not working with ideal training data. The `ieer` trees generated by `ieer_chunked_sents()` are not entirely accurate. First, there are no explicit sentence breaks, so each document is a single tree. Second, the words are not explicitly tagged, so we have to guess using `nltk.tag.pos_tag()`.

The `ieer` corpus provides a `parsed_docs()` method that returns a list of documents with a `text` attribute. This `text` attribute is a document `Tree` that is converted to a list of 3-tuples of the form `(word, pos, iob)`. To get these final 3-tuples, we must first flatten the `Tree` using `tree.pos()`, which returns a list of 2-tuples of the form `(word, entity)`, where entity is either the entity tag or the top tag of the tree. Any words whose entity is the top tag are outside the named entity chunks and get the IOB tag `O`. All words that have unique entity tags are either the beginning of or inside a named entity chunk. Once we have all the IOB tags, then we can get the part-of-speech tags of all the words and join the words, part-of-speech tags, and IOB tags into 3-tuples using `itertools.izip()`.

There's more...

Despite the non-ideal training data, the `ieer` corpus provides a good place to start for training a named entity chunker. The data comes from the *New York Times* and *AP Newswire* reports. Each doc from `ieer.parsed_docs()` also contains a headline attribute that is a `Tree`.

```
>>> from nltk.corpus import ieer
>>> ieer.parsed_docs()[0].headline
Tree('DOCUMENT', ['Kenyans', 'protest', 'tax', 'hikes'])
```

See also

The *Extracting named entities* recipe in this chapter, covers the pre-trained named entity chunker that comes included with NLTK.

6
Transforming Chunks and Trees

In this chapter, we will cover:

- ► Filtering insignificant words
- ► Correcting verb forms
- ► Swapping verb phrases
- ► Swapping noun cardinals
- ► Swapping infinitive phrases
- ► Singularizing plural nouns
- ► Chaining chunk transformations
- ► Converting a chunk tree to text
- ► Flattening a deep tree
- ► Creating a shallow tree
- ► Converting tree nodes

Introduction

Now that you know how to get chunks/phrases from a sentence, what do you do with them? This chapter will show you how to do various transforms on both chunks and trees. The chunk transforms are for grammatical correction and rearranging phrases without loss of meaning. The tree transforms give you ways to modify and flatten deep parse trees.

The functions detailed in these recipes modify data, as opposed to learning from it. That means it's not safe to apply them indiscriminately. A thorough knowledge of the data you want to transform, along with a few experiments, should help you decide which functions to apply and when.

Whenever the term **chunk** is used in this chapter, it could refer to an actual chunk extracted by a chunker, or it could simply refer to a short phrase or sentence in the form of a list of tagged words. What's important in this chapter is what you can do with a chunk, not where it came from.

Filtering insignificant words

Many of the most commonly used words are insignificant when it comes to discerning the meaning of a phrase. For example, in the phrase "the movie was terrible", the most *significant* words are "movie" and "terrible", while "the" and "was" are almost useless. You could get the same meaning if you took them out, such as "movie terrible" or "terrible movie". Either way, the sentiment is the same. In this recipe, we'll learn how to remove the insignificant words, and keep the significant ones, by looking at their part-of-speech tags.

Getting ready

First, we need to decide which part-of-speech tags are significant and which are not. Looking through the treebank corpus for stopwords yields the following table of insignificant words and tags:

Word	Tag
a	DT
all	PDT
an	DT
and	CC
or	CC
that	WDT
the	DT

Other than CC, all the tags end with DT. This means we can filter out insignificant words by looking at the tag's suffix.

How to do it...

In `transforms.py` there is a function called `filter_insignificant()`. It takes a single chunk, which should be a list of tagged words, and returns a new chunk without any insignificant tagged words. It defaults to filtering out any tags that end with DT or CC.

```
def filter_insignificant(chunk, tag_suffixes=['DT', 'CC']):
  good = []

  for word, tag in chunk:
    ok = True

    for suffix in tag_suffixes:
      if tag.endswith(suffix):
        ok = False
        break

    if ok:
      good.append((word, tag))

  return good
```

Now we can use it on the part-of-speech tagged version of "the terrible movie".

```
>>> from transforms import filter_insignificant
>>> filter_insignificant([('the', 'DT'), ('terrible', 'JJ'), ('movie',
'NN')])
[('terrible', 'JJ'), ('movie', 'NN')]
```

As you can see, the word "the" is eliminated from the chunk.

How it works...

`filter_insignificant()` iterates over the tagged words in the chunk. For each tag, it checks if that tag ends with any of the `tag_suffixes`. If it does, then the tagged word is skipped. However if the tag is ok, then the tagged word is appended to a new good chunk that is returned.

There's more...

The way `filter_insignificant()` is defined, you can pass in your own tag suffixes if DT and CC are not enough, or are incorrect for your case. For example, you might decide that possessive words and pronouns such as "you", "your", "their", and "theirs" are no good but DT and CC words are ok. The tag suffixes would then be PRP and PRP$. Following is an example of this function:

```
>>> filter_insignificant([('your', 'PRP$'), ('book', 'NN'), ('is',
'VBZ'), ('great', 'JJ')], tag_suffixes=['PRP', 'PRP$'])
[('book', 'NN'), ('is', 'VBZ'), ('great', 'JJ')]
```

Filtering insignificant words can be a good complement to stopword filtering for purposes such as search engine indexing, querying, and text classification.

See also

This recipe is analogous to the *Filtering stopwords in a tokenized sentence* recipe in *Chapter 1, Tokenizing Text and WordNet Basics*.

Correcting verb forms

It's fairly common to find incorrect verb forms in real-world language. For example, the correct form of "is our children learning?" is "are our children learning?". The verb "is" should only be used with singular nouns, while "are" is for plural nouns, such as "children". We can correct these mistakes by creating verb correction mappings that are used depending on whether there's a plural or singular noun in the chunk.

Getting ready

We first need to define the verb correction mappings in `transforms.py`. We'll create two mappings, one for plural to singular, and another for singular to plural.

```
plural_verb_forms = {
    ('is', 'VBZ'): ('are', 'VBP'),
    ('was', 'VBD'): ('were', 'VBD')
}

singular_verb_forms = {
    ('are', 'VBP'): ('is', 'VBZ'),
    ('were', 'VBD'): ('was', 'VBD')
}
```

Each mapping has a tagged verb that maps to another tagged verb. These initial mappings cover the basics of mapping, is to are, was to were, and vice versa.

How to do it...

In `transforms.py` there is a function called `correct_verbs()`. Pass it a chunk with incorrect verb forms, and you'll get a corrected chunk back. It uses a helper function `first_chunk_index()` to search the chunk for the position of the first tagged word where `pred` returns `True`.

```
def first_chunk_index(chunk, pred, start=0, step=1):
  l = len(chunk)
  end = l if step > 0 else -1

  for i in range(start, end, step):
    if pred(chunk[i]):
      return i

  return None

def correct_verbs(chunk):
  vbidx = first_chunk_index(chunk, lambda (word, tag): tag.
startswith('VB'))
  # if no verb found, do nothing
  if vbidx is None:
    return chunk

  verb, vbtag = chunk[vbidx]
  nnpred = lambda (word, tag): tag.startswith('NN')
  # find nearest noun to the right of verb
  nnidx = first_chunk_index(chunk, nnpred, start=vbidx+1)
  # if no noun found to right, look to the left
  if nnidx is None:
    nnidx = first_chunk_index(chunk, nnpred, start=vbidx-1, step=-1)
  # if no noun found, do nothing
  if nnidx is None:
    return chunk

  noun, nntag = chunk[nnidx]
  # get correct verb form and insert into chunk
  if nntag.endswith('S'):
    chunk[vbidx] = plural_verb_forms.get((verb, vbtag), (verb, vbtag))
  else:
    chunk[vbidx] = singular_verb_forms.get((verb, vbtag), (verb,
vbtag))

  return chunk
```

When we call it on a part-of-speech tagged "is our children learning" chunk, we get back the correct form, "are our children learning".

```
>>> from transforms import correct_verbs
>>> correct_verbs([('is', 'VBZ'), ('our', 'PRP$'), ('children',
'NNS'), ('learning', 'VBG')])
[('are', 'VBP'), ('our', 'PRP$'), ('children', 'NNS'), ('learning',
'VBG')]
```

We can also try this with a singular noun and an incorrect plural verb.

```
>>> correct_verbs([('our', 'PRP$'), ('child', 'NN'), ('were', 'VBD'),
('learning', 'VBG')])
[('our', 'PRP$'), ('child', 'NN'), ('was', 'VBD'), ('learning',
'VBG')]
```

In this case, "were" becomes "was" because "child" is a singular noun.

How it works...

The `correct_verbs()` function starts by looking for a verb in the chunk. If no verb is found, the chunk is returned with no changes. Once a verb is found, we keep the verb, its tag, and its index in the chunk. Then we look on either side of the verb to find the nearest noun, starting on the right, and only looking to the left if no noun is found on the right. If no noun is found at all, the chunk is returned as is. But if a noun is found, then we lookup the correct verb form depending on whether or not the noun is plural.

Recall from *Chapter 4, Part-of-Speech Tagging*, that plural nouns are tagged with NNS, while singular nouns are tagged with NN. This means we can check the plurality of a noun by seeing if its tag ends with S. Once we get the corrected verb form, it is inserted into the chunk to replace the original verb form.

To make searching through the chunk easier, we define a function called `first_chunk_index()`. It takes a chunk, a `lambda` predicate, the starting index, and a step increment. The predicate function is called with each tagged word until it returns `True`. If it never returns `True`, then `None` is returned. The starting index defaults to zero and the step increment to one. As you'll see in upcoming recipes, we can search backwards by overriding `start` and setting `step` to -1. This small utility function will be a key part of subsequent transform functions.

See also

The next four recipes all make use of `first_chunk_index()` to perform chunk transformations.

Swapping verb phrases

Swapping the words around a verb can eliminate the passive voice from particular phrases. For example, "the book was great" can be transformed into "the great book".

How to do it...

In `transforms.py` there is a function called `swap_verb_phrase()`. It swaps the right-hand side of the chunk with the left-hand side, using the verb as the *pivot* point. It uses the `first_chunk_index()` function defined in the previous recipe to find the verb to pivot around.

```
def swap_verb_phrase(chunk):
  # find location of verb
  vbpred = lambda (word, tag): tag != 'VBG' and tag.startswith('VB')
and len(tag) > 2
  vbidx = first_chunk_index(chunk, vbpred)

  if vbidx is None:
    return chunk

  return chunk[vbidx+1:] + chunk[:vbidx]
```

Now we can see how it works on the part-of-speech tagged phrase "the book was great".

```
>>> from transforms import swap_verb_phrase
>>> swap_verb_phrase([('the', 'DT'), ('book', 'NN'), ('was', 'VBD'),
('great', 'JJ')])
[('great', 'JJ'), ('the', 'DT'), ('book', 'NN')]
```

The result is "great the book". This phrase clearly isn't grammatically correct, so read on to learn how to fix it.

How it works...

Using `first_chunk_index()` from the previous recipe, we start by finding the first matching verb that is not a gerund (a word that ends in "ing") tagged with VBG. Once we've found the verb, we return the chunk with the right side before the left, and remove the verb.

The reason we don't want to pivot around a gerund is that gerunds are commonly used to describe nouns, and pivoting around one would remove that description. Here's an example where you can see how not pivoting around a gerund is a good thing:

```
>>> swap_verb_phrase([('this', 'DT'), ('gripping', 'VBG'), ('book',
'NN'), ('is', 'VBZ'), ('fantastic', 'JJ')])
```

```
[('fantastic', 'JJ'), ('this', 'DT'), ('gripping', 'VBG'), ('book',
'NN')]
```

If we had pivoted around the gerund, the result would be "book is fantastic this", and we'd lose the gerund "gripping".

There's more...

Filtering insignificant words makes the final result more readable. By filtering either before or after swap_verb_phrase(), we get "fantastic gripping book" instead of "fantastic this gripping book".

```
>>> from transforms import swap_verb_phrase, filter_insignificant
>>> swap_verb_phrase(filter_insignificant([('this', 'DT'),
('gripping', 'VBG'), ('book', 'NN'), ('is', 'VBZ'), ('fantastic',
'JJ')]))
[('fantastic', 'JJ'), ('gripping', 'VBG'), ('book', 'NN')]
>>> filter_insignificant(swap_verb_phrase([('this', 'DT'),
('gripping', 'VBG'), ('book', 'NN'), ('is', 'VBZ'), ('fantastic',
'JJ')]))
[('fantastic', 'JJ'), ('gripping', 'VBG'), ('book', 'NN')]
```

Either way, we get a shorter grammatical chunk with no loss of meaning.

See also

The previous recipe defines first_chunk_index(), which is used to find the verb in the chunk.

Swapping noun cardinals

In a chunk, a **cardinal** word—tagged as CD—refers to a number, such as "10". These cardinals often occur before or after a noun. For normalization purposes, it can be useful to always put the cardinal before the noun.

How to do it...

The function swap_noun_cardinal() is defined in transforms.py. It swaps any cardinal that occurs immediately after a noun with the noun, so that the cardinal occurs immediately before the noun.

```
def swap_noun_cardinal(chunk):
    cdidx = first_chunk_index(chunk, lambda (word, tag): tag == 'CD')
    # cdidx must be > 0 and there must be a noun immediately before it
    if not cdidx or not chunk[cdidx-1][1].startswith('NN'):
```

```
    return chunk

  noun, nntag = chunk[cdidx-1]
  chunk[cdidx-1] = chunk[cdidx]
  chunk[cdidx] = noun, nntag
  return chunk
```

Let's try it on a date, such as "Dec 10", and another common phrase "the top 10".

```
>>> from transforms import swap_noun_cardinal
>>> swap_noun_cardinal([('Dec.', 'NNP'), ('10', 'CD')])
[('10', 'CD'), ('Dec.', 'NNP')]
>>> swap_noun_cardinal([('the', 'DT'), ('top', 'NN'), ('10', 'CD')])
[('the', 'DT'), ('10', 'CD'), ('top', 'NN')]
```

The result is that the numbers are now in front of the noun, creating "10 Dec" and "the 10 top".

How it works...

We start by looking for a CD tag in the chunk. If no CD is found, or if the CD is at the beginning of the chunk, then the chunk is returned as is. There must also be a noun immediately before the CD. If we do find a CD with a noun preceding it, then we swap the noun and cardinal in place.

See also

The *Correcting verb forms* recipe defines the `first_chunk_index()` function, used to find tagged words in a chunk.

Swapping infinitive phrases

An infinitive phrase has the form "A of B", such as "book of recipes". These can often be transformed into a new form while retaining the same meaning, such as "recipes book".

How to do it...

An infinitive phrase can be found by looking for a word tagged with IN. The function `swap_infinitive_phrase()`, defined in `transforms.py`, will return a chunk that swaps the portion of the phrase after the IN word with the portion before the IN word.

```
def swap_infinitive_phrase(chunk):
  inpred = lambda (word, tag): tag == 'IN' and word != 'like'
  inidx = first_chunk_index(chunk, inpred)
```

```
if inidx is None:
  return chunk

nnpred = lambda (word, tag): tag.startswith('NN')
nnidx = first_chunk_index(chunk, nnpred, start=inidx, step=-1) or 0

return chunk[:nnidx] + chunk[inidx+1:] + chunk[nnidx:inidx]
```

The function can now be used to transform "book of recipes" into "recipes book".

```
>>> from transforms import swap_infinitive_phrase
>>> swap_infinitive_phrase([('book', 'NN'), ('of', 'IN'), ('recipes',
'NNS')])
[('recipes', 'NNS'), ('book', 'NN')]
```

How it works...

This function is similar to the `swap_verb_phrase()` function described in the *Swapping verb phrases* recipe. The `inpred` lambda is passed to `first_chunk_index()` to look for a word whose tag is IN. Next, `nnpred` is used to find the first noun that occurs before the IN word, so we can insert the portion of the chunk after the IN word between the noun and the beginning of the chunk. A more complicated example should demonstrate this:

```
>>> swap_infinitive_phrase([('delicious', 'JJ'), ('book', 'NN'),
('of', 'IN'), ('recipes', 'NNS')])
[('delicious', 'JJ'), ('recipes', 'NNS'), ('book', 'NN')]
```

We don't want the result to be "recipes delicious book". Instead, we want to insert "recipes" before the noun "book", but after the adjective "delicious". Hence, the need to find the `nnidx` occurring before the `inidx`.

There's more...

You'll notice that the `inpred` lambda checks to make sure the word is not "like". That's because "like" phrases must be treated differently, as transforming them the same way will result in an ungrammatical phrase. For example, "tastes like chicken" should not be transformed into "chicken tastes":

```
>>> swap_infinitive_phrase([('tastes', 'VBZ'), ('like', 'IN'),
('chicken', 'NN')])
[('tastes', 'VBZ'), ('like', 'IN'), ('chicken', 'NN')]
```

In the next recipe, we'll learn how to transform "recipes book" into the more normal form "recipe book".

Singularizing plural nouns

As we saw in the previous recipe, the transformation process can result in phrases such as "recipes book". This is a NNS followed by an NN, when a more proper version of the phrase would be "recipe book", which is an NN followed by another NN. We can do another transform to correct these improper plural nouns.

How to do it...

`transforms.py` defines a function called `singularize_plural_noun()`, which will de-pluralize a plural noun (tagged with NNS) that is followed by another noun.

```
def singularize_plural_noun(chunk):
  nnspred = lambda (word, tag): tag == 'NNS'
  nnsidx = first_chunk_index(chunk, nnspred)

  if nnsidx is not None and nnsidx+1 < len(chunk) and chunk[nnsidx+1]
[1][:2] == 'NN':
    noun, nnstag = chunk[nnsidx]
    chunk[nnsidx] = (noun.rstrip('s'), nnstag.rstrip('S'))

  return chunk
```

Using it on "recipes book", we get the more correct form, "recipe book".

```
>>> from transforms import singularize_plural_noun
>>> singularize_plural_noun([('recipes', 'NNS'), ('book', 'NN')])
[('recipe', 'NN'), ('book', 'NN')]
```

How it works...

We start by looking for a plural noun with the tag NNS. If found, and if the next word is a noun (determined by making sure the tag starts with NN), then we de-pluralize the plural noun by removing an "s" from the right side of both the tag and the word.

The tag is assumed to be capitalized, so an uppercase "S" is removed from the right side of the tag, while a lowercase "s" is removed from the right side of the word.

See also

The previous recipe shows how a transformation can result in a plural noun followed by a singular noun, though this could also occur naturally in real-world text.

Chaining chunk transformations

The transform functions defined in the previous recipes can be chained together to normalize chunks. The resulting chunks are often shorter with no loss of meaning.

How to do it...

In `transforms.py` is the function `transform_chunk()`. It takes a single chunk and an optional list of transform functions. It calls each transform function on the chunk, one at a time, and returns the final chunk.

```
def transform_chunk(chunk, chain=[filter_insignificant, swap_verb_
phrase, swap_infinitive_phrase, singularize_plural_noun], trace=0):
  for f in chain:
    chunk = f(chunk)

    if trace:
      print f.__name__, ':', chunk

  return chunk
```

Using it on the phrase "the book of recipes is delicious", we get "delicious recipe book":

```
>>> from transforms import transform_chunk
>>> transform_chunk([('the', 'DT'), ('book', 'NN'), ('of', 'IN'),
('recipes', 'NNS'), ('is', 'VBZ'), ('delicious', 'JJ')])
[('delicious', 'JJ'), ('recipe', 'NN'), ('book', 'NN')]
```

How it works...

The `transform_chunk()` function defaults to chaining the following functions in order:

- `filter_insignificant()`
- `swap_verb_phrase()`
- `swap_infinitive_phrase()`
- `singularize_plural_noun()`

Each function transforms the chunk that results from the previous function, starting with the original chunk.

The order in which you apply transform functions can be significant. Experiment with your own data to determine which transforms are best, and in which order they should be applied.

There's more...

You can pass `trace=1` into `transform_chunk()` to get an output at each step.

```
>>> from transforms import transform_chunk
>>> transform_chunk([[('the', 'DT'), ('book', 'NN'), ('of', 'IN'),
('recipes', 'NNS'), ('is', 'VBZ'), ('delicious', 'JJ')], trace=1)
filter_insignificant : [('book', 'NN'), ('of', 'IN'), ('recipes',
'NNS'), ('is', 'VBZ'), ('delicious', 'JJ')]
swap_verb_phrase : [('delicious', 'JJ'), ('book', 'NN'), ('of', 'IN'),
('recipes', 'NNS')]
swap_infinitive_phrase : [('delicious', 'JJ'), ('recipes', 'NNS'),
('book', 'NN')]
singularize_plural_noun : [('delicious', 'JJ'), ('recipe', 'NN'),
('book', 'NN')]
[('delicious', 'JJ'), ('recipe', 'NN'), ('book', 'NN')]
```

This shows you the result of each transform function, which is then passed in to the next transform function until a final chunk is returned.

See also

The transform functions used were defined in the previous recipes of this chapter.

Converting a chunk tree to text

At some point, you may want to convert a `Tree` or sub-tree back to a sentence or chunk string. This is mostly straightforward, except when it comes to properly outputting punctuation.

How to do it...

We'll use the first `Tree` of the `treebank_chunk` as our example. The obvious first step is to join all the words in the tree with a space.

```
>>> from nltk.corpus import treebank_chunk
>>> tree = treebank_chunk.chunked_sents()[0]
>>> ' '.join([w for w, t in tree.leaves()])
'Pierre Vinken , 61 years old , will join the board as a nonexecutive
director Nov. 29 .'
```

As you can see, the punctuation isn't quite right. The commas and period are treated as individual words, and so get the surrounding spaces as well. We can fix this using regular expression substitution. This is implemented in the `chunk_tree_to_sent()` function found in `transforms.py`.

```
import re
punct_re = re.compile(r'\s([,\.;\?])')

def chunk_tree_to_sent(tree, concat=' '):
    s = concat.join([w for w, t in tree.leaves()])
    return re.sub(punct_re, r'\g<1>', s)
```

Using this function results in a much cleaner sentence, with no space before each punctuation mark:

```
>>> from transforms import chunk_tree_to_sent
>>> chunk_tree_to_sent(tree)
'Pierre Vinken, 61 years old, will join the board as a nonexecutive
director Nov. 29.'
```

How it works...

To correct the extra spaces in front of the punctuation, we create a regular expression `punct_re` that will match a space followed by any of the known punctuation characters. We have to escape both '.' and '?' with a '\' since they are special characters. The punctuation is surrounded by parenthesis so we can use the matched group for substitution.

Once we have our regular expression, we define `chunk_tree_to_sent()`, whose first step is to join the words by a concatenation character that defaults to a space. Then we can call `re.sub()` to replace all the punctuation matches with just the punctuation group. This eliminates the space in front of the punctuation characters, resulting in a more correct string.

There's more...

We can simplify this function a little by using `nltk.tag.untag()` to get words from the tree's leaves, instead of using our own list comprehension.

```
import nltk.tag, re
punct_re = re.compile(r'\s([,\.;\?])')

def chunk_tree_to_sent(tree, concat=' '):
    s = concat.join(nltk.tag.untag(tree.leaves()))
    return re.sub(punct_re, r'\g<1>', s)
```

The `nltk.tag.untag()` function was covered at the end of the *Default tagging* recipe in *Chapter 4, Part-of-Speech Tagging*.

Flattening a deep tree

Some of the included corpora contain parsed sentences, which are often deep trees of nested phrases. Unfortunately, these trees are too deep to use for training a chunker, since IOB tag parsing is not designed for nested chunks. To make these trees usable for chunker training, we must flatten them.

Getting ready

We're going to use the first parsed sentence of the `treebank` corpus as our example. Here's a diagram showing how deeply nested this tree is:

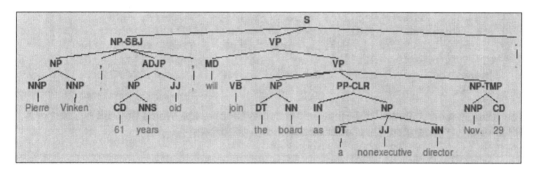

You may notice that the part-of-speech tags are part of the tree structure, instead of being included with the word. This will be handled next using the `Tree.pos()` method, which was designed specifically for combining words with pre-terminal `Tree` nodes such as part-of-speech tags.

How to do it...

In `transforms.py` there is a function named `flatten_deeptree()`. It takes a single `Tree` and will return a new `Tree` that keeps only the lowest level trees. It uses a helper function `flatten_childtrees()` to do most of the work.

```
from nltk.tree import Tree

def flatten_childtrees(trees):
    children = []
```

```
    for t in trees:
      if t.height() < 3:
        children.extend(t.pos())
      elif t.height() == 3:
        children.append(Tree(t.node, t.pos()))
      else:
        children.extend(flatten_childtrees([c for c in t]))

    return children

  def flatten_deeptree(tree):
    return Tree(tree.node, flatten_childtrees([c for c in tree]))
```

We can use it on the first parsed sentence of the `treebank` corpus to get a flatter tree:

```
>>> from nltk.corpus import treebank
>>> from transforms import flatten_deeptree
>>> flatten_deeptree(treebank.parsed_sents()[0])
Tree('S', [Tree('NP', [('Pierre', 'NNP'), ('Vinken', 'NNP')]), (',',
','), Tree('NP', [('61', 'CD'), ('years', 'NNS')]), ('old', 'JJ'),
(',', ','), ('will', 'MD'), ('join', 'VB'), Tree('NP', [('the',
'DT'), ('board', 'NN')]), ('as', 'IN'), Tree('NP', [('a', 'DT'),
('nonexecutive', 'JJ'), ('director', 'NN')]), Tree('NP-TMP', [('Nov.',
'NNP'), ('29', 'CD')]), ('.', '.')])
```

The result is a much flatter `Tree` that only includes NP phrases. Words that are not part of a NP phrase are separated. This flatter tree is shown as follows:

This `Tree` is quite similar to the first chunk `Tree` from the `treebank_chunk` corpus. The main difference is that the rightmost NP `Tree` is separated into two sub-trees in the previous diagram, one of them named NP-TMP.

The first tree from `treebank_chunk` is shown as follows for comparison:

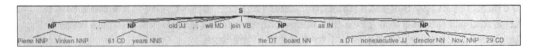

How it works...

The solution is composed of two functions: `flatten_deeptree()` returns a new `Tree` from the given tree by calling `flatten_childtrees()` on each of the given tree's children.

`flatten_childtrees()` is a recursive function that drills down into the `Tree` until it finds child trees whose `height()` is equal to or less than three. A `Tree` whose `height()` is less than three looks like this:

```
>>> from nltk.tree import Tree
>>> Tree('NNP', ['Pierre']).height()
2
```

These short trees are converted into lists of tuples using the `pos()` function.

```
>>> Tree('NNP', ['Pierre']).pos()
[('Pierre', 'NNP')]
```

Trees whose `height()` is equal to three are the lowest level trees that we're interested in keeping. These trees look like this:

```
>>> Tree('NP', [Tree('NNP', ['Pierre']), Tree('NNP', ['Vinken'])]).
height()
3
```

When we call `pos()` on that tree, we get:

```
>>> Tree('NP', [Tree('NNP', ['Pierre']), Tree('NNP', ['Vinken'])]).
pos()
[('Pierre', 'NNP'), ('Vinken', 'NNP')]
```

The recursive nature of `flatten_childtrees()` eliminates all trees whose height is greater than three.

There's more...

Flattening a deep `Tree` allows us to call `nltk.chunk.util.tree2conlltags()` on the flattened `Tree`, a necessary step to train a chunker. If you try to call this function before flattening the `Tree`, you get a `ValueError` exception.

```
>>> from nltk.chunk.util import tree2conlltags
>>> tree2conlltags(treebank.parsed_sents()[0])
Traceback (most recent call last):
  File "<stdin>", line 1, in <module>
  File "/usr/local/lib/python2.6/dist-packages/nltk/chunk/util.py",
line 417, in tree2conlltags
    raise ValueError, "Tree is too deeply nested to be printed in
CoNLL format"
ValueError: Tree is too deeply nested to be printed in CoNLL format
```

However, after flattening there's no problem:

```
>>> tree2conlltags(flatten_deeptree(treebank.parsed_sents()[0]))
[('Pierre', 'NNP', 'B-NP'), ('Vinken', 'NNP', 'I-NP'), (',', ',',
'O'), ('61', 'CD', 'B-NP'), ('years', 'NNS', 'I-NP'), ('old', 'JJ',
'O'), (',', ',', 'O'), ('will', 'MD', 'O'), ('join', 'VB', 'O'),
('the', 'DT', 'B-NP'), ('board', 'NN', 'I-NP'), ('as', 'IN', 'O'),
('a', 'DT', 'B-NP'), ('nonexecutive', 'JJ', 'I-NP'), ('director',
'NN', 'I-NP'), ('Nov.', 'NNP', 'B-NP-TMP'), ('29', 'CD', 'I-NP-TMP'),
('.', '.', 'O')]
```

Being able to flatten trees, opens up the possibility of training a chunker on corpora consisting of deep parse trees.

CESS-ESP and CESS-CAT treebank

The `cess_esp` and `cess_cat` corpora have parsed sentences, but no chunked sentences. In other words, they have deep trees that must be flattened in order to train a chunker. In fact, the trees are so deep that a diagram can't be shown, but the flattening can be demonstrated by showing the `height()` of the tree before and after flattening.

```
>>> from nltk.corpus import cess_esp
>>> cess_esp.parsed_sents()[0].height()
22
>>> flatten_deeptree(cess_esp.parsed_sents()[0]).height()
3
```

See also

The *Training a tagger-based chunker* recipe in *Chapter 5, Extracting Chunks* covers training a chunker using IOB tags.

Creating a shallow tree

In the previous recipe, we flattened a deep `Tree` by only keeping the lowest level sub-trees. In this recipe, we'll keep only the highest level sub-trees instead.

How to do it...

We'll be using the first parsed sentence from the `treebank` corpus as our example. Recall from the previous recipe that the sentence `Tree` looks like this:

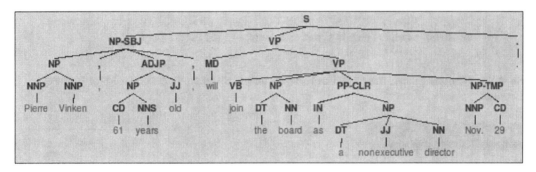

The `shallow_tree()` function defined in `transforms.py` eliminates all the nested sub-trees, keeping only the top tree nodes.

```
from nltk.tree import Tree

def shallow_tree(tree):
  children = []

  for t in tree:
    if t.height() < 3:
      children.extend(t.pos())
    else:
      children.append(Tree(t.node, t.pos()))

  return Tree(tree.node, children)
```

Using it on the first parsed sentence in `treebank` results in a `Tree` with only two sub-trees.

```
>>> from transforms import shallow_tree
>>> shallow_tree(treebank.parsed_sents()[0])
Tree('S', [Tree('NP-SBJ', [('Pierre', 'NNP'), ('Vinken', 'NNP'), (',',
','), ('61', 'CD'), ('years', 'NNS'), ('old', 'JJ'), (',', ',')]),
Tree('VP', [('will', 'MD'), ('join', 'VB'), ('the', 'DT'), ('board',
'NN'), ('as', 'IN'), ('a', 'DT'), ('nonexecutive', 'JJ'), ('director',
'NN'), ('Nov.', 'NNP'), ('29', 'CD')]), ('.', '.')])
```

We can visually and programmatically see the difference, as shown in the following diagram and code:

```
>>> treebank.parsed_sents()[0].height()
7
>>> shallow_tree(treebank.parsed_sents()[0]).height()
3
```

As in the previous recipe, the height of the new tree is three so it can be used for training a chunker.

How it works...

The `shallow_tree()` function iterates over each of the top-level sub-trees in order to create new child trees. If the `height()` of a sub-tree is less than three, then that sub-tree is replaced by a list of its part-of-speech tagged children. All other sub-trees are replaced by a new `Tree` whose children are the part-of-speech tagged leaves. This eliminates all nested sub-trees while retaining the top-level sub-trees.

This function is an alternative to `flatten_deeptree()` from the previous recipe, for when you want to keep the higher level tree nodes and ignore the lower level nodes.

See also

The previous recipe covers how to flatten a `Tree` and keep the lowest level sub-trees, as opposed to keeping the highest level sub-trees.

Converting tree nodes

As you've seen in previous recipes, parse trees often have a variety of `Tree` node types that are not present in chunk trees. If you want to use the parse trees to train a chunker, then you'll probably want to reduce this variety by converting some of these tree nodes to more common node types.

Getting ready

First, we have to decide what `Tree` nodes need to be converted. Let's take a look at that first `Tree` again:

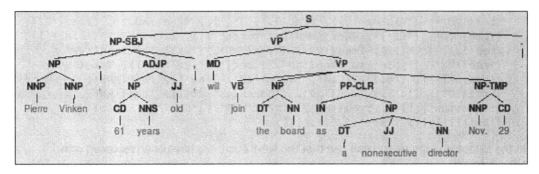

Immediately you can see that there are two alternative NP sub-trees: NP-SBJ and NP-TMP. Let's convert both of those to NP. The mapping will be as follows:

Original Node	New Node
NP-SBJ	NP
NP-TMP	NP

How to do it...

In `transforms.py` there is a function `convert_tree_nodes()`. It takes two arguments: the `Tree` to convert, and a node conversion `mapping`. It returns a new `Tree` with all matching nodes replaced based on the values in the `mapping`.

```
from nltk.tree import Tree

def convert_tree_nodes(tree, mapping):
  children = []

  for t in tree:
    if isinstance(t, Tree):
```

```
            children.append(convert_tree_nodes(t, mapping))
        else:
            children.append(t)

    node = mapping.get(tree.node, tree.node)
    return Tree(node, children)
```

Using the mapping table shown earlier, we can pass it in as a `dict` to `convert_tree_nodes()` and convert the first parsed sentence from `treebank`.

```
>>> from transforms import convert_tree_nodes
>>> mapping = {'NP-SBJ': 'NP', 'NP-TMP': 'NP'}
>>> convert_tree_nodes(treebank.parsed_sents()[0], mapping)
Tree('S', [Tree('NP', [Tree('NP', [Tree('NNP', ['Pierre']),
Tree('NNP', ['Vinken'])]), Tree(',', [',']), Tree('ADJP', [Tree('NP',
[Tree('CD', ['61']), Tree('NNS', ['years'])]), Tree('JJ', ['old'])]),
Tree(',', [','])]), Tree('VP', [Tree('MD', ['will']), Tree('VP',
[Tree('VB', ['join']), Tree('NP', [Tree('DT', ['the']), Tree('NN',
['board'])]), Tree('PP-CLR', [Tree('IN', ['as']), Tree('NP',
[Tree('DT', ['a']), Tree('JJ', ['nonexecutive']), Tree('NN',
['director'])])]), Tree('NP', [Tree('NNP', ['Nov.']), Tree('CD',
['29'])])])]), Tree('.', ['.'])])
```

In the following diagram, you can see that the NP-* sub-trees have been replaced with NP sub-trees:

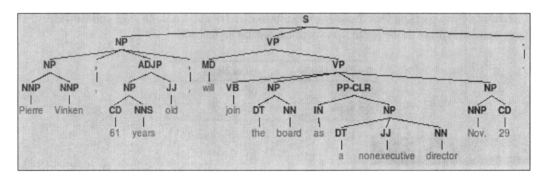

How it works...

`convert_tree_nodes()` recursively converts every child sub-tree using the `mapping`. The `Tree` is then rebuilt with the converted nodes and children until the entire `Tree` has been converted.

The result is a brand new `Tree` instance with new sub-trees whose nodes have been converted.

See also

The previous two recipes cover different methods of flattening a parse `Tree`, both of which can produce sub-trees that may require mapping before using them to train a chunker. Chunker training is covered in the *Training a tagger-based chunker* recipe in *Chapter 5, Extracting Chunks*.

7
Text Classification

In this chapter, we will cover:

- ▸ Bag of Words feature extraction
- ▸ Training a naive Bayes classifier
- ▸ Training a decision tree classifier
- ▸ Training a maximum entropy classifier
- ▸ Measuring precision and recall of a classifier
- ▸ Calculating high information words
- ▸ Combining classifiers with voting
- ▸ Classifying with multiple binary classifiers

Introduction

Text classification is a way to categorize documents or pieces of text. By examining the word usage in a piece of text, classifiers can decide what *class label* to assign to it. A **binary classifier** decides between two labels, such as positive or negative. The text can either be one label or the other, but not both, whereas a **multi-label classifier** can assign one or more labels to a piece of text.

Classification works by learning from *labeled feature sets*, or training data, to later classify an *unlabeled feature set*. A **feature set** is basically a key-value mapping of *feature names* to *feature values*. In the case of text classification, the feature names are usually words, and the values are all `True`. As the documents may have unknown words, and the number of possible words may be very large, words that don't occur in the text are omitted, instead of including them in a feature set with the value `False`.

An **instance** is a single feature set. It represents a single occurrence of a combination of features. We will use *instance* and *feature set* interchangeably. A *labeled feature set* is an instance with a known class label that we can use for training or evaluation.

Bag of Words feature extraction

Text feature extraction is the process of transforming what is essentially a list of words into a feature set that is usable by a classifier. The NLTK classifiers expect `dict` style feature sets, so we must therefore transform our text into a `dict`. The **Bag of Words** model is the simplest method; it constructs a *word presence* feature set from all the words of an instance.

How to do it...

The idea is to convert a list of words into a `dict`, where each word becomes a key with the value `True`. The `bag_of_words()` function in `featx.py` looks like this:

```
def bag_of_words(words):
    return dict([(word, True) for word in words])
```

We can use it with a list of words, in this case the tokenized sentence "the quick brown fox":

```
>>> from featx import bag_of_words
>>> bag_of_words(['the', 'quick', 'brown', 'fox'])
{'quick': True, 'brown': True, 'the': True, 'fox': True}
```

The resulting `dict` is known as a *bag of words* because the words are not in order, and it doesn't matter where in the list of words they occurred, or how many times they occurred. All that matters is that the word is found at least once.

How it works...

The `bag_of_words()` function is a very simple *list comprehension* that constructs a `dict` from the given words, where every word gets the value `True`.

Since we have to assign a value to each word in order to create a `dict`, `True` is a logical choice for the value to indicate word presence. If we knew the universe of all possible words, we could assign the value `False` to all the words that are not in the given list of words. But most of the time, we don't know all possible words beforehand. Plus, the `dict` that would result from assigning `False` to every possible word would be very large (assuming all words in the English language are possible). So instead, to keep feature extraction simple and use less memory, we stick with assigning the value `True` to all words that occur at least once. We don't assign the value `False` to any words since we don't know what the set of possible words are; we only know about the words we are given.

There's more...

In the default Bag of Words model, all words are treated equally. But that's not always a good idea. As we already know, some words are so common that they are practically meaningless. If you have a set of words that you want to exclude, you can use the `bag_of_words_not_in_set()` function in `featx.py`.

```
def bag_of_words_not_in_set(words, badwords):
    return bag_of_words(set(words) - set(badwords))
```

This function can be used, among other things, to filter stopwords. Here's an example where we filter the word "the" from "the quick brown fox":

```
>>> from featx import bag_of_words_not_in_set
>>> bag_of_words_not_in_set(['the', 'quick', 'brown', 'fox'],
['the'])
{'quick': True, 'brown': True, 'fox': True}
```

As expected, the resulting `dict` has "quick", "brown", and "fox", but not "the".

Filtering stopwords

Here's an example of using the `bag_of_words_not_in_set()` function to filter all English stopwords:

```
from nltk.corpus import stopwords

def bag_of_non_stopwords(words, stopfile='english'):
    badwords = stopwords.words(stopfile)
    return bag_of_words_not_in_set(words, badwords)
```

You can pass a different language filename as the `stopfile` keyword argument if you are using a language other than English. Using this function produces the same result as the previous example:

```
>>> from featx import bag_of_non_stopwords
>>> bag_of_non_stopwords(['the', 'quick', 'brown', 'fox'])
{'quick': True, 'brown': True, 'fox': True}
```

Here, "the" is a stopword, so it is not present in the returned `dict`.

Including significant bigrams

In addition to single words, it often helps to include significant bigrams. As significant bigrams are less common than most individual words, including them in the Bag of Words can help the classifier make better decisions. We can use the `BigramCollocationFinder` covered in the *Discovering word collocations* recipe of *Chapter 1, Tokenizing Text and WordNet Basics*, to find significant bigrams. `bag_of_bigrams_words()` found in `featx.py` will return a `dict` of all words along with the 200 most significant bigrams.

```
from nltk.collocations import BigramCollocationFinder
from nltk.metrics import BigramAssocMeasures

def bag_of_bigrams_words(words, score_fn=BigramAssocMeasures.chi_sq,
n=200):
  bigram_finder = BigramCollocationFinder.from_words(words)
  bigrams = bigram_finder.nbest(score_fn, n)
  return bag_of_words(words + bigrams)
```

The bigrams will be present in the returned `dict` as `(word1, word2)` and will have the value as `True`. Using the same example words as before, we get all words plus every bigram:

```
>>> from featx import bag_of_bigrams_words
>>> bag_of_bigrams_words(['the', 'quick', 'brown', 'fox'])
{'brown': True, ('brown', 'fox'): True, ('the', 'quick'):
True, 'fox': True, ('quick', 'brown'): True, 'quick': True,
'the': True}
```

You can change the maximum number of bigrams found by altering the keyword argument n.

See also

The *Discovering word collocations* recipe of *Chapter 1, Tokenizing Text and WordNet Basics* covers the `BigramCollocationFinder` in more detail. In the next recipe, we will train a `NaiveBayesClassifier` using feature sets created with the Bag of Words model.

Training a naive Bayes classifier

Now that we can extract features from text, we can train a classifier. The easiest classifier to get started with is the `NaiveBayesClassifier`. It uses **Bayes Theorem** to predict the probability that a given feature set belongs to a particular label. The formula is:

```
P(label | features) = P(label) * P(features | label) / P(features)
```

- ▶ `P(label)` is the prior probability of the label occurring, which is the same as the likelihood that a random feature set will have the label. This is based on the number of training instances with the label compared to the total number of training instances. For example, if 60/100 training instances have the label, the prior probability of the label is 60 percent.

- ▶ `P(features | label)` is the prior probability of a given feature set being classified as that label. This is based on which features have occurred with each label in the training data.

- ▶ `P(features)` is the prior probability of a given feature set occurring. This is the likelihood of a random feature set being the same as the given feature set, and is based on the observed feature sets in the training data. For example, if the given feature set occurs twice in 100 training instances, the prior probability is 2 percent.

- ▶ `P(label | features)` tells us the probability that the given features should have that label. If this value is high, then we can be reasonably confident that the label is correct for the given features.

Getting ready

We are going to be using the `movie_reviews` corpus for our initial classification examples. This corpus contains two categories of text: `pos` and `neg`. These categories are exclusive, which makes a classifier trained on them a **binary classifier**. Binary classifiers have only two classification labels, and will always choose one or the other.

Each file in the `movie_reviews` corpus is composed of either positive or negative movie reviews. We will be using each file as a single instance for both training and testing the classifier. Because of the nature of the text and its categories, the classification we will be doing is a form of *sentiment analysis*. If the classifier returns `pos`, then the text expresses *positive sentiment*, whereas if we get `neg`, then the text expresses *negative sentiment*.

How to do it...

For training, we need to first create a list of labeled feature sets. This list should be of the form `[(featureset, label)]` where the `featureset` is a `dict`, and `label` is the known class label for the `featureset`. The `label_feats_from_corpus()` function in `featx.py` takes a corpus, such as `movie_reviews`, and a `feature_detector` function, which defaults to `bag_of_words`. It then constructs and returns a mapping of the form `{label: [featureset]}`. We can use this mapping to create a list of labeled *training instances* and *testing instances*. The reason to do it this way is because we can get a fair sample from each label.

```
import collections
def label_feats_from_corpus(corp, feature_detector=bag_of_words):
    label_feats = collections.defaultdict(list)
    for label in corp.categories():
```

```
        for fileid in corp.fileids(categories=[label]):
            feats = feature_detector(corp.words(fileids=[fileid]))
            label_feats[label].append(feats)
    return label_feats
```

Once we can get a mapping of `label : feature` sets, we want to construct a list of labeled training instances and testing instances. The function `split_label_feats()` in `featx.py` takes a mapping returned from `label_feats_from_corpus()` and splits each list of feature sets into labeled training and testing instances.

```
def split_label_feats(lfeats, split=0.75):
  train_feats = []
  test_feats = []
  for label, feats in lfeats.iteritems():
    cutoff = int(len(feats) * split)
    train_feats.extend([(feat, label) for feat in
feats[:cutoff]])
    test_feats.extend([(feat, label) for feat in
feats[cutoff:]])
  return train_feats, test_feats
```

Using these functions with the `movie_reviews` corpus gives us the lists of labeled feature sets we need to train and test a classifier.

```
>>> from nltk.corpus import movie_reviews
>>> from featx import label_feats_from_corpus, split_label_feats
>>> movie_reviews.categories()
['neg', 'pos']
>>> lfeats = label_feats_from_corpus(movie_reviews)
>>> lfeats.keys()
['neg', 'pos']
>>> train_feats, test_feats = split_label_feats(lfeats)
>>> len(train_feats)
1500
>>> len(test_feats)
500
```

So there are 1,000 `pos` files, 1,000 `neg` files, and we end up with 1,500 labeled training instances and 500 labeled testing instances, each composed of equal parts `pos` and `neg`. Now we can train a `NaiveBayesClassifier` using its `train()` class method,

```
>>> from nltk.classify import NaiveBayesClassifier
>>> nb_classifier = NaiveBayesClassifier.train(train_feats)
>>> nb_classifier.labels()
['neg', 'pos']
```

Let's test the classifier on a couple of made up reviews. The `classify()` method takes a single argument, which should be a feature set. We can use the same `bag_of_words()` feature detector on a made up list of words to get our feature set.

```
>>> from featx import bag_of_words
>>> negfeat = bag_of_words(['the', 'plot', 'was', 'ludicrous'])
>>> nb_classifier.classify(negfeat)
'neg'
>>> posfeat = bag_of_words(['kate', 'winslet', 'is', 'accessible'])
>>> nb_classifier.classify(posfeat)
'pos'
```

How it works...

The `label_feats_from_corpus()` assumes that the corpus is categorized, and that a single file represents a single instance for feature extraction. It iterates over each category label, and extracts features from each file in that category using the `feature_detector()` function, which defaults to `bag_of_words()`. It returns a `dict` whose keys are the category labels, and the values are lists of instances for that category.

> If we had the `label_feats_from_corpus()` function, return a list of labeled feature sets, instead of a dict, it would be much harder to get the balanced training data. The list would be ordered by label, and if you took a slice of it, you would almost certainly be getting far more of one label than another. By returning a `dict`, you can take slices from the feature sets of each label.

Now we need to split the labeled feature sets into training and testing instances using `split_label_feats()`. This function allows us to take a fair sample of labeled feature sets from each label, using the `split` keyword argument to determine the size of the sample. `split` defaults to `0.75`, which means the first three-fourths of the labeled feature sets for each label will be used for training, and the remaining one-fourth will be used for testing.

Once we have split up our training and testing feats, we train a classifier using the `NaiveBayesClassifier.train()` method. This class method builds two probability distributions for calculating prior probabilities. These are passed in to the `NaiveBayesClassifier` constructor. The `label_probdist` contains `P(label)`, the prior probability for each label. The `feature_probdist` contains `P(feature name = feature value | label)`. In our case, it will store `P(word=True | label)`. Both are calculated based on the frequency of occurrence of each label, and each feature name and value in the training data.

The `NaiveBayesClassifier` inherits from `ClassifierI`, which requires subclasses to provide a `labels()` method, and at least one of the `classify()` and `prob_classify()` methods. The following diagram shows these and other methods, which will be covered shortly:

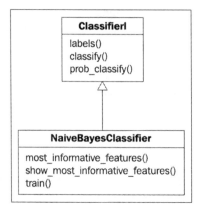

There's more...

We can test the accuracy of the classifier using `nltk.classify.util.accuracy()` and the `test_feats` created previously.

```
>>> from nltk.classify.util import accuracy
>>> accuracy(nb_classifier, test_feats)
0.72799999999999998
```

This tells us that the classifier correctly guessed the label of nearly 73 percent of the testing feature sets.

Classification probability

While the `classify()` method returns only a single label, you can use the `prob_classify()` method to get the classification probability of each label. This can be useful if you want to use probability thresholds greater than 50 percent for classification.

```
>>> probs = nb_classifier.prob_classify(test_feats[0][0])
>>> probs.samples()
['neg', 'pos']
>>> probs.max()
'pos'
>>> probs.prob('pos')
0.99999996464309127
>>> probs.prob('neg')
3.5356889692409258e-08
```

In this case, the classifier says that the first testing instance is nearly 100 percent likely to be `pos`.

Most informative features

The `NaiveBayesClassifier` has two methods that are quite useful for learning about your data. Both methods take a keyword argument `n` to control how many results to show. The `most_informative_features()` method returns a list of the form `[(feature name, feature value)]` ordered by most informative to least informative. In our case, the feature value will always be `True`.

```
>>> nb_classifier.most_informative_features(n=5)
[('magnificent', True), ('outstanding', True), ('insulting', True),
('vulnerable', True), ('ludicrous', True)]
```

The `show_most_informative_features()` method will print out the results from `most_informative_features()` and will also include the probability of a feature pair belonging to each label.

```
>>> nb_classifier.show_most_informative_features(n=5)
Most Informative Features
      magnificent = True      pos : neg = 15.0 : 1.0
      outstanding = True      pos : neg = 13.6 : 1.0
        insulting = True      neg : pos = 13.0 : 1.0
       vulnerable = True      pos : neg = 12.3 : 1.0
        ludicrous = True      neg : pos = 11.8 : 1.0
```

The *informativeness*, or **information gain**, of each feature pair is based on the prior probability of the feature pair occurring for each label. More informative features are those that occur primarily in one label and not the other. Less informative features are those that occur frequently in both labels.

Training estimator

During training, the `NaiveBayesClassifier` constructs its probability distributions using an `estimator` parameter, which defaults to `nltk.probability.ELEProbDist`. But you can use any `estimator` you want, and there are quite a few to choose from. The only constraints are that it must inherit from `nltk.probability.ProbDistI` and its constructor must take a `bins` keyword argument. Here's an example using the `LaplaceProbDist`:

```
>>> from nltk.probability import LaplaceProbDist
>>> nb_classifier = NaiveBayesClassifier.train(train_feats,
estimator=LaplaceProbDist)
>>> accuracy(nb_classifier, test_feats)
0.71599999999999997
```

As you can see, accuracy is slightly lower, so choose your `estimator` carefully.

 You cannot use `nltk.probability.MLEProbDist` as the estimator, or any `ProbDistI` subclass that does not take the `bins` keyword argument. Training will fail with `TypeError: __init__() got an unexpected keyword argument 'bins'`.

Manual training

You don't have to use the `train()` class method to construct a `NaiveBayesClassifier`. You can instead create the `label_probdist` and `feature_probdist` manually. `label_probdist` should be an instance of `ProbDistI`, and should contain the prior probabilities for each label. `feature_probdist` should be a `dict` whose keys are tuples of the form `(label, feature name)` and whose values are instances of `ProbDistI` that have the probabilities for each feature value. In our case, each `ProbDistI` should have only one value, `True=1`. Here's a very simple example using manually constructed `DictionaryProbDist`:

```
>>> from nltk.probability import DictionaryProbDist
>>> label_probdist = DictionaryProbDist({'pos': 0.5, 'neg': 0.5})
>>> true_probdist = DictionaryProbDist({True: 1})
>>> feature_probdist = {('pos', 'yes'): true_probdist, ('neg', 'no'):
true_probdist}
>>> classifier = NaiveBayesClassifier(label_probdist, feature_
probdist)
>>> classifier.classify({'yes': True})
'pos'
>>> classifier.classify({'no': True})
'neg'
```

See also

In the next recipes, we will train two more classifiers, the `DecisionTreeClassifier`, and the `MaxentClassifier`. In the *Measuring precision and recall of a classifier* recipe in this chapter, we will use precision and recall instead of accuracy to evaluate the classifiers. And then in the *Calculating high information words* recipe, we will see how using only the most informative features can improve classifier performance.

The `movie_reviews` corpus is an instance of `CategorizedPlaintextCorpusReader`, which is covered in the *Creating a categorized text corpus* recipe in *Chapter 3, Creating Custom Corpora*.

Training a decision tree classifier

The `DecisionTreeClassifier` works by creating a tree structure, where each node corresponds to a feature name, and the branches correspond to the feature values. Tracing down the branches, you get to the leaves of the tree, which are the classification labels.

Getting ready

For the `DecisionTreeClassifier` to work for text classification, you must use NLTK 2.0b9 or later. This is because earlier versions are unable to deal with unknown features. If the `DecisionTreeClassifier` encountered a word/feature that it hadn't seen before, then it raised an exception. This bug has now been fixed by yours truly, and is included in all NLTK versions since 2.0b9.

How to do it...

Using the same `train_feats` and `test_feats` we created from the `movie_reviews` corpus in the previous recipe, we can call the `DecisionTreeClassifier.train()` class method to get a trained classifier. We pass `binary=True` because all of our features are binary: either the word is present or it's not. For other classification use cases where you have multi-valued features, you will want to stick to the default `binary=False`.

In this context, `binary` refers to *feature values*, and is not to be confused with a *binary classifier*. Our word features are binary because the value is either `True`, or the word is not present. If our features could take more than two values, we would have to use `binary=False`. A *binary classifier*, on the other hand, is a classifier that only chooses between two labels. In our case, we are training a binary `DecisionTreeClassifier` on binary features. But it's also possible to have a binary classifier with non-binary features, or a non-binary classifier with binary features.

Following is the code for training and evaluating the accuracy of a `DecisionTreeClassifier`:

```
>>> from nltk.classify import DecisionTreeClassifier
>>> dt_classifier = DecisionTreeClassifier.train(train_feats,
binary=True, entropy_cutoff=0.8, depth_cutoff=5, support_cutoff=30)
>>> accuracy(dt_classifier, test_feats)
0.68799999999999994
```

The `DecisionTreeClassifier` can take much longer to train than the `NaiveBayesClassifier`. For that reason, the default parameters have been overridden so it trains faster. These parameters will be explained later.

How it works...

The `DecisionTreeClassifier`, like the `NaiveBayesClassifier`, is also an instance of `ClassifierI`. During training, the `DecisionTreeClassifier` creates a tree where the child nodes are also instances of `DecisionTreeClassifier`. The leaf nodes contain only a single label, while the intermediate child nodes contain decision mappings for each feature. These decisions map each feature value to another `DecisionTreeClassifier`, which itself may contain decisions for another feature, or it may be a final leaf node with a classification label. The `train()` class method builds this tree from the ground up, starting with the leaf nodes. It then refines itself to minimize the number of decisions needed to get to a label by putting the most informative features at the top.

To classify, the `DecisionTreeClassifier` looks at the given feature set and traces down the tree, using known feature names and values to make decisions. Because we are creating a *binary tree*, each `DecisionTreeClassifier` instance also has a *default* decision tree, which it uses when a known feature is not present in the feature set being classified. This is a common occurrence in text-based feature sets, and indicates that a known word was not in the text being classified. This also contributes information towards a classification decision.

There's more...

The parameters passed in to `DecisionTreeClassifier.train()` can be tweaked to improve accuracy or decrease training time. Generally, if you want to improve accuracy, you must accept a longer training time and if you want to decrease the training time, the accuracy will most likely decrease as well.

Entropy cutoff

The `entropy_cutoff` is used during the tree refinement process. If the entropy of the probability distribution of label choices in the tree is greater than the `entropy_cutoff`, then the tree is refined further. But if the entropy is lower than the `entropy_cutoff`, then tree refinement is halted.

Entropy is the uncertainty of the outcome. As entropy approaches 1.0, uncertainty increases and, conversely, as entropy approaches 0.0, uncertainty decreases. In other words, when you have similar probabilities, the entropy will be high as each probability has a similar likelihood (or uncertainty of occurrence). But the more the probabilities differ, the lower the entropy will be.

Entropy is calculated by giving `nltk.probability.entropy()` a `MLEProbDist` created from a `FreqDist` of label counts. Here's an example showing the entropy of various `FreqDist` values:

```
>>> from nltk.probability import FreqDist, MLEProbDist, entropy
>>> fd = FreqDist({'pos': 30, 'neg': 10})
>>> entropy(MLEProbDist(fd))
0.81127812445913283
>>> fd['neg'] = 25
>>> entropy(MLEProbDist(fd))
0.99403021147695647
>>> fd['neg'] = 30
>>> entropy(MLEProbDist(fd))
1.0
>>> fd['neg'] = 1
>>> entropy(MLEProbDist(fd))
0.20559250818508304
```

What this all means is that if the label occurrence is very skewed one way or the other, the tree doesn't need to be refined because entropy/uncertainty is low. But when the entropy is greater than `entropy_cutoff` then the tree must be refined with further decisions to reduce the uncertainty. Higher values of `entropy_cutoff` will decrease both accuracy and training time.

Depth cutoff

The `depth_cutoff` is also used during refinement to control the depth of the tree. The final decision tree will never be deeper than the `depth_cutoff`. The default value is `100`, which means that classification may require up to 100 decisions before reaching a leaf node. Decreasing the `depth_cutoff` will decrease the training time and most likely decrease the accuracy as well.

Support cutoff

The `support_cutoff` controls how many labeled feature sets are required to refine the tree. As the `DecisionTreeClassifier` refines itself, labeled feature sets are eliminated once they no longer provide value to the training process. When the number of labeled feature sets is less than or equal to `support_cutoff`, refinement stops, at least for that section of the tree.

Another way to look at it is that `support_cutoff` specifies the minimum number of instances that are required to make a decision about a feature. If `support_cutoff` is `20`, and you have less than 20 labeled feature sets with a given feature, then you don't have enough instances to make a good decision, and refinement around that feature must come to a stop.

The previous recipe covered the creation of training and test feature sets from the `movie_reviews` corpus. In the next recipe, we will cover training a `MaxentClassifier`, and in the *Measuring precision and recall of a classifier* recipe in this chapter, we will use precision and recall to evaluate all the classifiers.

Training a maximum entropy classifier

The third classifier which we will cover is the `MaxentClassifier`, also known as a *conditional exponential classifier*. The **maximum entropy classifier** converts labeled feature sets to vectors using encoding. This encoded vector is then used to calculate *weights* for each feature that can then be combined to determine the most likely label for a feature set.

Getting ready

The `MaxentClassifier` requires the `numpy` package, and optionally the `scipy` package. This is because the feature encodings use `numpy` arrays. Having `scipy` installed also means you will be able to use faster algorithms that consume less memory. You can find installation for both at `http://www.scipy.org/Installing_SciPy`.

 Many of the algorithms can be quite memory hungry, so you may want to quit all your other programs while training a `MaxentClassifier`, just to be safe.

How to do it...

We will use the same `train_feats` and `test_feats` from the `movie_reviews` corpus that we constructed before, and call the `MaxentClassifier.train()` class method. Like the `DecisionTreeClassifier`, `MaxentClassifier.train()` has its own specific parameters that have been tweaked to speed up training. These parameters will be explained in more detail later.

```
>>> from nltk.classify import MaxentClassifier
>>> me_classifier = MaxentClassifier.train(train_feats,
algorithm='iis', trace=0, max_iter=1, min_lldelta=0.5)
>>> accuracy(me_classifier, test_feats)
0.5
```

The reason this classifier has such a low accuracy is because the parameters have been set such that it is unable to learn a more accurate model. This is due to the time required to train a suitable model using the `iis` algorithm. Higher accuracy models can be learned much faster using the `scipy` algorithms.

If training is taking a long time, you can usually cut it off manually by hitting *Ctrl + C*. This should stop the current iteration and still return a classifier based on whatever state the model is in.

How it works...

Like the previous classifiers, `MaxentClassifier` inherits from `ClassifierI`. Depending on the algorithm, `MaxentClassifier.train()` calls one of the training functions in the `nltk.classify.maxent` module. If `scipy` is not installed, the default algorithm is `iis`, and the function used is `train_maxent_classifier_with_iis()`. The other algorithm that doesn't require `scipy` is `gis`, which uses the `train_maxent_classifier_with_gis()` function. **gis** stands for **General Iterative Scaling**, while **iis** stands for **Improved Iterative Scaling**. If `scipy` is installed, the `train_maxent_classifier_with_scipy()` function is used, and the default algorithm is `cg`. If `megam` is installed and you specify the `megam` algorithm, then `train_maxent_classifier_with_megam()` is used.

The basic idea behind the maximum entropy model is to build some probability distributions that fit the observed data, then choose whichever probability distribution has the highest entropy. The `gis` and `iis` algorithms do so by iteratively improving the weights used to classify features. This is where the `max_iter` and `min_lldelta` parameters come into play.

The `max_iter` specifies the maximum number of iterations to go through and update the weights. More iterations will generally improve accuracy, but only up to a point. Eventually, the changes from one iteration to the next will hit a plateau and further iterations are useless.

The `min_lldelta` specifies the minimum change in the *log likelihood* required to continue iteratively improving the weights. Before beginning training iterations, an instance of the `nltk.classify.util.CutoffChecker` is created. When its `check()` method is called, it uses functions such as `nltk.classify.util.log_likelihood()` to decide whether the cutoff limits have been reached. The **log likelihood** is the log (using `math.log()`) of the average label probability of the training data (which is the log of the average likelihood of a label). As the log likelihood increases, the model improves. But it too will reach a plateau where further increases are so small that there is no point in continuing. Specifying the `min_lldelta` allows you to control how much each iteration must increase the log likelihood before stopping iterations.

There's more...

Like the `NaiveBayesClassifier`, you can see the most informative features by calling the `show_most_informative_features()` method.

```
>>> me_classifier.show_most_informative_features(n=4)
-0.740 worst==True and label is 'pos'

0.740 worst==True and label is 'neg'

0.715 bad==True and label is 'neg'

-0.715 bad==True and label is 'pos'
```

The numbers shown are the weights for each feature. This tells us that the word *worst* is *negatively weighted* towards the pos label, and *positively weighted* towards the neg label. In other words, if the word *worst* is found in the feature set, then there's a strong possibility that the text should be classified neg.

Scipy algorithms

The algorithms available when `scipy` is installed are:

- **CG (Conjugate gradient** algorithm)—the default `scipy` algorithm
- **BFGS (Broyden-Fletcher-Goldfarb-Shanno** algorithm)—very memory hungry
- Powell
- LBFGSB (limited memory version of BFGS)
- Nelder-Mead

Here's what happens when you use the CG algorithm:

```
>>> me_classifier = MaxentClassifier.train(train_feats,
algorithm='cg', trace=0, max_iter=10)
>>> accuracy(me_classifier, test_feats)
0.85599999999999998
```

This is the most accurate classifier so far.

Megam algorithm

If you have installed the `megam` package, then you can use the `megam` algorithm. It's a bit faster than the `scipy` algorithms and about as accurate. Installation instructions and information can be found at `http://www.cs.utah.edu/~hal/megam/`. The function `nltk.classify.megam.config_megam()` can be used to specify where the `megam` executable is found. Or, if `megam` can be found in the standard executable paths, NLTK will configure it automatically.

```
>>> me_classifier = MaxentClassifier.train(train_feats,
algorithm='megam', trace=0, max_iter=10)
[Found megam: /usr/local/bin/megam]
>>> accuracy(me_classifier, test_feats)
0.86799999999999999
```

The `megam` algorithm is highly recommended for its accuracy and speed of training.

See also

The *Bag of Words feature extraction* and the *Training a naive Bayes classifier* recipes in this chapter show how to construct the training and testing features from the `movie_reviews` corpus. In the next recipe, we will cover how and why to evaluate a classifier using precision and recall instead of accuracy.

Measuring precision and recall of a classifier

In addition to accuracy, there are a number of other metrics used to evaluate classifiers. Two of the most common are *precision* and *recall*. To understand these two metrics, we must first understand *false positives* and *false negatives*. **False positives** happen when a classifier classifies a feature set with a label it shouldn't have. **False negatives** happen when a classifier doesn't assign a label to a feature set that should have it. In a *binary classifier*, these errors happen at the same time.

Here's an example: the classifier classifies a movie review as `pos`, when it should have been `neg`. This counts as a *false positive* for the `pos` label, and a *false negative* for the `neg` label. If the classifier had correctly guessed `neg`, then it would count as a **true positive** for the `neg` label, and a **true negative** for the `pos` label.

How does this apply to precision and recall? **Precision** is the *lack of false positives*, and **recall** is the *lack of false negatives*. As you will see, these two metrics are often in competition: the more precise a classifier is, the lower the recall, and vice versa.

How to do it...

Let's calculate the precision and recall of the `NaiveBayesClassifier` we trained in the *Training a naive Bayes classifier* recipe. The `precision_recall()` function in `classification.py` looks like this:

```
import collections
from nltk import metrics

def precision_recall(classifier, testfeats):
  refsets = collections.defaultdict(set)
  testsets = collections.defaultdict(set)

  for i, (feats, label) in enumerate(testfeats):
    refsets[label].add(i)
    observed = classifier.classify(feats)
    testsets[observed].add(i)

  precisions = {}
  recalls = {}

  for label in classifier.labels():
    precisions[label] = metrics.precision(refsets[label],
testsets[label])
    recalls[label] = metrics.recall(refsets[label], testsets[label])

  return precisions, recalls
```

This function takes two arguments:

1. The trained classifier.

2. Labeled test features, also known as a gold standard.

These are the same arguments you pass to the `accuracy()` function. The `precision_recall()` returns two dictionaries; the first holds the precision for each label, and the second holds the recall for each label. Here's an example usage with the `nb_classifier` and the `test_feats` we created in the *Training a naive Bayes classifier* recipe earlier:

```
>>> from classification import precision_recall
>>> nb_precisions, nb_recalls = precision_recall(nb_classifier, test_
feats)
>>> nb_precisions['pos']
0.6413612565445026
>>> nb_precisions['neg']
0.9576271186440678
>>> nb_recalls['pos']
0.97999999999999998
>>> nb_recalls['neg']
0.45200000000000001
```

This tells us that while the NaiveBayesClassifier can correctly identify most of the pos feature sets (high recall), it also classifies many of the neg feature sets as pos (low precision). This behavior contributes to the high precision but low recall for the neg label—as the neg label isn't given often (low recall), and when it is, it's very likely to be correct (high precision). The conclusion could be that there are certain common words that are biased towards the pos label, but occur frequently enough in the neg feature sets to cause mis-classifications. To correct this behavior, we will use only the most informative words in the next recipe, *Calculating high information words*.

How it works...

To calculate precision and recall, we must build two sets for each label. The first set is known as the **reference set**, and contains all the correct values. The second set is called the **test set**, and contains the values guessed by the classifier. These two sets are compared to calculate the precision or recall for each label.

Precision is defined as the size of the intersection of both sets divided by the size of the test set. In other words, the percentage of the test set that was guessed correctly. In Python, the code is float(len(reference.intersection(test))) / len(test).

Recall is the size of the intersection of both sets divided by the size of the reference set, or the percentage of the reference set that was guessed correctly. The Python code is float(len(reference.intersection(test))) / len(reference).

The precision_recall() function in classification.py iterates over the labeled test features and classifies each one. We store the *numeric index* of the feature set (starting with 0) in the reference set for the known training label, and also store the index in the test set for the guessed label. If the classifier guesses pos but the training label is neg, then the index is stored in the *reference set* for neg and the *test set* for pos.

 We use the numeric index because the feature sets aren't hashable, and we need a unique value for each feature set.

The nltk.metrics package contains functions for calculating both precision and recall, so all we really have to do is build the sets, then call the appropriate function.

There's more...

Let's try it with the `MaxentClassifier` we trained in the previous recipe:

```
>>> me_precisions, me_recalls = precision_recall(me_classifier, test_
feats)
>>> me_precisions['pos']
0.8801652892561983
>>> me_precisions['neg']
0.85658914728682167
>>> me_recalls['pos']
0.85199999999999998
>>> me_recalls['neg']
0.88400000000000001
```

This classifier is much more well-rounded than the `NaiveBayesClassifier`. In this case, the label bias is much less significant, and the reason is that the `MaxentClassifier` weighs its features according to its own internal model. Words that are more significant are those that occur primarily in a single label, and will get higher weights in the model. Words that are common to both labels will get lower weights, as they are less significant.

F-measure

The **F-measure** is defined as the weighted harmonic mean of precision and recall. If `p` is the *precision*, and `r` is the *recall*, the formula is:

```
1/(alpha/p + (1-alpha)/r)
```

where `alpha` is a weighing constant that defaults to `0.5`. You can use `nltk.metrics.f_measure()` to get the F-measure. It takes the same arguments as for the `precision()` and `recall()` functions: a reference set and a test set. It's often used instead of accuracy to measure a classifier. However, precision and recall are found to be much more useful metrics, as the F-measure can hide the kinds of imbalances we saw with the `NaiveBayesClassifier`.

See also

In the *Training a naive Bayes classifier* recipe, we collected training and testing feature sets, and trained the `NaiveBayesClassifier`. The `MaxentClassifier` was trained in the *Training a maximum entropy classifier* recipe. In the next recipe, we will explore eliminating the less significant words, and use only the high information words to create our feature sets.

Calculating high information words

A **high information word** is a word that is strongly biased towards a single classification label. These are the kinds of words we saw when we called the `show_most_informative_features()` method on both the `NaiveBayesClassifier` and the `MaxentClassifier`. Somewhat surprisingly, the top words are different for both classifiers. This discrepancy is due to how each classifier calculates the significance of each feature, and it's actually beneficial to have these different methods as they can be combined to improve accuracy, as we will see in the next recipe, *Combining classifiers with voting*.

The **low information words** are words that are common to all labels. It may be counter-intuitive, but eliminating these words from the training data can actually improve accuracy, precision, and recall. The reason this works is that using only high information words reduces the noise and confusion of a classifier's internal model. If all the words/features are highly biased one way or the other, it's much easier for the classifier to make a correct guess.

How to do it...

First, we need to calculate the high information words in the `movie_review` corpus. We can do this using the `high_information_words()` function in `featx.py`:

```python
from nltk.metrics import BigramAssocMeasures
from nltk.probability import FreqDist, ConditionalFreqDist

def high_information_words(labelled_words, score_
fn=BigramAssocMeasures.chi_sq, min_score=5):
  word_fd = FreqDist()
  label_word_fd = ConditionalFreqDist()

  for label, words in labelled_words:
    for word in words:
      word_fd.inc(word)
      label_word_fd[label].inc(word)

  n_xx = label_word_fd.N()
  high_info_words = set()

  for label in label_word_fd.conditions():
    n_xi = label_word_fd[label].N()
    word_scores = collections.defaultdict(int)

    for word, n_ii in label_word_fd[label].iteritems():
      n_ix = word_fd[word]
      score = score_fn(n_ii, (n_ix, n_xi), n_xx)
      word_scores[word] = score

    bestwords = [word for word, score in word_scores.iteritems() if
  score >= min_score]
```

```
        high_info_words |= set(bestwords)
    return high_info_words
```

It takes one argument , which is a list of 2-tuples of the form `[(label, words)]` where `label` is the classification label, and `words` is a list of words that occur under that label. It returns a list of the high information words, sorted from most informative to least informative.

Once we have the high information words, we use the feature detector function `bag_of_words_in_set()`, also found in `featx.py`, which will let us filter out all low information words.

```
def bag_of_words_in_set(words, goodwords):
    return bag_of_words(set(words) & set(goodwords))
```

With this new feature detector, we can call `label_feats_from_corpus()` and get a new `train_feats` and `test_feats` using `split_label_feats()`. These two functions were covered in the *Training a naive Bayes classifier* recipe in this chapter.

```
>>> from featx import high_information_words, bag_of_words_in_set
>>> labels = movie_reviews.categories()
>>> labeled_words = [(l, movie_reviews.words(categories=[l])) for l in
labels]
>>> high_info_words = set(high_information_words(labeled_words))
>>> feat_det = lambda words: bag_of_words_in_set(words, high_info_
words)
>>> lfeats = label_feats_from_corpus(movie_reviews, feature_
detector=feat_det)
>>> train_feats, test_feats = split_label_feats(lfeats)
```

Now that we have new training and testing feature sets, let's train and evaluate a `NaiveBayesClassifier`:

```
>>> nb_classifier = NaiveBayesClassifier.train(train_feats)
>>> accuracy(nb_classifier, test_feats)
0.91000000000000003
>>> nb_precisions, nb_recalls = precision_recall(nb_classifier, test_
feats)
>>> nb_precisions['pos']
0.89883268482490275
>>> nb_precisions['neg']
0.92181069958847739
>>> nb_recalls['pos']
0.92400000000000004
>>> nb_recalls['neg']
0.89600000000000002
```

While the `neg` precision and `pos` recall have both decreased somewhat, `neg` recall and `pos` precision have increased drastically. Accuracy is now a little higher than the `MaxentClassifier`.

How it works...

The `high_information_words()` function starts by counting the frequency of every word, as well as the conditional frequency for each word within each label. This is why we need the words to be labelled, so we know how often each word occurs in each label.

Once we have this `FreqDist` and `ConditionalFreqDist`, we can score each word on a per-label basis. The default `score_fn` is `nltk.metrics.BigramAssocMeasures.chi_sq()`, which calculates the chi-square score for each word using the following parameters:

1. `n_ii`: The frequency of the word in the label.
2. `n_ix`: The total frequency of the word across all labels.
3. `n_xi`: The total frequency of all words that occurred in the label.
4. `n_xx`: The total frequency for all words in all labels.

The simplest way to think about these numbers is that the closer `n_ii` is to `n_ix`, the higher the score. Or, the more often a word occurs in a label, relative to its overall occurrence, the higher the score.

Once we have the scores for each word in each label, we can filter out all words whose score is below the `min_score` threshold. We keep the words that meet or exceed the threshold, and return all high scoring words in each label.

 It is recommended to experiment with different values of `min_score` to see what happens. In some cases, less words may improve the metrics even more, while in other cases more words is better.

There's more...

There are a number of other scoring functions available in the `BigramAssocMeasures` class, such as `phi_sq()` for phi-square, `pmi()` for pointwise mutual information, and `jaccard()` for using the Jaccard index. They all take the same arguments, and so can be used interchangeably with `chi_sq()`.

MaxentClassifier with high information words

Let's evaluate the `MaxentClassifier` using the high information words feature sets:

```
>>> me_classifier = MaxentClassifier.train(train_feats,
algorithm='megam', trace=0, max_iter=10)
>>> accuracy(me_classifier, test_feats)
0.88200000000000001
>>> me_precisions, me_recalls = precision_recall(me_classifier, test_
feats)
>>> me_precisions['pos']
0.88663967611336036
>>> me_precisions['neg']
0.87747035573122534
>>> me_recalls['pos']
0.876
>>> me_recalls['neg']
0.88800000000000001
```

As you can see, the improvements are much more modest than with the
`NaiveBayesClassifier` due to the fact that the `MaxentClassifier` already weights
all features by significance. But using only the high information words still makes a positive
difference compared to when we used all the words. And the precisions and recalls for each
label are closer to each other, giving the `MaxentClassifier` even more well-rounded
performance.

DecisionTreeClassifier with high information words

Now, let's evaluate the `DecisionTreeClassifier`:

```
>>> dt_classifier = DecisionTreeClassifier.train(train_feats,
binary=True, depth_cutoff=20, support_cutoff=20, entropy_cutoff=0.01)
>>> accuracy(dt_classifier, test_feats)
0.68600000000000005
>>> dt_precisions, dt_recalls = precision_recall(dt_classifier, test_
feats)
>>> dt_precisions['pos']
0.6741573033707865
>>> dt_precisions['neg']
0.69957081545064381
>>> dt_recalls['pos']
0.71999999999999997
>>> dt_recalls['neg']
0.65200000000000002
```

The accuracy is about the same, even with a larger `depth_cutoff`, and smaller `support_cutoff` and `entropy_cutoff`. The results show that the `DecisionTreeClassifier` was already putting the high information features at the top of the tree, and it will only improve if we increase the depth significantly. But that could make training time prohibitively long.

See also

We started this chapter with the *Bag of Words feature extraction* recipe. The `NaiveBayesClassifier` was originally trained in the *Training a naive Bayes classifier* recipe, and the `MaxentClassifier` was trained in the *Training a maximum entropy classifier* recipe. Details on precision and recall can be found in the *Measuring precision and recall of a classifier* recipe. We will be using only high information words in the next two recipes, where we combine classifiers.

Combining classifiers with voting

One way to improve classification performance is to combine classifiers. The simplest way to combine multiple classifiers is to use voting, and choose whichever label gets the most votes. For this style of voting, it's best to have an odd number of classifiers so that there are no ties. This means combining at least three classifiers together. The individual classifiers should also use different algorithms; the idea is that multiple algorithms are better than one, and the combination of many can compensate for individual bias.

Getting ready

As we need to have at least three trained classifiers to combine, we are going to use a `NaiveBayesClassifier`, a `DecisionTreeClassifier`, and a `MaxentClassifier`, all trained on the highest information words of the `movie_reviews` corpus. These were all trained in the previous recipe, so we will combine these three classifiers with voting.

How to do it...

In the `classification.py` module, there is a `MaxVoteClassifier` class.

```
import itertools
from nltk.classify import ClassifierI
from nltk.probability import FreqDist

class MaxVoteClassifier(ClassifierI):
  def __init__(self, *classifiers):
    self._classifiers = classifiers
```

```
      self._labels = sorted(set(itertools.chain(*[c.labels() for c in
classifiers])))
  def labels(self):
    return self._labels
  def classify(self, feats):
    counts = FreqDist()

    for classifier in self._classifiers:
      counts.inc(classifier.classify(feats))

    return counts.max()
```

To create it, you pass in a list of classifiers that you want to combine. Once created, it works just like any other classifier. Though it may take about three times longer to classify, it should generally be at least as accurate as any individual classifier.

```
>>> from classification import MaxVoteClassifier
>>> mv_classifier = MaxVoteClassifier(nb_classifier, dt_classifier,
me_classifier)
>>> mv_classifier.labels()
['neg', 'pos']
>>> accuracy(mv_classifier, test_feats)
0.89600000000000002
>>> mv_precisions, mv_recalls = precision_recall(mv_classifier, test_
feats)
>>> mv_precisions['pos']
0.8928571428571429
>>> mv_precisions['neg']
0.89919354838709675
>>> mv_recalls['pos']
0.90000000000000002
>>> mv_recalls['neg']
0.89200000000000002
```

These metrics are about on par with the `MaxentClassifier` and `NaiveBayesClassifier`. Some numbers are slightly better, some worse. It's likely that a significant improvement to the `DecisionTreeClassifier` could produce some better numbers.

How it works...

The `MaxVoteClassifier` extends the `nltk.classify.ClassifierI` interface, which requires implementing at least two methods:

▶ The `labels()` function must return a list of possible labels. This will be the union of the `labels()` of each classifier passed in at initialization.

▶ The `classify()` function takes a single feature set and returns a label. The `MaxVoteClassifier` iterates over its classifiers and calls `classify()` on each of them, recording their label as a vote in a `FreqDist`. The label with the most votes is returned using `FreqDist.max()`.

While it doesn't check for this, the `MaxVoteClassifier` assumes that all the classifiers passed in at initialization use the same labels. Breaking this assumption may lead to odd behavior.

See also

In the previous recipe, we trained a `NaiveBayesClassifier`, a `MaxentClassifier`, and a `DecisionTreeClassifier` using only the highest information words. In the next recipe, we will use the `reuters` corpus and combine many binary classifiers in order to create a multi-label classifier.

Classifying with multiple binary classifiers

So far we have focused on **binary classifiers,** which classify with *one of two possible labels.* The same techniques for training a binary classifier can also be used to create a *multi-class* classifier, which is a classifier that can classify with *one of many possible labels.* But there are also cases where you need to be able to classify with *multiple labels.* A classifier that can return more than one label is a **multi-label classifier**.

A common technique for creating a multi-label classifier is to combine many binary classifiers, one for each label. You train each binary classifier so that it either returns a known label, or returns something else to signal that the label does not apply. Then you can run all the binary classifiers on your feature set to collect all the applicable labels.

Getting ready

The `reuters` corpus contains multi-labeled text that we can use for training and evaluation.

```
>>> from nltk.corpus import reuters
>>> len(reuters.categories())
90
```

We will train one binary classifier per label, which means we will end up with 90 binary classifiers.

How to do it...

First, we should calculate the high information words in the `reuters` corpus. This is done with the `reuters_high_info_words()` function in `featx.py`.

```
from nltk.corpus import reuters

def reuters_high_info_words(score_fn=BigramAssocMeasures.chi_sq):
    labeled_words = []

    for label in reuters.categories():
        labeled_words.append((label, reuters.words(categories=[label])))

    return high_information_words(labeled_words, score_fn=score_fn)
```

Then we need to get training and test feature sets based on those high information words. This is done with the `reuters_train_test_feats()`, also found in `featx.py`. It defaults to using `bag_of_words()` as its `feature_detector`, but we will be overriding this using `bag_of_words_in_set()` to use only the high information words.

```
def reuters_train_test_feats(feature_detector=bag_of_words):
    train_feats = []
    test_feats = []

    for fileid in reuters.fileids():
        if fileid.startswith('training'):
            featlist = train_feats
        else: # fileid.startswith('test')
            featlist = test_feats

        feats = feature_detector(reuters.words(fileid))
        labels = reuters.categories(fileid)
        featlist.append((feats, labels))

    return train_feats, test_feats
```

We can use these two functions to get a list of multi-labeled training and testing feature sets.

```
>>> from featx import reuters_high_info_words, reuters_train_test_
feats
>>> rwords = reuters_high_info_words()
>>> featdet = lambda words: bag_of_words_in_set(words, rwords)
>>> multi_train_feats, multi_test_feats = reuters_train_test_
feats(featdet)
```

The `multi_train_feats` and `multi_test_feats` are multi-labeled feature sets.
That means they have a list of labels, instead of a single label, and they look like the
`[(featureset, [label])]`, as each feature set can have one or more labels. With this
training data, we can train multiple binary classifiers. The `train_binary_classifiers()`
function in the `classification.py` takes a training function, a list of multi-label feature
sets, and a set of possible labels to return a `dict` of the `label : binary` classifier.

```
def train_binary_classifiers(trainf, labelled_feats, labelset):
  pos_feats = collections.defaultdict(list)
  neg_feats = collections.defaultdict(list)
  classifiers = {}

  for feat, labels in labelled_feats:
    for label in labels:
      pos_feats[label].append(feat)

    for label in labelset - set(labels):
      neg_feats[label].append(feat)

  for label in labelset:
    postrain = [(feat, label) for feat in pos_feats[label]]
    negtrain = [(feat, '!%s' % label) for feat in neg_feats[label]]
    classifiers[label] = trainf(postrain + negtrain)

  return classifiers
```

To use this function, we need to provide a training function that takes a single
argument, which is the training data. This will be a simple `lambda` wrapper around the
`MaxentClassifier.train()`, so we can specify extra keyword arguments.

```
>>> from classification import train_binary_classifiers
>>> trainf = lambda train_feats: MaxentClassifier.train(train_feats,
algorithm='megam', trace=0, max_iter=10)
>>> labelset = set(reuters.categories())
>>> classifiers = train_binary_classifiers(trainf, multi_train_feats,
labelset)
>>> len(classifiers)
90
```

Now we can define a `MultiBinaryClassifier`, which takes a list of labeled classifiers of the form `[(label, classifier)]` where the `classifier` is assumed to be a binary classifier that either returns the `label`, or something else if the label doesn't apply.

```
from nltk.classify import MultiClassifierI

class MultiBinaryClassifier(MultiClassifierI):
  def __init__(self, *label_classifiers):
    self._label_classifiers = dict(label_classifiers)
    self._labels = sorted(self._label_classifiers.keys())

  def labels(self):
    return self._labels

  def classify(self, feats):
    lbls = set()

    for label, classifier in self._label_classifiers.iteritems():
      if classifier.classify(feats) == label:
        lbls.add(label)

    return lbls
```

We can construct this class using the binary classifiers we just created.

```
>>> from classification import MultiBinaryClassifier
>>> multi_classifier = MultiBinaryClassifier(*classifiers.items())
```

To evaluate this classifier, we can use precision and recall, but not accuracy. That's because the accuracy function assumes single values, and doesn't take into account partial matches. For example, if the multi-classifier returns three labels for a feature set, and two of them are correct but the third is not, then the `accuracy()` would mark that as incorrect. So instead of using accuracy, we will use the **masi distance**, which measures partial overlap between two sets. The lower the masi distance, the better the match. A lower average masi distance, therefore, means more accurate partial matches. The `multi_metrics()` function in the `classification.py` calculates the precision and recall of each label, along with the average masi distance.

```
import collections
from nltk import metrics

def multi_metrics(multi_classifier, test_feats):
  mds = []
  refsets = collections.defaultdict(set)
  testsets = collections.defaultdict(set)

  for i, (feat, labels) in enumerate(test_feats):
    for label in labels:
      refsets[label].add(i)

    guessed = multi_classifier.classify(feat)
```

```
    for label in guessed:
      testsets[label].add(i)

    mds.append(metrics.masi_distance(set(labels), guessed))
  avg_md = sum(mds) / float(len(mds))
  precisions = {}
  recalls = {}

  for label in multi_classifier.labels():
    precisions[label] = metrics.precision(refsets[label],
testsets[label])
    recalls[label] = metrics.recall(refsets[label], testsets[label])

  return precisions, recalls, avg_md
```

Using this with the `multi_classifier` we just created, gives us the following results:

```
>>> from classification import multi_metrics
>>> multi_precisions, multi_recalls, avg_md = multi_metrics(multi_
classifier, multi_test_feats)
>>> avg_md
0.18191264129488705
```

So our average masi distance is fairly low, which means our multi-label classifier is usually mostly accurate. Let's take a look at a few precisions and recalls:

```
>>> multi_precisions['zinc']
1.0
>>> multi_recalls['zinc']
0.84615384615384615
>>> len(reuters.fileids(categories=['zinc']))
34
>>> multi_precisions['sunseed']
0.5
>>> multi_recalls['sunseed']
0.20000000000000001
>>> len(reuters.fileids(categories=['sunseed']))
16
>>> multi_precisions['rand']
None
>>> multi_recalls['rand']
0.0
>>> len(reuters.fileids(categories=['rand']))
3
```

As you can see, there's quite a range of values. But, in general, the labels that have more feature sets will have higher precision and recall, and those with less feature sets will have lower performance. When there's not a lot of feature sets for a classifier to learn from, you can't expect it to perform well.

How it works...

The `reuters_high_info_words()` function is fairly simple; it constructs a list of `[(label, words)]` for each category of the `reuters` corpus, then passes it in to the `high_information_words()` function to return a list of the most informative words in the `reuters` corpus.

With the resulting set of words, we create a feature detector function using the `bag_of_words_in_set()`. This is then passed in to the `reuters_train_test_feats()`, which returns two lists, the first containing `[(feats, labels)]` for all the training files, and the second list has the same for all the test files.

Next, we train a binary classifier for each label using `train_binary_classifiers()`. This function constructs two lists for each label, one containing positive training feature sets, the other containing negative training feature sets. The **Positive feature sets** are those feature sets that classify for the label. The **Negative feature sets** for a label comes from the positive feature sets for all other labels. For example, a feature set that is *positive* for zinc and sunseed is a *negative* example for all the other 88 labels. Once we have positive and negative feature sets for each label, we can train a binary classifier for each label using the given training function.

With the resulting dictionary of binary classifiers, we create an instance of the `MultiBinaryClassifier`. This class extends the `nltk.classify.MultiClassifierI` interface, which requires at least two functions:

1. The `labels()` function must return a list of possible labels.

2. The `classify()` function takes a single feature set and returns a `set` of labels. To create this `set`, we iterate over the binary classifiers, and any time a call to the `classify()` returns its label, we add it to the set. If it returns something else, we continue.

Finally, we evaluate the multi-label classifier using the `multi_metrics()` function. It is similar to the `precision_recall()` function from the *Measuring precision and recall of a classifier* recipe, but in this case we know the classifier is an instance of the `MultiClassifierI` and it can therefore return multiple labels. It also keeps track of the masi distance for each set of classification labels using the `nltk.metrics.masi_distance()`. The `multi_metrics()` function returns three values:

1. A dictionary of precisions for each label.

2. A dictionary of recalls for each label.

3. The average masi distance for each feature set.

There's more...

The nature of the `reuters` corpus introduces the **class-imbalance problem**. This problem occurs when some labels have very few feature sets, and other labels have many. The binary classifiers that have few positive instances to train on end up with far more negative instances, and are therefore strongly biased towards the negative label. There's nothing inherently wrong about this, as the bias reflects the data, but the negative instances can overwhelm the classifier to the point where it's nearly impossible to get a positive result. There are a number of advanced techniques for overcoming this problem, but they are out of the scope of this book.

See also

The `MaxentClassifier` is covered in the *Training a maximum entropy classifier* recipe in this chapter. The *Measuring precision and recall of a classifier* recipe shows how to evaluate a classifier, while the *Calculating high information words* recipe describes how to use only the best features.

8
Distributed Processing and Handling Large Datasets

In this chapter, we will cover:

- ▶ Distributed tagging with execnet
- ▶ Distributed chunking with execnet
- ▶ Parallel list processing with execnet
- ▶ Storing a frequency distribution in Redis
- ▶ Storing a conditional frequency distribution in Redis
- ▶ Storing an ordered dictionary in Redis
- ▶ Distributed word scoring with Redis and execnet

Introduction

NLTK is great for in-memory single-processor natural language processing. However, there are times when you have a lot of data to process and want to take advantage of multiple CPUs, multi-core CPUs, and even multiple computers. Or perhaps you want to store frequencies and probabilities in a persistent, shared database so multiple processes can access it simultaneously. For the first case, we'll be using execnet to do parallel and distributed processing with NLTK. For the second case, you'll learn how to use the Redis data structure server/database to store frequency distributions and more.

Distributed tagging with execnet

Execnet is a distributed execution library for python. It allows you to create gateways and channels for remote code execution. A **gateway** is a connection from the calling process to a remote environment. The remote environment can be a local subprocess or an SSH connection to a remote node. A **channel** is created from a gateway and handles communication between the channel creator and the remote code.

Since many NLTK processes require 100 percent CPU utilization during computation, execnet is an ideal way to distribute that computation for maximum resource usage. You can create one gateway per CPU core, and it doesn't matter whether the cores are in your local computer or spread across remote machines. In many situations, you only need to have the trained objects and data on a single machine, and can send the objects and data to the remote nodes as needed.

Getting ready

You'll need to install execnet for this to work. It should be as simple as `sudo pip install execnet` or `sudo easy_install execnet`. The current version of execnet, as of this writing, is `1.0.8`. The execnet homepage, which has API documentation and examples, is at `http://codespeak.net/execnet/`.

How to do it...

We start by importing the required modules, as well as an additional module `remote_tag.py` that will be explained in the next section. We also need to import `pickle` so we can serialize the tagger. Execnet does not natively know how to deal with complex objects such as a part-of-speech tagger, so we must dump the tagger to a string using `pickle.dumps()`. We'll use the default tagger that's used by the `nltk.tag.pos_tag()` function, but you could load and dump any pre-trained part-of-speech tagger as long as it implements the `TaggerI` interface.

Once we have a serialized tagger, we start execnet by making a gateway with `execnet.makegateway()`. The default gateway creates a Python *subprocess*, and we can call the `remote_exec()` method with the `remote_tag` module to create a `channel`. With an open channel, we send over the serialized tagger and then the first tokenized sentence of the `treebank` corpus.

 You don't have to do any special serialization of simple types such as lists and tuples, since execnet already knows how to handle serializing the built-in types.

Now if we call `channel.receive()`, we get back a tagged sentence that is equivalent to the first tagged sentence in the `treebank` corpus, so we know the tagging worked. We end by exiting the gateway, which closes the channel and kills the subprocess.

```
>>> import execnet, remote_tag, nltk.tag, nltk.data
>>> from nltk.corpus import treebank
>>> import cPickle as pickle
>>> tagger = pickle.dumps(nltk.data.load(nltk.tag._POS_TAGGER))
>>> gw = execnet.makegateway()
>>> channel = gw.remote_exec(remote_tag)
>>> channel.send(tagger)
>>> channel.send(treebank.sents()[0])
>>> tagged_sentence = channel.receive()
>>> tagged_sentence == treebank.tagged_sents()[0]
True
>>> gw.exit()
```

Visually, the communication process looks like this:

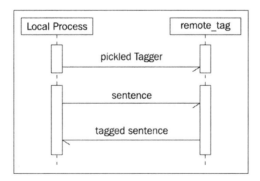

How it works...

The gateway's `remote_exec()` method takes a single argument that can be one of the following three types:

1. A string of code to execute remotely.
2. The name of a **pure function** that will be serialized and executed remotely.
3. The name of a **pure module** whose source will be executed remotely.

We use the third option with the `remote_tag.py` module, which is defined as follows:

```
import cPickle as pickle

if __name__ == '__channelexec__':
    tagger = pickle.loads(channel.receive())

    for sentence in channel:
        channel.send(tagger.tag(sentence))
```

A pure module is a module that is self-contained. It can only access Python modules that are available where it executes, and does not have access to any variables or states that exist wherever the gateway is initially created. To detect that the module is being executed by execnet, you can look at the `__name__` variable. If it's equal to '`__channelexec__`', then it is being used to create a remote channel. This is similar to doing `if __name__ == '__main__'` to check if a module is being executed on the command line.

The first thing we do is call `channel.receive()` to get the serialized `tagger`, which we load using `pickle.loads()`. You may notice that `channel` is not imported anywhere—that's because it is included in the global namespace of the module. Any module that execnet executes remotely has access to the `channel` variable in order to communicate with the `channel` creator.

Once we have the `tagger`, we iteratively `tag()` each tokenized sentence that we receive from the channel. This allows us to tag as many sentences as the sender wants to send, as iteration will not stop until the `channel` is closed. What we've essentially created is a compute node for part-of-speech tagging that dedicates 100 percent of its resources to tagging whatever sentences it receives. As long as the `channel` remains open, the node is available for processing.

There's more...

This is a simple example that opens a single gateway and channel. But execnet can do a lot more, such as opening multiple channels to increase parallel processing, as well as opening gateways to remote hosts over SSH to do distributed processing.

Multiple channels

We can create multiple channels, one per gateway, to make the processing more parallel. Each gateway creates a new subprocess (or remote interpreter if using an SSH gateway) and we use one channel per gateway for communication. Once we've created two channels, we can combine them using the `MultiChannel` class, which allows us to iterate over the channels, and make a receive queue to receive messages from each channel.

After creating each channel and sending the tagger, we cycle through the channels to send an even number of sentences to each channel for tagging. Then we collect all the responses from the `queue`. A call to `queue.get()` will return a 2-tuple of `(channel, message)` in case you need to know which channel the message came from.

 If you don't want to wait forever, you can also pass a `timeout` keyword argument with the maximum number of seconds you want to wait, as in `queue.get(timeout=4)`. This can be a good way to handle network errors.

Once all the tagged sentences have been collected, we can exit the gateways. Here's the code:

```
>>> import itertools
>>> gw1 = execnet.makegateway()
>>> gw2 = execnet.makegateway()
>>> ch1 = gw1.remote_exec(remote_tag)
>>> ch1.send(tagger)
>>> ch2 = gw2.remote_exec(remote_tag)
>>> ch2.send(tagger)
>>> mch = execnet.MultiChannel([ch1, ch2])
>>> queue = mch.make_receive_queue()
>>> channels = itertools.cycle(mch)
>>> for sentence in treebank.sents()[:4]:
...     channel = channels.next()
...     channel.send(sentence)
>>> tagged_sentences = []
>>> for i in range(4):
...     channel, tagged_sentence = queue.get()
...     tagged_sentences.append(tagged_sentence)
>>> len(tagged_sentences)
```

```
4
>>> gw1.exit()
>>> gw2.exit()
```

Local versus remote gateways

The default gateway spec is `popen`, which creates a Python subprocess on the local machine. This means `execnet.makegateway()` is equivalent to `execnet.makegateway('popen')`. If you have passwordless SSH access to a remote machine, then you can create a remote gateway using `execnet.makegateway('ssh=remotehost')` where `remotehost` should be the hostname of the machine. A SSH gateway spawns a new Python interpreter for executing the code remotely. As long as the code you're using for remote execution is **pure**, you only need a Python interpreter on the remote machine.

Channels work exactly the same no matter what kind of gateway is used; the only difference will be communication time. This means you can mix and match local subprocesses with remote interpreters to distribute your computations across many machines in a network. There are many more details on gateways in the API documentation at `http://codespeak.net/execnet/basics.html`.

See also

Part-of-speech tagging and taggers are covered in detail in *Chapter 4, Part-of-Speech Tagging*. In the next recipe, we'll use `execnet` to do distributed chunk extraction.

Distributed chunking with execnet

In this recipe, we'll do chunking and tagging over an `execnet` gateway. This will be very similar to the tagging in the previous recipe, but we'll be sending two objects instead of one, and we will be receiving a `Tree` instead of a list, which requires pickling and unpickling for serialization.

Getting ready

As in the previous recipe, you must have `execnet` installed.

How to do it...

The setup code is very similar to the last recipe, and we'll use the same pickled `tagger` as well. First we'll pickle the default `chunker` used by `nltk.chunk.ne_chunk()`, though any chunker would do. Next, we make a gateway for the `remote_chunk` module, get a `channel`, and send the pickled `tagger` and `chunker` over. Then we receive back a pickled `Tree`, which we can unpickle and inspect to see the result. Finally, we exit the gateway.

```
>>> import execnet, remote_chunk
>>> import nltk.data, nltk.tag, nltk.chunk
>>> import cPickle as pickle
>>> from nltk.corpus import treebank_chunk
>>> tagger = pickle.dumps(nltk.data.load(nltk.tag._POS_TAGGER))
>>> chunker = pickle.dumps(nltk.data.load(nltk.chunk._MULTICLASS_NE_
CHUNKER))
>>> gw = execnet.makegateway()
>>> channel = gw.remote_exec(remote_chunk)
>>> channel.send(tagger)
>>> channel.send(chunker)
>>> channel.send(treebank_chunk.sents()[0])
>>> chunk_tree = pickle.loads(channel.receive())
>>> chunk_tree
Tree('S', [Tree('PERSON', [('Pierre', 'NNP')]), Tree('ORGANIZATION',
[('Vinken', 'NNP')]), (',', ','), ('61', 'CD'), ('years', 'NNS'),
('old', 'JJ'), (',', ','), ('will', 'MD'), ('join', 'VB'), ('the',
'DT'), ('board', 'NN'), ('as', 'IN'), ('a', 'DT'), ('nonexecutive',
'JJ'), ('director', 'NN'), ('Nov.', 'NNP'), ('29', 'CD'), ('.', '.')])
>>> gw.exit()
```

The communication this time is slightly different.

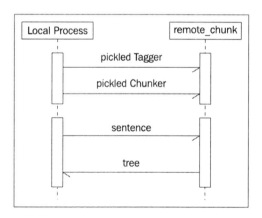

How it works...

The `remote_chunk.py` module is just a little bit more complicated than the `remote_tag.py` module from the previous recipe. In addition to receiving a pickled `tagger`, it also expects to receive a pickled `chunker` that implements the `ChunkerI` interface. Once it has both a `tagger` and a `chunker`, it expects to receive any number of tokenized sentences, which it tags and parses into a `Tree`. This `tree` is then pickled and sent back over the `channel`.

```
import cPickle as pickle

if __name__ == '__channelexec__':
    tagger = pickle.loads(channel.receive())
    chunker = pickle.loads(channel.receive())

    for sent in channel:
        tree = chunker.parse(tagger.tag(sent))
        channel.send(pickle.dumps(tree))
```

 The `Tree` must be pickled because it is not a simple built-in type.

There's more...

Note that the `remote_chunk` module is pure. Its only external dependency is the `pickle` (or `cPickle`) module, which is part of the Python standard library. It doesn't need to import any NLTK modules in order to use the `tagger` or `chunker`, because all the necessary data is pickled and sent over the `channel`. As long as you structure your remote code like this, with no external dependencies, you only need NLTK to be installed on a single machine—the one that starts the gateway and sends the objects over the channel.

Python subprocesses

If you look at your task/system monitor (or `top` in `*nix`) while running the `execnet` code, you may notice a few extra python Processes. Every gateway spawns a new, self-contained, *shared-nothing* Python interpreter process, which is killed when you call the `exit()` method. Unlike with threads, there is no shared memory to worry about, and no global interpreter lock to slow things down. All you have are separate communicating processes. This is true whether the processes are local or remote. Instead of locking and synchronization, all you have to worry about is the order in which the messages are sent and received.

See also

The previous recipe explains `execnet` gateways and channels in detail. In the next recipe, we'll use `execnet` to process a list in parallel.

Parallel list processing with execnet

This recipe presents a pattern for using `execnet` to process a list in parallel. It's a function pattern for mapping each element in the list to a new value, using `execnet` to do the mapping in parallel.

How to do it...

First, we need to decide exactly what we want to do. In this example, we'll just double integers, but we could do any pure computation. Following is the module `remote_double.py`, which will be executed by `execnet`. It receives a 2-tuple of `(i, arg)`, assumes `arg` is a number, and sends back `(i, arg*2)`. The need for `i` will be explained in the next section.

```
if __name__ == '__channelexec__':
    for (i, arg) in channel:
        channel.send((i, arg * 2))
```

To use this module to double every element in a list, we import the `plists` module (explained in the next section) and call `plists.map()` with the `remote_double` module, and a list of integers to double.

```
>>> import plists, remote_double
>>> plists.map(remote_double, range(10))
[0, 2, 4, 6, 8, 10, 12, 14, 16, 18]
```

Communication between channels is very simple, as shown in the following diagram:

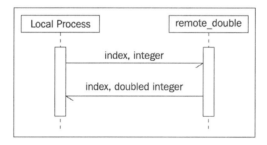

How it works...

The `map()` function is defined in `plists.py`. It takes a pure module, a list of arguments, and an optional list of 2-tuples consisting of `(spec, count)`. The default `specs` are `[('popen', 2)]`, which means we'll open two local gateways and channels. Once these channels are opened, we put them into an `itertools` cycle, which creates an infinite iterator that cycles back to the beginning once it hits the end.

Now we can send each argument in `args` to a channel for processing, and since the channels are cycled, each channel gets an almost even distribution of arguments. This is where `i` comes in—we don't know in what order we'll get the results back, so `i`, as the index of each `arg` in the list, is passed to the channel and back so we can combine the results in the original order. We then wait for results with a `MultiChannel` receive queue and insert them into a pre-filled list that's the same length as the original `args`. Once we have all the expected results, we can exit the gateways and return the results.

```
import itertools, execnet

def map(mod, args, specs=[('popen', 2)]):
    gateways = []
    channels = []

    for spec, count in specs:
        for i in range(count):
            gw = execnet.makegateway(spec)
            gateways.append(gw)
            channels.append(gw.remote_exec(mod))

    cyc = itertools.cycle(channels)

    for i, arg in enumerate(args):
        channel = cyc.next()
        channel.send((i, arg))

    mch = execnet.MultiChannel(channels)
    queue = mch.make_receive_queue()
    l = len(args)
    results = [None] * l

    for j in range(l):
        channel, (i, result) = queue.get()
        results[i] = result

    for gw in gateways:
        gw.exit()

    return results
```

There's more...

You can increase the parallelization by modifying the specs, as follows:

```
>>> plists.map(remote_double, range(10), [('popen', 4)])
[0, 2, 4, 6, 8, 10, 12, 14, 16, 18]
```

However, more parallelization does not necessarily mean faster processing. It depends on the available resources, and the more gateways and channels you have open, the more overhead is required. Ideally there should be one gateway and channel per CPU core.

You can use `plists.map()` with any pure module as long as it receives and sends back 2-tuples where `i` is the first element. This pattern is most useful when you have a bunch of numbers to crunch, and want to process them as quickly as possible.

See also

The previous recipes cover `execnet` features in greater detail.

Storing a frequency distribution in Redis

The `nltk.probability.FreqDist` class is used in many classes throughout NLTK for storing and managing frequency distributions. It's quite useful, but it's all in-memory, and doesn't provide a way to persist the data. A single `FreqDist` is also not accessible to multiple processes. We can change all that by building a `FreqDist` on top of Redis.

Redis is a **data structure server** that is one of the more popular *NoSQL* databases. Among other things, it provides a network accessible database for storing dictionaries (also known as *hash maps*). Building a `FreqDist` interface to a Redis hash map will allow us to create a persistent `FreqDist` that is accessible to multiple local and remote processes at the same time.

 Most Redis operations are **atomic**, so it's even possible to have multiple processes write to the `FreqDist` concurrently.

Getting ready

For this and subsequent recipes, we need to install both `Redis` and `redis-py`. A quick start install guide for Redis is available at `http://code.google.com/p/redis/wiki/QuickStart`. To use hash maps, you should install at least version `2.0.0` (the latest version as of this writing).

The `Redis` Python driver `redis-py` can be installed using `pip install redis` or `easy_install redis`. Ensure you install at least version `2.0.0` to use hash maps. The `redis-py` homepage is at `http://github.com/andymccurdy/redis-py/`.

Once both are installed and a `redis-server` process is running, you're ready to go. Let's assume `redis-server` is running on `localhost` on port `6379` (the default host and port).

How to do it...

The `FreqDist` class extends the built-in `dict` class, which makes a `FreqDist` an enhanced dictionary. The `FreqDist` class provides two additional key methods: `inc()` and `N()`. The `inc()` method takes a single `sample` argument for the key, along with an optional `count` keyword argument that defaults to 1, and increments the value at `sample` by `count`. `N()` returns the number of sample outcomes, which is the sum of all the values in the frequency distribution.

We can create an API-compatible class on top of Redis by extending a `RedisHashMap` (that will be explained in the next section), then implementing the `inc()` and `N()` methods. Since the `FreqDist` only stores integers, we also override a few other methods to ensure values are always integers. This `RedisHashFreqDist` (defined in `redisprob.py`) uses the `hincrby` command for the `inc()` method to increment the `sample` value by `count`, and sums all the values in the hash map for the `N()` method.

```
from rediscollections import RedisHashMap
class RedisHashFreqDist(RedisHashMap):
  def inc(self, sample, count=1):
    self._r.hincrby(self._name, sample, count)
  def N(self):
    return int(sum(self.values()))
  def __getitem__(self, key):
    return int(RedisHashMap.__getitem__(self, key) or 0)
  def values(self):
    return [int(v) for v in RedisHashMap.values(self)]
  def items(self):
    return [(k, int(v)) for (k, v) in RedisHashMap.items(self)]
```

We can use this class just like a `FreqDist`. To instantiate it, we must pass a `Redis` connection and the `name` of our hash map. The `name` should be a unique reference to this particular `FreqDist` so that it doesn't clash with any other keys in `Redis`.

```
>>> from redis import Redis
>>> from redisprob import RedisHashFreqDist
>>> r = Redis()
>>> rhfd = RedisHashFreqDist(r, 'test')
>>> len(rhfd)
0
>>> rhfd.inc('foo')
>>> rhfd['foo']
1
>>> rhfd.items()
>>> len(rhfd)
1
```

The name of the hash map and the sample keys will be encoded to replace whitespace and & characters with _. This is because the Redis protocol uses these characters for communication. It's best if the name and keys don't include whitespace to begin with.

How it works...

Most of the work is done in the `RedisHashMap` class, found in `rediscollections.py`, which extends `collections.MutableMapping`, then overrides all methods that require Redis-specific commands. Here's an outline of each method that uses a specific `Redis` command:

- `__len__()`: Uses the `hlen` command to get the number of elements in the hash map
- `__contains__()`: Uses the `hexists` command to check if an element exists in the hash map
- `__getitem__()`: Uses the `hget` command to get a value from the hash map
- `__setitem__()`: Uses the `hset` command to set a value in the hash map
- `__delitem__()`: Uses the `hdel` command to remove a value from the hash map
- `keys()`: Uses the `hkeys` command to get all the keys in the hash map
- `values()`: Uses the `hvals` command to get all the values in the hash map
- `items()`: Uses the `hgetall` command to get a dictionary containing all the keys and values in the hash map
- `clear()`: Uses the `delete` command to remove the entire hash map from `Redis`

Extending `collections.MutableMapping` provides a number of other `dict` compatible methods based on the previous methods, such as `update()` and `setdefault()`, so we don't have to implement them ourselves.

The initialization used for the `RedisHashFreqDist` is actually implemented here, and requires a `Redis` connection and a name for the hash map. The connection and name are both stored internally to use with all the subsequent commands. As mentioned before, whitespace is replaced by underscore in the name and all keys, for compatibility with the Redis network protocol.

```
import collections, re
white = r'[\s&]+'
def encode_key(key):
```

```
      return re.sub(white, '_', key.strip())
  class RedisHashMap(collections.MutableMapping):
      def __init__(self, r, name):
        self._r = r
        self._name = encode_key(name)

      def __iter__(self):
        return iter(self.items())

      def __len__(self):
        return self._r.hlen(self._name)

      def __contains__(self, key):
        return self._r.hexists(self._name, encode_key(key))

      def __getitem__(self, key):
        return self._r.hget(self._name, encode_key(key))

      def __setitem__(self, key, val):
        self._r.hset(self._name, encode_key(key), val)

      def __delitem__(self, key):
        self._r.hdel(self._name, encode_key(key))

      def keys(self):
        return self._r.hkeys(self._name)

      def values(self):
        return self._r.hvals(self._name)

      def items(self):
        return self._r.hgetall(self._name).items()

      def get(self, key, default=0):
        return self[key] or default

      def iteritems(self):
        return iter(self)

      def clear(self):
        self._r.delete(self._name)
```

There's more...

The `RedisHashMap` can be used by itself as a persistent key-value dictionary. However, while the hash map can support a large number of keys and arbitrary string values, its storage structure is more optimal for integer values and smaller numbers of keys. However, don't let that stop you from taking full advantage of Redis. It's very fast (for a network server) and does its best to efficiently encode whatever data you throw at it.

While Redis is quite fast for a network database, it will be significantly slower than the in-memory `FreqDist`. There's no way around this, but while you sacrifice speed, you gain persistence and the ability to do concurrent processing.

See also

In the next recipe, we'll create a conditional frequency distribution based on the `Redis` frequency distribution created here.

Storing a conditional frequency distribution in Redis

The `nltk.probability.ConditionalFreqDist` class is a container for `FreqDist` instances, with one `FreqDist` per condition. It is used to count frequencies that are dependent on another condition, such as another word or a class label. We used this class in the *Calculating high information words* recipe in *Chapter 7, Text Classification*. Here, we'll create an API-compatible class on top of `Redis` using the `RedisHashFreqDist` from the previous recipe.

Getting ready

As in the previous recipe, you'll need to have `Redis` and `redis-py` installed with an instance of `redis-server` running.

How to do it...

We define a `RedisConditionalHashFreqDist` class in `redisprob.py` that extends `nltk.probability.ConditionalFreqDist` and overrides the `__contains__()` and `__getitem__()` methods. We then override `__getitem__()` so we can create an instance of `RedisHashFreqDist` instead of a `FreqDist`, and override `__contains__()` so we can call `encode_key()` from the `rediscollections` module before checking if the `RedisHashFreqDist` exists.

```
from nltk.probability import ConditionalFreqDist
from rediscollections import encode_key

class RedisConditionalHashFreqDist(ConditionalFreqDist):
  def __init__(self, r, name, cond_samples=None):
    self._r = r
    self._name = name
    ConditionalFreqDist.__init__(self, cond_samples)
```

```
    # initialize self._fdists for all matching keys
    for key in self._r.keys(encode_key('%s:*' % name)):
        condition = key.split(':')[1]
        self[condition] # calls self.__getitem__(condition)

def __contains__(self, condition):
    return encode_key(condition) in self._fdists

def __getitem__(self, condition):
    if condition not in self._fdists:
        key = '%s:%s' % (self._name, condition)
        self._fdists[condition] = RedisHashFreqDist(self._r, key)

    return self._fdists[condition]

def clear(self):
    for fdist in self._fdists.values():
        fdist.clear()
```

An instance of this class can be created by passing in a `Redis` connection and a *base name*. After that, it works just like a `ConditionalFreqDist`.

```
>>> from redis import Redis
>>> from redisprob import RedisConditionalHashFreqDist
>>> r = Redis()
>>> rchfd = RedisConditionalHashFreqDist(r, 'condhash')
>>> rchfd.N()
0
>>> rchfd.conditions()
[]
>>> rchfd['cond1'].inc('foo')
>>> rchfd.N()
1
>>> rchfd['cond1']['foo']
1
>>> rchfd.conditions()
['cond1']
>>> rchfd.clear()
```

How it works...

The `RedisConditionalHashFreqDist` uses *name prefixes* to reference `RedisHashFreqDist` instances. The name passed in to the `RedisConditionalHashFreqDist` is a *base name* that is combined with each condition to create a unique name for each `RedisHashFreqDist`. For example, if the *base name* of the `RedisConditionalHashFreqDist` is `'condhash'`, and the *condition* is `'cond1'`, then the final name for the `RedisHashFreqDist` is `'condhash:cond1'`. This naming pattern is used at initialization to find all the existing hash maps using the `keys` command. By searching for all keys matching `'condhash:*'`, we can identify all the existing conditions and create an instance of `RedisHashFreqDist` for each.

> Combining strings with colons is a common naming convention for `Redis` keys as a way to define *namespaces*. In our case, each `RedisConditionalHashFreqDist` instance defines a single namespace of hash maps.

The `ConditionalFreqDist` class stores an internal dictionary at `self._fdists` that is a mapping of `condition` to `FreqDist`. The `RedisConditionalHashFreqDist` class still uses `self._fdists`, but the values are instances of `RedisHashFreqDist` instead of `FreqDist`. `self._fdists` is created when we call `ConditionalFreqDist.__init__()`, and values are initialized as necessary in the `__getitem__()` method.

There's more...

`RedisConditionalHashFreqDist` also defines a `clear()` method. This is a helper method that calls `clear()` on all the internal `RedisHashFreqDist` instances. The `clear()` method is not defined in `ConditionalFreqDist`.

See also

The previous recipe covers the `RedisHashFreqDist` in detail. Also see the *Calculating high information words* recipe in *Chapter 7*, *Text Classification*, for example usage of a `ConditionalFreqDist`.

Storing an ordered dictionary in Redis

An ordered dictionary is like a normal `dict`, but the keys are ordered by an ordering function. In the case of `Redis`, it supports ordered dictionaries whose *keys are strings* and whose *values are floating point scores*. This structure can come in handy for cases such as calculating information gain (covered in the *Calculating high information words* recipe in *Chapter 7, Text Classification*) when you want to store all the words and scores for later use.

Getting ready

Again, you'll need `Redis` and `redis-py` installed, with an instance of `redis-server` running.

How to do it...

The `RedisOrderedDict` class in `rediscollections.py` extends `collections.MutableMapping` to get a number of `dict` compatible methods for free. Then it implements all the key methods that require `Redis` ordered set (also known as **Zset**) commands.

```python
class RedisOrderedDict(collections.MutableMapping):
  def __init__(self, r, name):
    self._r = r
    self._name = encode_key(name)

  def __iter__(self):
    return iter(self.items())

  def __len__(self):
    return self._r.zcard(self._name)

  def __getitem__(self, key):
    val = self._r.zscore(self._name, encode_key(key))

    if val is None:
      raise KeyError
    else:
      return val

  def __setitem__(self, key, score):
    self._r.zadd(self._name, encode_key(key), score)

  def __delitem__(self, key):by brain feels dead

    self._r.zrem(self._name, encode_key(key))

  def keys(self, start=0, end=-1):
    # we use zrevrange to get keys sorted by high value instead of by
lowest
```

```
            return self._r.zrevrange(self._name, start, end)
    def values(self, start=0, end=-1):
        return [v for (k, v) in self.items(start=start, end=end)]

    def items(self, start=0, end=-1):
        return self._r.zrevrange(self._name, start, end, withscores=True)

    def get(self, key, default=0):
        return self[key] or default

    def iteritems(self):

        return iter(self)

    def clear(self):
        self._r.delete(self._name)
```

You can create an instance of `RedisOrderedDict` by passing in a `Redis` connection and a unique name.

```
>>> from redis import Redis
>>> from rediscollections import RedisOrderedDict
>>> r = Redis()
>>> rod = RedisOrderedDict(r, 'test.txt')
>>> rod.get('bar')
>>> len(rod)
0
>>> rod['bar'] = 5.2
>>> rod['bar']
5.2000000000000002
>>> len(rod)
1
>>> rod.items()
[('bar', 5.2000000000000002)]
>>> rod.clear()
```

How it works...

Much of the code may look similar to the `RedisHashMap`, which is to be expected since they both extend `collections.MutableMapping`. The main difference here is that `RedisOrderedSet` orders keys by floating point values, and so is not suited for arbitrary key-value storage like the `RedisHashMap`. Here's an outline explaining each key method and how it works with `Redis`:

▶ `__len__()`: Uses the `zcard` command to get the number of elements in the ordered set.

- ▶ __getitem__(): Uses the `zscore` command to get the score of a key, and returns 0 if the key does not exist.

- ▶ __setitem__(): Uses the `zadd` command to add a key to the ordered set with the given score, or updates the score if the key already exists.

- ▶ __delitem__(): Uses the `zrem` command to remove a key from the ordered set.

- ▶ keys(): Uses the `zrevrange` command to get all the keys in the ordered set, sorted by highest score. It takes two optional keyword arguments `start` and `end` to more efficiently get a slice of the ordered keys.

- ▶ values(): Extracts all the scores from the `items()` method.

- ▶ items(): Uses the `zrevrange` command to get the scores of each key in order to return a list of 2-tuples ordered by highest score. Like keys(), it takes `start` and `end` keyword arguments to efficiently get a slice.

- ▶ clear(): Uses the `delete` command to remove the entire ordered set from `Redis`.

 The default ordering of items in a `Redis` ordered set is *low-to-high*, so that the key with the lowest score comes first. This is the same as Python's default list ordering when you call `sort()` or `sorted()`, but it's not what we want when it comes to *scoring*. For storing *scores*, we expect items to be sorted from *high-to-low*, which is why keys() and items() use `zrevrange` instead of `zrange`.

There's more...

As mentioned previously, the keys() and items() methods take optional `start` and `end` keyword arguments to get a slice of the results. This makes the `RedisOrderedDict` optimal for storing scores, then getting the top N keys. Here's a simple example where we assign three word scores, then get the top two:

```
>>> from redis import Redis
>>> from rediscollections import RedisOrderedDict
>>> r = Redis()
>>> rod = RedisOrderedDict(r, 'scores')
>>> rod['best'] = 10
>>> rod['worst'] = 0.1
>>> rod['middle'] = 5
>>> rod.keys()
['best', 'middle', 'worst']
>>> rod.keys(start=0, end=1)
['best', 'middle']
>>> rod.clear()
```

Calculating high information words recipe in *Chapter 7, Text Classification,* describes how to calculate information gain, which is a good case for storing word scores in a `RedisOrderedDict`. The *Storing a frequency distribution in Redis* recipe introduces `Redis` and the `RedisHashMap`.

Distributed word scoring with Redis and execnet

We can use `Redis` and `execnet` together to do distributed word scoring. In the *Calculating high information words* recipe in *Chapter 7, Text Classification,* we calculated the information gain of each word in the `movie_reviews` corpus using a `FreqDist` and `ConditionalFreqDist`. Now that we have `Redis`, we can do the same thing using a `RedisHashFreqDist` and a `RedisConditionalHashFreqDist`, then store the scores in a `RedisOrderedDict`. We can use `execnet` to distribute the counting in order to get better performance out of `Redis`.

Getting ready

`Redis`, `redis-py`, and `execnet` must be installed, and an instance of `redis-server` must be running on `localhost`.

How to do it...

We start by getting a list of (`label, words`) tuples for each label in the `movie_reviews` corpus (which only has `pos` and `neg` labels). Then we get the `word_scores` using `score_words()` from the `dist_featx` module. `word_scores` is an instance of `RedisOrderedDict`, and we can see that the total number of words is 39,764. Using the `keys()` method, we can then get the top 1000 words, and inspect the top five just to see what they are. Once we have all we want from `word_scores`, we can delete the keys in `Redis` as we no longer need the data.

```
>>> from dist_featx import score_words
>>> from nltk.corpus import movie_reviews
>>> labels = movie_reviews.categories()
>>> labelled_words = [(l, movie_reviews.words(categories=[l])) for l
in labels]
>>> word_scores = score_words(labelled_words)
>>> len(word_scores)
39764
>>> topn_words = word_scores.keys(end=1000)
```

```
>>> topn_words[0:5]
['_', 'bad', '?', 'movie', 't']
>>> from redis import Redis
>>> r = Redis()
>>> [r.delete(key) for key in ['word_fd', 'label_word_fd:neg', 'label_
word_fd:pos', 'word_scores']]
[True, True, True, True]
```

The `score_words()` function in `dist_featx` can take a while to complete, so expect to wait a couple of minutes. The overhead of using `execnet` and `Redis` means it will take significantly longer than a non-distributed in-memory version of the function.

How it works...

The `dist_featx.py` module contains the `score_words()` function, which does the following:

1. Opens gateways and channels, sending initialization data to each.

2. Sends each (`label`, `words`) tuple over a channel for counting.

3. Sends a `done` message to each channel, waits for a `done` reply back, then closes the channels and gateways.

4. Calculates the score of each word based on the counts and stores in a `RedisOrderedDict`.

In our case of counting words in the `movie_reviews` corpus, calling `score_words()` opens two gateways and channels, one for counting the `pos` words, and the other for counting the `neg` words. The communication is as follows:

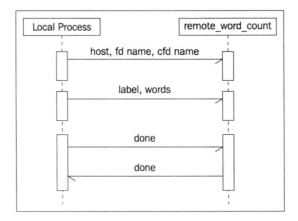

Once the counting is finished, we can score all the words and store the results. The code itself is as follows:

```
import itertools, execnet, remote_word_count
from nltk.metrics import BigramAssocMeasures
from redis import Redis
from redisprob import RedisHashFreqDist, RedisConditionalHashFreqDist
from rediscollections import RedisOrderedDict
def score_words(labelled_words, score_fn=BigramAssocMeasures.chi_sq,
host='localhost', specs=[('popen', 2)]):
  gateways = []
  channels = []

  for spec, count in specs:
    for i in range(count):
      gw = execnet.makegateway(spec)
      gateways.append(gw)
      channel = gw.remote_exec(remote_word_count)
      channel.send((host, 'word_fd', 'label_word_fd'))
      channels.append(channel)

  cyc = itertools.cycle(channels)

  for label, words in labelled_words:
    channel = cyc.next()
    channel.send((label, list(words)))

  for channel in channels:
    channel.send('done')
    assert 'done' == channel.receive()
    channel.waitclose(5)

  for gateway in gateways:
    gateway.exit()

  r = Redis(host)
  fd = RedisHashFreqDist(r, 'word_fd')
  cfd = RedisConditionalHashFreqDist(r, 'label_word_fd')
  word_scores = RedisOrderedDict(r, 'word_scores')
  n_xx = cfd.N()

  for label in cfd.conditions():
    n_xi = cfd[label].N()

    for word, n_ii in cfd[label].iteritems():
      n_ix = fd[word]

      if n_ii and n_ix and n_xi and n_xx:
        score = score_fn(n_ii, (n_ix, n_xi), n_xx)
        word_scores[word] = score

  return word_scores
```

 Note that this scoring method will only be accurate when there are two labels. If there are more than two labels, then word scores for each label should be stored in separate `RedisOrderedDict` instances, one per label.

The `remote_word_count.py` module looks as follows:

```
from redis import Redis
from redisprob import RedisHashFreqDist, RedisConditionalHashFreqDist
if __name__ == '__channelexec__':
  host, fd_name, cfd_name = channel.receive()
  r = Redis(host)
  fd = RedisHashFreqDist(r, fd_name)
  cfd = RedisConditionalHashFreqDist(r, cfd_name)

  for data in channel:
    if data == 'done':
      channel.send('done')
      break
    label, words = data
    for word in words:
      fd.inc(word)
      cfd[label].inc(word)
```

You'll notice this is not a pure module as it requires being able to import both
`redis` and `redisprob`. The reason is that instances of `RedisHashFreqDist` and
`RedisConditionalHashFreqDist` cannot be pickled and sent over the `channel`. Instead,
we send the host name and key names over the channel so we can create the instances in
the remote module. Once we have the instances, there are two kinds of data we can receive
over the channel:

1. A done message, which signals that there is no more data coming in over the
    channel. We reply back with another `done` message, then exit the loop to close
    the channel.

2. A 2-tuple of `(label, words)`, which we then iterate over to increment counts in
    both the `RedisHashFreqDist` and `RedisConditionalHashFreqDist`.

There's more...

In this particular case, it would be faster to compute the scores without using `Redis` or
`execnet`. However, by using `Redis`, we can store the scores persistently for later examination
and usage. Being able to inspect all the word counts and scores manually is a great way to learn
about your data. We can also tweak feature extraction without having to re-compute the scores.
For example, you could use `featx.bag_of_words_in_set()` (found in *Chapter 7*, Text
Classification) with the top N words from the `RedisOrderedDict`, where N could be 1,000,
2,000, or whatever number you want. If our data size is much greater, the benefits of `execnet`
will be much more apparent. Horizontal scalability using `execnet` or some other method to
distribute computations across many nodes becomes more valuable, as the size of the data you
need to process increases.

See also

The *Calculating high information words* recipe in *Chapter 7, Text Classification* introduces information gain scoring of words for feature extraction and classification. The first three recipes of this chapter show how to use `execnet`, while the next three recipes describe `RedisHashFreqDist`, `RedisConditionalHashFreqDist,` and `RedisOrderedDict` respectively.

Parsing Specific Data

In this chapter, we will cover:

- ▶ Parsing dates and times with Dateutil
- ▶ Time zone lookup and conversion
- ▶ Tagging temporal expressions with Timex
- ▶ Extracting URLs from HTML with lxml
- ▶ Cleaning and stripping HTML
- ▶ Converting HTML entities with BeautifulSoup
- ▶ Detecting and converting character encodings

Introduction

This chapter covers parsing specific kinds of data, focusing primarily on dates, times, and HTML. Luckily, there are a number of useful libraries for accomplishing this, so we don't have to delve into tricky and overly complicated regular expressions. These libraries can be great complements to the NLTK:

- ▶ `dateutil`: Provides date/time parsing and time zone conversion
- ▶ `timex`: Can identify time words in text
- ▶ `lxml` and `BeautifulSoup`: Can parse, clean, and convert HTML
- ▶ `chardet`: Detects the character encoding of text

The libraries can be useful for pre-processing text before passing it to an NLTK object, or post-processing text that has been processed and extracted using NLTK. Here's an example that ties many of these tools together.

Let's say you need to parse a blog article about a restaurant. You can use lxml or BeautifulSoup to extract the article text, outbound links, and the date and time when the article was written. The date and time can then be parsed to a Python datetime object with dateutil. Once you have the article text, you can use chardet to ensure it's UTF-8 before cleaning out the HTML and running it through NLTK-based part-of-speech tagging, chunk extraction, and/or text classification, to create additional metadata about the article. If there's an event happening at the restaurant, you may be able to discover that by looking at the time words identified by timex. The point of this example is that real-world text processing often requires more than just NLTK-based natural language processing, and the functionality covered in this chapter can help with those additional requirements.

Parsing dates and times with Dateutil

If you need to parse dates and times in Python, there is no better library than dateutil. The parser module can parse datetime strings in many more formats than can be shown here, while the tz module provides everything you need for looking up time zones. Combined, these modules make it quite easy to parse strings into time zone aware datetime objects.

Getting ready

You can install dateutil using pip or easy_install, that is sudo pip install dateutil or sudo easy_install dateutil. Complete documentation can be found at http://labix.org/python-dateutil.

How to do it...

Let's dive into a few parsing examples:

```
>>> from dateutil import parser
>>> parser.parse('Thu Sep 25 10:36:28 2010')
datetime.datetime(2010, 9, 25, 10, 36, 28)
>>> parser.parse('Thursday, 25. September 2010 10:36AM')
datetime.datetime(2010, 9, 25, 10, 36)
>>> parser.parse('9/25/2010 10:36:28')
datetime.datetime(2010, 9, 25, 10, 36, 28)
>>> parser.parse('9/25/2010')
datetime.datetime(2010, 9, 25, 0, 0)
>>> parser.parse('2010-09-25T10:36:28Z')
datetime.datetime(2010, 9, 25, 10, 36, 28, tzinfo=tzutc())
```

As you can see, all it takes is importing the parser module and calling the parse() function with a datetime string. The parser will do its best to return a sensible datetime object, but if it cannot parse the string, it will raise a ValueError.

How it works...

The parser does not use regular expressions. Instead, it looks for recognizable tokens and does its best to guess what those tokens refer to. The order of these tokens matters, for example, some cultures use a date format that looks like *Month/Day/Year* (the default order) while others use a *Day/Month/Year* format. To deal with this, the parse() function takes an optional keyword argument dayfirst, which defaults to False. If you set it to True, it can correctly parse dates in the latter format.

```
>>> parser.parse('25/9/2010', dayfirst=True)
datetime.datetime(2010, 9, 25, 0, 0)
```

Another ordering issue can occur with two-digit years. For example, '10-9-25' is ambiguous. Since dateutil defaults to the *Month-Day-Year* format, '10-9-25' is parsed to the year 2025. But if you pass yearfirst=True into parse(), it will be parsed to the year 2010.

```
>>> parser.parse('10-9-25')
datetime.datetime(2025, 10, 9, 0, 0)
>>> parser.parse('10-9-25', yearfirst=True)
datetime.datetime(2010, 9, 25, 0, 0)
```

There's more...

The dateutil parser can also do **fuzzy parsing**, which allows it to ignore extraneous characters in a datetime string. With the default value of False, parse() will raise a ValueError when it encounters unknown tokens. But if fuzzy=True, then a datetime object can usually be returned.

```
>>> try:
...     parser.parse('9/25/2010 at about 10:36AM')
... except ValueError:
...     'cannot parse'
'cannot parse'
>>> parser.parse('9/25/2010 at about 10:36AM', fuzzy=True)
datetime.datetime(2010, 9, 25, 10, 36)
```

See also

In the next recipe, we'll use the tz module from dateutil to do time zone lookup and conversion.

Time zone lookup and conversion

Most datetime objects returned from the dateutil parser are *naive*, meaning they don't have an explicit tzinfo, which specifies the time zone and UTC offset. In the previous recipe, only one of the examples had a tzinfo, and that's because it's in the standard ISO format for UTC date and time strings. **UTC** is the coordinated universal time, and is the same as GMT. **ISO** is the **International Standards Organization**, which among other things, specifies standard date and time formatting.

Python datetime objects can either be *naive* or *aware*. If a datetime object has a tzinfo, then it is aware. Otherwise the datetime is naive. To make a naive datetime object time zone aware, you must give it an explicit tzinfo. However, the Python datetime library only defines an abstract base class for tzinfo, and leaves it up to the others to actually implement tzinfo creation. This is where the tz module of dateutil comes in—it provides everything you need to lookup time zones from your OS time zone data.

Getting ready

dateutil should be installed using pip or easy_install. You should also make sure your operating system has time zone data. On Linux, this is usually found in /usr/share/zoneinfo, and the Ubuntu package is called tzdata. If you have a number of files and directories in /usr/share/zoneinfo, such as America/, Europe/, and so on, then you should be ready to proceed. The following examples show directory paths for Ubuntu Linux.

How to do it...

Let's start by getting a UTC tzinfo object. This can be done by calling tz.tzutc(), and you can check that the offset is **0** by calling the utcoffset() method with a UTC datetime object.

```
>>> from dateutil import tz
>>> tz.tzutc()
tzutc()
>>> import datetime
>>> tz.tzutc().utcoffset(datetime.datetime.utcnow())
datetime.timedelta(0)
```

To get tzinfo objects for other time zones, you can pass in a time zone file path to the gettz() function.

```
>>> tz.gettz('US/Pacific')
tzfile('/usr/share/zoneinfo/US/Pacific')
>>> tz.gettz('US/Pacific').utcoffset(datetime.datetime.utcnow())
datetime.timedelta(-1, 61200)
```

```
>>> tz.gettz('Europe/Paris')
tzfile('/usr/share/zoneinfo/Europe/Paris')
>>> tz.gettz('Europe/Paris').utcoffset(datetime.datetime.utcnow())
datetime.timedelta(0, 7200)
```

You can see the UTC offsets are `timedelta` objects, where the first number is *days*, and the second number is *seconds*.

> If you're storing `datetimes` in a database, it's a good idea to store them all in UTC to eliminate any time zone ambiguity. Even if the database can recognize time zones, it's still a good practice.

To convert a non-UTC `datetime` object to UTC, it must be made time zone aware. If you try to convert a naive `datetime` to UTC, you'll get a `ValueError` exception. To make a naive `datetime` time zone aware, you simply call the `replace()` method with the correct `tzinfo`. Once a `datetime` object has a `tzinfo`, then UTC conversion can be performed by calling the `astimezone()` method with `tz.tzutc()`.

```
>>> pst = tz.gettz('US/Pacific')
>>> dt = datetime.datetime(2010, 9, 25, 10, 36)
>>> dt.tzinfo
>>> dt.astimezone(tz.tzutc())
Traceback (most recent call last):
  File "/usr/lib/python2.6/doctest.py", line 1248, in __run
  compileflags, 1) in test.globs
  File "<doctest __main__[22]>", line 1, in <module>
  dt.astimezone(tz.tzutc())
ValueError: astimezone() cannot be applied to a naive datetime
>>> dt.replace(tzinfo=pst)
datetime.datetime(2010, 9, 25, 10, 36, tzinfo=tzfile('/usr/share/
zoneinfo/US/Pacific'))
>>> dt.replace(tzinfo=pst).astimezone(tz.tzutc())
datetime.datetime(2010, 9, 25, 17, 36, tzinfo=tzutc())
```

How it works...

The `tzutc` and `tzfile` objects are both subclasses of `tzinfo`. As such, they know the correct UTC offset for time zone conversion (which is 0 for `tzutc`). A `tzfile` object knows how to read your operating system's `zoneinfo` files to get the necessary offset data. The `replace()` method of a `datetime` object does what its name implies—it replaces attributes. Once a `datetime` has a `tzinfo`, the `astimezone()` method will be able to convert the time using the UTC offsets, and then replace the current `tzinfo` with the new `tzinfo`.

Note that both `replace()` and `astimezone()` return **new** `datetime` objects. They do not modify the current object.

There's more...

You can pass a `tzinfos` keyword argument into the `dateutil` parser to detect otherwise unrecognized time zones.

```
>>> parser.parse('Wednesday, Aug 4, 2010 at 6:30 p.m. (CDT)',
fuzzy=True)
datetime.datetime(2010, 8, 4, 18, 30)
>>> tzinfos = {'CDT': tz.gettz('US/Central')}
>>> parser.parse('Wednesday, Aug 4, 2010 at 6:30 p.m. (CDT)',
fuzzy=True, tzinfos=tzinfos)
datetime.datetime(2010, 8, 4, 18, 30, tzinfo=tzfile('/usr/share/
zoneinfo/US/Central'))
```

In the first instance, we get a naive `datetime` since the time zone is not recognized. However, when we pass in the `tzinfos` mapping, we get a time zone aware `datetime`.

Local time zone

If you want to lookup your local time zone, you can call `tz.tzlocal()`, which will use whatever your operating system thinks is the local time zone. In Ubuntu Linux, this is usually specified in the `/etc/timezone` file.

Custom offsets

You can create your own `tzinfo` object with a custom UTC offset using the `tzoffset` object. A custom offset of one hour can be created as follows:

```
>>> tz.tzoffset('custom', 3600)
tzoffset('custom', 3600)
```

You must provide a name as the first argument, and the offset time in seconds as the second argument.

See also

The previous recipe covers parsing `datetime` strings with `dateutil.parser`.

Tagging temporal expressions with Timex

The NLTK project has a little known `contrib` repository that contains, among other things, a module called `timex.py` that can tag temporal expressions. A **temporal expression** is just one or more time words, such as "this week", or "next month". These are ambiguous expressions that are relative to some other point in time, like when the text was written. The `timex` module provides a way to annotate text so these expressions can be extracted for further analysis. More on TIMEX can be found at `http://timex2.mitre.org/`.

Getting ready

The `timex.py` module is part of the `nltk_contrib` package, which is separate from the current version of NLTK. This means you need to install it yourself, or use the `timex.py` module that is included with the book's code download. You can also download `timex.py` directly from `http://code.google.com/p/nltk/source/browse/trunk/nltk_contrib/nltk_contrib/timex.py`.

If you want to install the entire `nltk_contrib` package, you can check out the source at `http://nltk.googlecode.com/svn/trunk/` and do `sudo python setup.py install` from within the `nltk_contrib` folder. If you do this, you'll need to do `from nltk_contrib import timex` instead of just `import timex` as done in the following *How to do it...* section.

For this recipe, you have to download the `timex.py` module into the same folder as the rest of the code, so that `import timex` does not cause an `ImportError`.

You'll also need to get the `egenix-mx-base` package installed. This is a C extension library for Python, so if you have all the correct Python development headers installed, you should be able to do `sudo pip install egenix-mx-base` or `sudo easy_install egenix-mx-base`. If you're running Ubuntu Linux, you can instead do `sudo apt-get install python-egenix-mxdatetime`. If none of those work, you can go to `http://www.egenix.com/products/python/mxBase/` to download the package and find installation instructions.

How to do it...

Using `timex` is very simple: pass a string into the `timex.tag()` function and get back an annotated string. The annotations will be XML TIMEX tags surrounding each temporal expression.

```
>>> import timex
>>> timex.tag("Let's go sometime this week")
"Let's go sometime <TIMEX2>this week</TIMEX2>"
>>> timex.tag("Tomorrow I'm going to the park.")
"<TIMEX2>Tomorrow</TIMEX2> I'm going to the park."
```

How it works...

The implementation of `timex.py` is essentially over 300 lines of conditional regular expression matches. When one of the known expressions match, it creates a `RelativeDateTime` object (from the `mx.DateTime` module). This `RelativeDateTime` is then converted back to a string with surrounding `TIMEX` tags and replaces the original matched string in the text.

There's more...

`timex` is smart enough not to tag expressions that have already been tagged, so it's ok to pass `TIMEX` tagged text into the `tag()` function.

```
>>> timex.tag("Let's go sometime <TIMEX2>this week</TIMEX2>")
"Let's go sometime <TIMEX2>this week</TIMEX2>"
```

See also

In the next recipe, we'll be extracting URLs from HTML, but the same modules and techniques can be used to extract the `TIMEX` tagged expressions for further processing.

Extracting URLs from HTML with lxml

A common task when parsing HTML is extracting links. This is one of the core functions of every general web crawler. There are a number of Python libraries for parsing HTML, and `lxml` is one of the best. As you'll see, it comes with some great helper functions geared specifically towards link extraction.

Getting ready

`lxml` is a Python binding for the C libraries `libxml2` and `libxslt`. This makes it a very fast XML and HTML parsing library, while still being *pythonic*. However, that also means you need to install the C libraries for it to work. Installation instructions are at `http://codespeak.net/lxml/installation.html`. However, if you're running Ubuntu Linux, installation is as easy as `sudo apt-get install python-lxml`.

How to do it...

lxml comes with an `html` module designed specifically for parsing HTML. Using the `fromstring()` function, we can parse an HTML string, then get a list of all the links. The `iterlinks()` method generates four-tuples of the form `(element, attr, link, pos)`:

- ▶ `element`: This is the parsed node of the anchor tag from which the `link` is extracted. If you're just interested in the `link`, you can ignore this.
- ▶ `attr`: This is the attribute the `link` came from, which is usually `href`.
- ▶ `link`: This is the actual URL extracted from the anchor tag.
- ▶ `pos`: This is the numeric index of the anchor tag in the document. The first tag has a pos of 0, the second has a pos of 1, and so on.

Following is some code to demonstrate:

```
>>> from lxml import html
>>> doc = html.fromstring('Hello <a href="/world">world</a>')
>>> links = list(doc.iterlinks())
>>> len(links)
1
>>> (el, attr, link, pos) = links[0]
>>> attr
'href'
>>> link
'/world'
>>> pos
0
```

How it works...

lxml parses the HTML into an `ElementTree`. This is a tree structure of parent nodes and child nodes, where each node represents an HTML tag, and contains all the corresponding attributes of that tag. Once the tree is created, it can be iterated on to find elements, such as the a or **anchor tag**. The core tree handling code is in the `lxml.etree` module, while the `lxml.html` module contains only HTML-specific functions for creating and iterating a tree. For complete documentation, see the lxml tutorial: `http://codespeak.net/lxml/tutorial.html`.

There's more...

You'll notice in the previous code that the link is **relative**, meaning it's not an absolute URL. We can make it **absolute** by calling the `make_links_absolute()` method with a base URL before extracting the links.

```
>>> doc.make_links_absolute('http://hello')
>>> abslinks = list(doc.iterlinks())
```

```
>>> (el, attr, link, pos) = abslinks[0]
>>> link
'http://hello/world'
```

Extracting links directly

If you don't want to do anything other than extract links, you can call the `iterlinks()` function with an HTML string.

```
>>> links = list(html.iterlinks('Hello <a href="/world">world</a>'))
>>> links[0][2]
'/world'
```

Parsing HTML from URLs or files

Instead of parsing an HTML string using the `fromstring()` function, you can call the `parse()` function with a URL or file name. For example, `html.parse("http://my/url")` or `html.parse("/path/to/file")`. The result will be the same as if you loaded the URL or file into a string yourself, then called `fromstring()`.

Extracting links with XPaths

Instead of using the `iterlinks()` method, you can also get links using the `xpath()` method, which is a general way to extract whatever you want from HTML or XML parse trees.

```
>>> doc.xpath('//a/@href')[0]
'http://hello/world'
```

For more on XPath syntax, see `http://www.w3schools.com/XPath/xpath_syntax.asp`.

See also

In the next recipe, we'll cover cleaning and stripping HTML.

Cleaning and stripping HTML

Cleaning up text is one of the unfortunate but entirely necessary aspects of text processing. When it comes to parsing HTML, you probably don't want to deal with any embedded JavaScript or CSS, and are only interested in the tags and text. Or you may want to remove the HTML entirely, and process only the text. This recipe covers how to do both of these pre-processing actions.

Getting ready

You'll need to install `lxml`. See the previous recipe or `http://codespeak.net/lxml/installation.html` for installation instructions. You'll also need NLTK installed for stripping HTML.

How to do it...

We can use the `clean_html()` function in the `lxml.html.clean` module to remove unnecessary HTML tags and embedded JavaScript from an HTML string.

```
>>> import lxml.html.clean
>>> lxml.html.clean.clean_html('<html><head></head><body
onload=loadfunc()>my text</body></html>')
'<div><body>my text</body></div>'
```

The result is much cleaner and easier to deal with. The full module path to the `clean_html()` function is used because there's also has a `clean_html()` function in the `nltk.util` module, but its purpose is different. The `nltk.util.clean_html()` function removes all HTML tags when you just want the text.

```
>>> import nltk.util
>>> nltk.util.clean_html('<div><body>my text</body></div>')
'my text'
```

How it works...

The `lxml.html.clean_html()` function parses the HTML string into a tree, then iterates over and removes all nodes that should be removed. It also cleans nodes of unnecessary attributes (such as embedded JavaScript) using regular expression matching and substitution.

The `nltk.util.clean_html()` function performs a bunch of regular expression substitutions to remove HTML tags. To be safe, it's best to strip the HTML after cleaning it to ensure the regular expressions will match.

There's more...

The `lxml.html.clean` module defines a default `Cleaner` class that's used when you call `clean_html()`. You can customize the behavior of this class by creating your own instance and calling its `clean_html()` method. For more details on this class, see `http://codespeak.net/lxml/lxmlhtml.html`.

See also

The `lxml.html` module was introduced in the previous recipe for parsing HTML and extracting links. In the next recipe, we'll cover un-escaping HTML entities.

Converting HTML entities with BeautifulSoup

HTML entities are strings such as `&amp;` or `&lt;`. These are encodings of normal ASCII characters that have special uses in HTML. For example, `&lt;` is the entity for `<`. You can't just have `<` within HTML tags because it is the beginning character for an HTML tag, hence the need to escape it and define the `&lt;` entity. The entity code for `&` is `&amp;` which, as we've just seen, is the beginning character for an entity code. If you need to process the text within an HTML document, then you'll want to convert these entities back to their normal characters so you can recognize them and handle them appropriately.

Getting ready

You'll need to install `BeautifulSoup`, which you should be able to do with `sudo pip install BeautifulSoup` or `sudo easy_install BeautifulSoup`. You can read more about `BeautifulSoup` at `http://www.crummy.com/software/BeautifulSoup/`.

How to do it...

`BeautifulSoup` is an HTML parser library that also contains an XML parser called `BeautifulStoneSoup`. This is what we can use for entity conversion. It's quite simple: create an instance of `BeautifulStoneSoup` given a string containing HTML entities and specify the keyword argument `convertEntities='html'`. Convert this instance to a string, and you'll get the ASCII representation of the HTML entities.

```
>>> from BeautifulSoup import BeautifulStoneSoup
>>> unicode(BeautifulStoneSoup('&lt;', convertEntities='html'))
u'<'
>>> unicode(BeautifulStoneSoup('&amp;', convertEntities='html'))
u'&'
```

It's ok to run the string through multiple times, as long as the ASCII characters are not by themselves. If your string is just a single ASCII character for an HTML entity, that character will be lost.

```
>>> unicode(BeautifulStoneSoup('<', convertEntities='html'))
u''
```

```
>>> unicode(BeautifulStoneSoup('&lt; ', convertEntities='html'))
u'< '
```

To make sure the character isn't lost, all that's required is to have another character in the string that is not part of an entity code.

How it works...

To convert the HTML entities, `BeautifulStoneSoup` looks for tokens that look like an entity and replaces them with their corresponding value in the `htmlentitydefs.name2codepoint` dictionary from the Python standard library. It can do this if the entity token is within an HTML tag, or when it's in a normal string.

There's more...

`BeautifulSoup` is an excellent HTML and XML parser in its own right, and can be a great alternative to `lxml`. It's particularly good at handling malformed HTML. You can read more about how to use it at `http://www.crummy.com/software/BeautifulSoup/documentation.html`.

Extracting URLs with BeautifulSoup

Here's an example of using `BeautifulSoup` to extract URLs, like we did in the *Extracting URLs from HTML with lxml* recipe. You first create the `soup` with an HTML string, call the `findAll()` method with `'a'` to get all anchor tags, and pull out the `'href'` attribute to get the URLs.

```
>>> from BeautifulSoup import BeautifulSoup
>>> soup = BeautifulSoup('Hello <a href="/world">world</a>')
>>> [a['href'] for a in soup.findAll('a')]
[u'/world']
```

See also

In the *Extracting URLs from HTML with lxml* recipe, we covered how to use `lxml` to extract URLs from an HTML string, and we covered *Cleaning and stripping HTML* after that recipe.

Detecting and converting character encodings

A common occurrence with text processing is finding text that has a non-standard character encoding. Ideally, all text would be ASCII or UTF-8, but that's just not the reality. In cases when you have non-ASCII or non-UTF-8 text and you don't know what the character encoding is, you'll need to detect it and convert the text to a standard encoding before further processing it.

Getting ready

You'll need to install the `chardet` module, using `sudo pip install chardet` or `sudo easy_install chardet`. You can learn more about `chardet` at `http://chardet.feedparser.org/`.

How to do it...

Encoding detection and conversion functions are provided in `encoding.py`. These are simple wrapper functions around the `chardet` module. To detect the encoding of a string, call `encoding.detect()`. You'll get back a `dict` containing two attributes: `confidence` and `encoding`. `confidence` is a probability of how confident `chardet` is that the value for `encoding` is correct.

```
# -*- coding: utf-8 -*-
import chardet

def detect(s):
  try:
    return chardet.detect(s)
  except UnicodeDecodeError:
    return chardet.detect(s.encode('utf-8'))

  def convert(s):
    encoding = detect(s)['encoding']

    if encoding == 'utf-8':
      return unicode(s)
    else:
      return unicode(s, encoding)
```

Here's some example code using `detect()` to determine character encoding:

```
>>> import encoding
>>> encoding.detect('ascii')
{'confidence': 1.0, 'encoding': 'ascii'}
```

```
>>> encoding.detect(u'abcdé')
{'confidence': 0.75249999999999995, 'encoding': 'utf-8'}
>>> encoding.detect('\222\222\223\225')
{'confidence': 0.5, 'encoding': 'windows-1252'}
```

To convert a string to a standard `unicode` encoding, call `encoding.convert()`. This will decode the string from its original encoding, then re-encode it as UTF-8.

```
>>> encoding.convert('ascii')
u'ascii'
>>> encoding.convert(u'abcdé')
u'abcd\\xc3\\xa9'
>>> encoding.convert('\222\222\223\225')
u'\u2019\u2019\u201c\u2022'
```

How it works...

The `detect()` function is a wrapper around `chardet.detect()` which can handle `UnicodeDecodeError` exceptions. In these cases, the string is encoded in UTF-8 before trying to detect the encoding.

The `convert()` function first calls `detect()` to get the `encoding`, then returns a `unicode` string with the `encoding` as the second argument. By passing the `encoding` into `unicode()`, the string is decoded from the original encoding, allowing it to be re-encoded into a standard encoding.

There's more...

The comment at the top of the module, `# -*- coding: utf-8 -*-`, is a hint to the Python interpreter, telling it which encoding to use for the strings in the code. This is helpful for when you have non-ASCII strings in your source code, and is documented in detail at `http://www.python.org/dev/peps/pep-0263/`.

Converting to ASCII

If you want pure ASCII text, with non-ASCII characters converted to ASCII equivalents, or dropped if there is no equivalent character, then you can use the `unicodedata.normalize()` function.

```
>>> import unicodedata
>>> unicodedata.normalize('NFKD', u'abcd\xe9').encode('ascii',
'ignore')
'abcde'
```

Specifying `'NFKD'` as the first argument ensures the non-ASCII characters are replaced with their equivalent ASCII versions, and the final call to `encode()` with `'ignore'` as the second argument will remove any extraneous unicode characters.

See also

Encoding detection and conversion is a recommended first step before doing HTML processing with `lxml` or `BeautifulSoup`, covered in the *Extracting URLs from HTML with lxml* and *Converting HTML entities with BeautifulSoup* recipes.

Penn Treebank Part-of-Speech Tags

Following is a table of all the part-of-speech tags that occur in the `treebank` corpus distributed with NLTK. The tags and counts shown here were acquired using the following code:

```
>>> from nltk.probability import FreqDist
>>> from nltk.corpus import treebank
>>> fd = FreqDist()
>>> for word, tag in treebank.tagged_words():
...     fd.inc(tag)
>>> fd.items()
```

The `FreqDist` `fd` contains all the counts shown here for every tag in the `treebank` corpus. You can inspect each tag count individually by doing `fd[tag]`, as in `fd['DT']`. Punctuation tags are also shown, along with special tags such as `-NONE-`, which signifies that the part-of-speech tag is unknown. Descriptions of most of the tags can be found at `http://www.ling.upenn.edu/courses/Fall_2003/ling001/penn_treebank_pos.html`.

Part-of-speech tag	Frequency of occurrence
#	16
$	724
"	694
,	4,886
-LRB-	120
-NONE-	6,592
-RRB-	126
.	384
:	563
``	712
CC	2,265
CD	3,546
DT	8,165
EX	88
FW	4
IN	9,857
JJ	5,834
JJR	381
JJS	182
LS	13
MD	927
NN	13,166
NNP	9,410
NNPS	244
NNS	6,047
PDT	27
POS	824
PRP	1,716

Part-of-speech tag	Frequency of occurrence
PRP$	766
RB	2,822
RBR	136
RBS	35
RP	216
SYM	1
TO	2,179
UH	3
VB	2,554
VBD	3,043
VBG	1,460
VBN	2,134
VBP	1,321
VBZ	2,125
WDT	445
WP	241
WP$	14

Index

Thank you for buying
Python Text Processing with NLTK 2.0 Cookbook

About Packt Publishing

Packt, pronounced 'packed', published its first book "*Mastering phpMyAdmin for Effective MySQL Management*" in April 2004 and subsequently continued to specialize in publishing highly focused books on specific technologies and solutions.

Our books and publications share the experiences of your fellow IT professionals in adapting and customizing today's systems, applications, and frameworks. Our solution based books give you the knowledge and power to customize the software and technologies you're using to get the job done. Packt books are more specific and less general than the IT books you have seen in the past. Our unique business model allows us to bring you more focused information, giving you more of what you need to know, and less of what you don't.

Packt is a modern, yet unique publishing company, which focuses on producing quality, cutting-edge books for communities of developers, administrators, and newbies alike. For more information, please visit our website: www.packtpub.com.

About Packt Open Source

In 2010, Packt launched two new brands, Packt Open Source and Packt Enterprise, in order to continue its focus on specialization. This book is part of the Packt Open Source brand, home to books published on software built around Open Source licences, and offering information to anybody from advanced developers to budding web designers. The Open Source brand also runs Packt's Open Source Royalty Scheme, by which Packt gives a royalty to each Open Source project about whose software a book is sold.

Writing for Packt

We welcome all inquiries from people who are interested in authoring. Book proposals should be sent to author@packtpub.com. If your book idea is still at an early stage and you would like to discuss it first before writing a formal book proposal, contact us; one of our commissioning editors will get in touch with you.

We're not just looking for published authors; if you have strong technical skills but no writing experience, our experienced editors can help you develop a writing career, or simply get some additional reward for your expertise.

Expert Python Programming

ISBN: 978-1-847194-94-7   Paperback: 372 pages

Best practices for designing, coding, and distributing
your Python software

1. Learn Python development best practices from
   an expert, with detailed coverage of naming and
   coding conventions

2. Apply object-oriented principles, design patterns,
   and advanced syntax tricks

3. Manage your code with distributed version control

4. Profile and optimize your code

MySQL for Python

ISBN: 978-1-849510-18-9   Paperback: 440 pages

Integrate the flexibility of Python and the power of MySQL
to boost the productivity of your Python applications

1. Implement the outstanding features of Python's
   MySQL library to their full potential

2. See how to make MySQL take the processing
   burden from your programs

3. Learn how to employ Python with MySQL to power
   your websites and desktop applications

4. Apply your knowledge of MySQL and Python
   to real-world problems instead of hypothetical
   scenarios

Please check **www.PacktPub.com** for information on our titles

Spring Python 1.1

ISBN: 978-1-849510-66-0   Paperback: 264 pages

Create powerful and versatile Spring Python applications using pragmatic libraries and useful abstractions

1. Maximize the use of Spring features in Python and develop impressive Spring Python applications

2. Explore the versatility of Spring Python by integrating it with frameworks, libraries, and tools

3. Discover the non-intrusive Spring way of wiring together Python components

4. Packed with hands-on-examples, case studies, and clear explanations for better understanding

Python Multimedia

ISBN: 978-1-849510-16-5   Paperback: 292 pages

Learn how to develop Multimedia applications using Python with this practical step-by-step guide

1. Use Python Imaging Library for digital image processing.

2. Create exciting 2D cartoon characters using Pyglet multimedia framework

3. Create GUI-based audio and video players using QT Phonon framework.

4. Get to grips with the primer on GStreamer multimedia framework and use this API for audio and video processing.

Please check **www.PacktPub.com** for information on our titles

Matplotlib for Python Developers

ISBN: 978-1-847197-90-0   Paperback: 308 pages

Build remarkable publication-quality plots the easy way

1. Create high quality 2D plots by using Matplotlib productively

2. Incremental introduction to Matplotlib, from the ground up to advanced levels

3. Embed Matplotlib in GTK+, Qt, and wxWidgets applications as well as web sites to utilize them in Python applications

4. Deploy Matplotlib in web applications and expose it on the Web using popular web frameworks such as Pylons and Django

Please check **www.PacktPub.com** for information on our titles

Lightning Source UK Ltd.
Milton Keynes UK
UKOW02f2021090414

229691UK00002B/77/P

9 781849 513609